A Dash of Hope

A Dash of Hope

The Life of Aditya P. Dash

BLACK EAGLE BOOKS
Dublin, USA | Bhubaneswar, India

 Black Eagle Books
USA address:
7464 Wisdom Lane
Dublin, OH 43016

India address:
E/312, Trident Galaxy, Kalinga Nagar,
Bhubaneswar-751003, Odisha, India

E-mail: info@blackeaglebooks.org
Website: www.blackeaglebooks.org

First International Edition Published by
Black Eagle Books, 2025

A DASH OF HOPE: The Life of Aditya P. Dash
by Aditya Prasad Dash

Copyright © **Aditya P. Dash**

All rights reserved. No part of this publication may be reproduced, stored in a retrieval system, or transmitted, in any form or by any means, electronic, mechanical, photocopying, recording or otherwise without the prior permission of the publisher.

Cover Design: **Dr Francis Barclay**
Interior Design: Ezy's Publication

ISBN- 978-1-64560-747-2 (Paperback)

Printed in the United States of America

CONTENTS

Forwards	07
Acknowledgements	19
A colourful start	21
Growing up in Nandapur where soul of India lies	23
Meeting Mosquitoes and malaria	27
The barefoot journey begins	29
The accidental Duryodhan	33
Youth and waywardness	34
Education and erudition	36
Men of honour and those without	42
A new dawn at Utkal University	45
Research and revival	49
The Keonjhar project	58
The wedlock	64
The field days	73
Shaping the scientist	75
Surge of the scientist	80
Flight to Maroua	87
From Pondy to Trivandrum	93
Birth of NAVBD	99
A challenging life at Institute of Life Sciences	104

Back to ICMR	132
An Unexpected call from the UN	193
Around hundred-thousand Tulips	222
A Stately honour in Thailand	224
Another stint with the WHO	227
Coming to Temple town	342
A (new beginning): AARAMBH	247
A Spell bounding spell at CUTN	251
Reaching New Heights	267
Transforming CUTN	269
Malpractice in Indian Science	290
A decade of CUTN	306
CUTN during COVID 19	307
Signing off with satisfaction	313
Another Innings	319
Looking back	336
Padma Politics	342
Nobel laureates of Indian Origin/connection	347
The CSIR Connection	350
Vanishing Scientists	354
Experiencing Spiritualism	359
On Deck – Post Retirement	365
Witness to history: The Ram Mandir Consecration ceremony	373
Annexures	377

Forewords

11th October 2024

I had the privilege of knowing Prof. Aditya Prasad Dash over two decades, during which I have been impressed with his dedication and remarkable professional journey. With Ph.D. and D.Sc. degrees, he has made significant contribution in the fields of Vector Borne and Neglected Tropical Diseases (NTDs) and Climate Change and Tropical Diseases Research (TDR) while working with WHO.

Dr Dash's leadership and expertise have been exceptional, and his autobiography offers an engaging account of his personal and professional experiences, providing valuable insights into the challenges he faced and overcame and achievements he made throughout his career. This book relates the inspiring story of a boy from a remote Indian village who rose to prominence in global public health, leading national laboratories and contributing significantly to disease control.

As the Regional Adviser for Neglected and Tropical Diseases at the WHO South-East Asia Regional Office, I have personally seen his pivotal role in supporting countries like Maldives, Sri Lanka, Thailand, and Bangladesh to eliminate lymphatic filariasis, as well as his efforts to reduce the NTD burden in India. He was also instrumental in shaping policies for the control and elimination of several other vector borne diseases such as dengue, kala-azar, and malaria. Moreover, Dr Dash played a crucial role in developing generic protocols to study the health impacts of climate change and fostering collaborations among institutions working on tropical diseases.

In addition to his work in public health, Dr Dash served as Vice Chancellor of the Central University of Tamil Nadu and the Asian Institute of Public Health University, significantly contributing to education and research. Leading five national laboratories and two universities is no easy task, but his leadership and perseverance made it possible. This book provides his candid reflections on the challenges he faced in higher education and research in India. His insights and experiences navigating these obstacles make it an essential read for anyone interested in the field.

Recognized with the prestigious Padma Shri in Science & Engineering in 2022, Dr Dash's achievements are truly exceptional. I am confident this autobiography will inspire readers from diverse fields and backgrounds.

Dr Poonam Khetrapal Singh
First Indian elected Regional Director (2014 -2023)
World Health Organisation (South East Asia Region)

1st October, 2024

Professor Aditya P Dash gives his personal, frank, perspective on every institution and area he has experienced in his long and chequered career.

This memoir opens a window to health sciences research in areas such as in malaria as well as the challenges in leading major institutions.

Dr K. VijayRaghavan, FRS
Ex- Principal Scientific Adviser to Government of India
Former Secretary, Department of Biotechnology,
Government of India

12th September2024

Dr A. P. Dash comes from a very distinguished with a strong religious background and his wife is a daughter of the first DG, Police of Odisha. He has distinguished himself in the area of Vector Borne Diseases and Public Health which is a very heady mix, where basic science, applied science as well as public health mixes itself for a common public good. His work has been cited in the first 10 distinguished publications in Biomedical sciences. His work has a huge impact on control of Malaria in India and South East Asia. He started his career in the Regional Medical Research Centre (ICMR), Bhubaneshwar and then moved to develop Institute of Life Sciences (ILS), Bhubaneshwar and saw its transition from a State funded organisation to a Government of India, DBT institute. Today ILS stands proud as one of the most distinguished institutes under DBT umbrella.

He headed the National Institute for Research on Tribal Health, Jabalpur; Centre for Research in Medical Entomology, Madurai; National Institute of Malaria Research, New Delhi and Desert Medicine Research Centre, Jodhpur. Wherever he went, he has put his signature and let these institutes to the pinnacle of glory. He joined the World Health Organisation, as the Regional Advisor of vector borne and neglected tropical diseases, wherein he strengthened the subject in the entire South East Asia region. After his retirement he joined as a Vice Chancellor of Central University of Tamil Nadu and was again responsible for its stellar growth. His latest assignment has been as a Vice Chancellor of Asian Institute of Public Health University, Odisha; from where he retired last year. This is a rare example of institute builder and a builder of large national work force. Each one of them have made its own mark and have left a global foot print. He was awarded *Padamshree* for his work apart from numerous national and international awards. As a human being he is very pleasant, humble as well as has an ability to easily mix with his co-workers as well as senior administrative management and other luminaries. This is one of the secrets of his success. He is an out and out family man, devoted husband, father and grandfather. I have had a long association with him which was professional as well as very personal. So, this autobiography does not completely describe him. To really know him you need to interact with him at closed quarters.

Professor Nirmal Kumar Ganguly
M.B.B.S., M.D., FRCP (London), Fellow, Imperial College
(London), FAMS, FNA (Ind. Med.)
FNASc, FTWAS (Italy), FIACS (Canada), FIMSA
Former Director General – Indian Council of Medical Research
Ex- President, JIPMER, Pondicherry
(PADMABHUSAN AWARDEE)

12th October 2024

It has been a pleasure to have known and interact with Prof. A. P. Dash (AP) for nearly two decades in various leadership capacities in India. AP's scientific contributions to the field of neglected tropical diseases (NTDs) and vector-borne infectious diseases (VBDs) are countless as evident from hundreds of research publications. He has served in leadership capacities in so many national institutions of higher learning and for his outstanding and regionally relevant scientific contributions, AP was honored with one of the highest civilian awards (Padma Shree) by the Government of India in 2022.

Apart from his outstanding scientific contributions, AP has mentored and inspired numerous young scientists in India. In my personal interactions with AP in several scientific meetings, I observed him to be surrounded by dozens of young scientists, and it is remarkable that he was so easily approachable and made time to guide them and satisfy their scientific curiosities as if he drove his own inspiration from them.

AP's memoir "A Dash of Hope" will serve as a reminder of ongoing challenges in the areas of NTDs and VBDs that affect hundreds of millions of people globally. It also demonstrates that nothing is impossible if you work hard with passion and dedication. I have no doubt that AP's exceptional contributions summarized in the memoir will continue to inspire future generation of scientists in India.

Nirbhay Kumar, PhD, FAAAS, FAAM, FASTMH
*Professor of Global Health,
George Washington University, Washington DC, USA
(Former Professor and Chair of Tropical Medicine, and Director of Vector-Borne Infectious Diseases Research Center, Tulane University, New Orleans, LA, USA)
(Former Professor of Molecular Microbiology and Immunology, and Deputy Director of Johns Hopkins Malaria Research Institute, Baltimore, MD, USA)*

7th November 2024

I have had the privilege to know Prof. A. P. Dash for more than 20 years since he first invited me to attend the International Conference on Malaria "Laveran to Genomics" in New Delhi, Nov 4-6, 2005. This conference commemorated 125 years of malaria research since the discovery of the *Plasmodium* parasite by Laveran, and it was my first visit and introduction to India. At that time, Prof. Dash was the Director of the National Institute for Malaria Research (NIMR), an Indian Council of Medical Research (ICMR) institute. My visit to India was pivotal and life-changing and changed the course of my career. Prof. Dash was instrumental in introducing me to Indian scientists and to facilitating collaborations between my research lab at New York University and researchers at ICMR-NIMR, as well as with scientists at other institutions in India. These initial introductions led to highly productive, long-term partnerships and significant advances in malaria research over the years. For example, our jointly authored paper published in 2012 describes how the malaria parasite *Plasmodium vivax* exhibits greater genetic diversity than *Plasmodium falciparum* and was published as the front-cover paper in *Nature Genetics*. As a direct results of Prof. Dash's encouragement, input, and assistance, ICMR-NIMR in collaboration with my lab was awarded two highly prestigious U.S.A. National Institutes of Health grants, a

Fogarty Research and Training grant, and an International Centre of Excellence for Malaria Research which has been continually funded for more than 15 years.

Prof Dash's other contributions are too numerous to list here and are not limited to malaria. Rather, his portfolio shows a breadth and depth on a range of vector-borne diseases rarely seen among scientists. Acknowledgment of his pivotal role in Indian infectious disease research, policy development, and public health have included his election as Fellow of the National Academy of Sciences, Allahabad in 2000, as Fellow of the Academy of Medical Sciences, Delhi in 2007, and Fellow of the National Environmental Science Academy of India. In 2022 he was recognized with the highly prestigious Padma Shri in Science & Engineering in recognition of his distinguished contribution to science.

I am thrilled that Prof. Dash has written his autobiography so that others may be inspired, uplifted, and encouraged from a life well lived. His achievements and accomplishments are truly remarkable and thought-provoking, and it has been my great fortune to know him.

Professor Jane M. Carlton
Director, Johns Hopkins Malaria Research Institute
Founding Director,
NIH International Centre of Excellence for Malaria in India
Former Director, Centre for Genomics & Systems Biology,
New York University

Acknowledgements

To my wife Vijaylakshmi: Thank you for many years of friendship, love, care, and support. Your belief in me and in what we could achieve together has made our happy life possible. I am deeply grateful for your guidance, and I appreciate you being both my critic and my adviser. I also owe a great debt of gratitude to my parents—may their souls rest in peace—and to my elder brother, Er Girija Prasad Dash, for his unwavering support. I bow to all who have illuminated my path and touched my life, whether with joy or with pain.

CHAPTER-1

A Colourful Start

My story begins on a bright Sunday afternoon in 1951, just a few days before the vibrant festival of Holi, in the serene town of Hindol, nestled in the Dhenkanal district of Odisha, India. I am the fourth child in a large family. My father, late Lokanath Dash, had once served as a royal employee in the Hindol Princely State. However, his life took a turn when he was abruptly dismissed in the early 1940s, possibly due to his involvement in the *"Praja Mandal Andolana,"* a local freedom movement (started in 1937 in *Dudurkote*, Hindol). After losing his job under the reign of Late Naba Kishor Chandra Mardaraj Jagdev, he secured work at the Titagarh Paper Mills in Angul. Despite being educated, he declined a government job offer after India gained independence, choosing instead to move our family back to our ancestral village, Nandapur.

My father often shared stories about Hindol, which was once a princely state in Orissa during the British Raj. After the East India Company occupied Orissa in 1803, treaties were established with various estates in the region, including Hindol. Following India's independence in 1947, Hindol merged with the newly formed nation. In 1948, when all the princely states, including Hindol, formally integrated with the province of Orissa, the region became part of what is now the Dhenkanal district.

My father's family hails from the Dash lineage of Nandapur village in the Dhenkanal district of Odisha, located about 45 kilometers from Dhenkanal town. My grandfather, the late Dr Somanath Dash, was the first doctor in the Hindol kingdom. He left Nandapur to settle in Hindol, where he tended to the health needs of the community. Tragically, my grandfather passed away at a young age, leaving behind his wife and four children. I have been told that he succumbed to typhoid or pneumonia, and at that time, antibiotics were not available. Had they been accessible, his death might have been prevented.

My father, late Lokanath Dash, lost his father when he was only ten years old. Despite the hardships he faced, he worked diligently to complete his high school education in Dhenkanal, often walking the 45 kilometers each way. Fortunately, the King of Hindol took responsibility for my father's education. My grandmother, Chanduri Devi, had a deep affection for me. The night before I was born, she dreamt that a son would arrive on the following Sunday, which inspired my parents to name me "Aditya," after the Sun God, symbolizing hope and new beginnings.

After my father left the royal service, he quickly secured a job in Angul, prompting our entire family to return to our native village, Nandapur, where my uncle and his family resided. Growing up with four brothers and many sisters was not easy, especially in a large joint family. With my father working in Angul, which was about 25 kilometers away—a considerable distance at the time—we often had to manage daily life without his presence. Yet, even amid the difficulties, a sense of togetherness and resilience coloured our early years.

CHAPTER- 2

GROWING UP IN NANDAPUR, WHERE THE SOUL OF INDIA LIES

My early childhood, until the age of nine, was spent in my village. It is often said that the soul of India resides in its villages, and Nandapur exemplified this notion with its peaceful lifestyle, calmness, and quietude. The village featured expansive open areas surrounded by trees, creating a harmonious and eco-friendly environment. Most houses were constructed with thatched roofs and adorned with mud plaster, which the villagers would refresh on festive occasions. Our home was situated in the heart of the village.

Born in the early 1950s, I have vivid memories of a small sign drawn in chalk on the upper corner of our house's exterior wall, indicating the date of the DDT spray carried out under the National Malaria Eradication Programme, the largest disease eradication initiative in history. Nandapur was primarily a *Brahmin* settlement. The cultural heritage of the village, with its Brahmin traditions and religious practices, have added a unique dimension to our family's legacy. The place had a strong connection to spirituality and community life, given the role of *Brahmins* in rituals and temple services. A vast network of *Brahmins* is vital for the worship of the Lord, representing all *Vedas* and *Gotras*.

According to legendary accounts, elite Brahmins were brought to Odisha from *Kanyakubja* or *Ujjain*, with some arriving from *Varanasi*. They were granted land and other endowments in exchange for their dedication to ritualistic responsibilities. My father told me that our family hailed from Varanasi (*Kashi*) many years ago. We also learned that we belong to the "*Batshashya Gotra*," the *Gotra* of Lord Parshuram, the sixth incarnation of Lord Vishnu, as outlined in *Hindu* scriptures.

Few families owned land for cultivation, and farmers relied on bulls for ploughing and other field activities. The village comprised two distinct hamlets, clearly marked on either side: *Kandha Sahi* and *Pana (Harijan) Sahi*. Alongside the *Brahmin* households, there were a few homes belonging to *Malis*, who were responsible for worshipping the village deity. The educational status of the villagers was relatively low; in fact, there were hardly six or seven educated families, including ours. Each *Brahmin* household in the village had its unique characteristics. The verandas were elevated, requiring one to climb a few steps to enter the house.

My village had a school, known as Nandapur Lower Primary School (now upgraded to Upper Primary School). I began my education there, although at that time, there was no Nursery, LKG, or UKG. When I was five years old, I enrolled in Class I. Before starting school, my mother taught me the basics at home. I completed my studies up to Class III in the village school. I remember my teacher, the late Gati Krishna Dash, who was also from the village and known for his strictness. Although he was familiar with our family, he never pampered us or made exceptions to the rules. The walls of the school were adorned with slogans promoting a noble path in life, which we read daily. At that time, the Indian education system placed significant emphasis on human values, culture, and heritage, as well as nurturing discipline. Our textbooks included many moral lessons, and the teachers were upright and honest, exhibiting high integrity. This focus on values and discipline may have been the guiding principle that shaped our character.

The village had a *"Shiva"* temple that attracted many visitors from nearby villages. My uncle regularly attended the temple for daily rituals. Every year, on *Kartik Poornima*, a special festival took place, drawing all the villagers to the temple to celebrate. At home, each evening, we would wash our faces, hands, and feet before gathering together to recite our daily prayers, which were followed by study time. This routine became a cherished part of our lives and continued until I completed my high school education, which at that time was up to Class XI.

In primary school, every school day was my favourite. When I returned home with my bag slung over my shoulder, two important women in my life awaited my arrival: my grandmother and my mother. Like most siblings, we often competed for our grandmother's attention, and I believe I succeeded in that regard. She had a fondness for all of us, but I sensed she held a special place in her heart for me, perhaps because she saw me as a replacement for her deceased son, my uncle, who had departed for the heavenly abode at an early age, after completing a Law degree.

My other uncle, who lived in the village with us, did not have any children when I was in primary school. He was very fond of my siblings and me and took care of our landed properties in the village, including some in a neighbouring village called *Barisingha*. The rice fields in *Barisingha* were more fertile than those in our own village. I recall that we had four to six employees assisting us in the village and several pairs of bulls for cultivation work, with paddy being the main crop.

On Sundays and holidays, my uncle would take my younger brother Babula (Bhabani Prasad) and me to the fields to familiarize us with our land. While I had little interest in these matters, Babula had a natural affinity for them. He could identify each of our fields by name. One of our largest fields was filled with several big mango trees, each with its own name. Summer vacations were a true delight for us. In the mango field, we built a temporary hut where we would watch the mangoes fall, running to pick them up and gather them in one place. There was a huge variety of mangoes, making it a joyful experience.

CHAPTER-3

Meeting Mosquitoes and Malaria

During my schooling in the village, I suffered from bouts of fever that my father referred to as malaria, for which I was given antimalarial tablets. At that time, government health staff visited our village regularly and meticulously, going from house to house to collect mosquitoes. I remember seeing a health worker collect mosquitoes in a test tube, using a suction tube to capture them. I was fascinated as I watched the mosquitoes futilely trying to escape inside the test tube. I learned that my fevers were often caused by bites from these insects.

Behind our house, there was a large piece of land where, during the harvesting season, all the paddy plants were cut and brought. At that time, there were no machines to separate the paddy from the dried plants, so the bulls were made to walk over the harvested crop at night. By morning, the paddy would be separated, and it was fascinating to sit and watch this process from evening until dinner. During that time, employees were not paid in cash; instead, my uncle provided them with an equal amount of paddy each month. Looking back at my childhood, I realize how much

I enjoyed being in nature, despite the other challenges we faced. It truly was a happy early childhood. The beginning of my life was simple, much like that of many others in remote villages in India.

CHAPTER – 4

The Bare-Foot Journey Begins

After completing Class III, I had to enrol in the nearby Middle English School for Class IV, which was about 3 to 4 kilometers from our village. Every day, I walked barefoot to school with my peers, as wearing shoes or slippers was not customary in remote villages like ours. To shorten the distance, we often took a shortcut through the rice fields. I was not very happy with my teacher at that school. My father, who worked in Angul, would come to the village on weekends. One day, he took me to Angul to continue my studies. Angul was a small town in Dhenkanal district (now a district in its own right). I was admitted to Class IV at *Bazarpada* Upper Primary School, where I studied until Class V. This school was located across from Angul High School, which was well-reputed in Odisha. The head teacher at *Bazarpada* School was a tall man with an imposing personality. He was familiar with my father and took a particular interest in my studies, providing me with special care and attention. As I said earlier, the education system at that time in India placed significant emphasis on human values, culture, and heritage, as well as nurturing discipline.

After completing Class V, I easily gained admission

to Class VI at Angul High School, a prestigious institution known for its many capable teachers. Stepping into this school marked one of the most exciting chapters of my life. I can clearly recall my early days in high school.

I recall that I achieved the highest marks in the Class VI examination in my section, which made me very happy. After the results were declared, summer vacation began, and I used to visit my native village during every break to relish village life. Of course, I equally enjoyed my time in the small town of Angul. At that time, Angul was a charming, small town with a cinema hall called "Shankar Cinema," where we occasionally watched mythological films. I loved Angul, and even now, hearing the name brings me excitement. At one end of the town, there was the *Lingara* River, and nearby was a weekly market, known as 'Hat,' that took place every Sunday. Additionally, there was a daily market behind Angul High School, where we could buy fresh vegetables and seasonal local fruits. Visiting the daily market was often a delightful experience.

There were no malls in those days, just several shops in the Angul market. One store worth mentioning was 'The Pattnayak Store,' a variety shop where almost everything was available. The Anglo-Indian colony in Angul relied on this store for their necessities, and we often bought biscuits and other commodities from there.

In the early 1960s, I was in Angul with my father when we received the distressing news that our grandmother, who lived with our extended family in our native village, was very sick. We rushed back to the village, but by the time we arrived, our grandmother had passed away. My heart felt heavy with sorrow; I was deeply saddened. For every child, a mother is the most precious possession. Yet, when I reflect on it now, I realize I was even more attached to my grandmother. Her love, care, and possessiveness are still vivid in my memory.

Angul was also famous for the *"Bajiraut Chhatravas" (Bajiraut* Hostel), popularly known as the *"Malati Choudhury Ashram."* On weekends, we would cycle to this peaceful place, and I felt a deep attachment to it. Malati Devi Choudhury was a civil rights and freedom activist and a follower of Gandhian principles. She was profoundly influenced by both Rabindranath Tagore and Mahatma Gandhi. Malati Choudhury began her education in Santiniketan in 1921, where she was classmates with Amita Sen, the mother of Professor Amartya Sen. During this time, a young man named Naba Krushna Choudhuri, from a prominent family in Odisha, also attended Santiniketan after being invited by Gandhiji, and they eventually married. Naba krushna Choudhuri later became the Chief Minister of Odisha in 1927 and again in 1951. As activists, the Choudhurys applied educational principles to create a nurturing environment for *Satyagraha*. Even before Independence, Malati Choudhury established the *"Bajiraut Chhatravas"* in Angul in 1946 and the *Utkal Navajeevan Mandal* in 1948. The *"Bajiraut Chhatravas,"* or *"Malati Choudhury Ashram,"* still stands in Angul today, and I have a strong desire to revisit this meaningful place.

CHAPTER – 5

The Accidental Duryodhan

My father had a sister who was happily married and lived in a village about 12 kilometres from Angul. Her husband's elder brother was a well-known figure in the area. He had been affected by polio and was affectionately known as *"Chhota Pisa"* among our sibling's. He had a fondness for my father, and we always received an open invitation to visit their village every weekend. At that time, there was no bus service, so we travelled by bicycle. My father would often take me along, and sometimes my elder brother would join us. Every visit was enjoyable. As soon as we arrived at their home, I would rush inside to greet my father's sister, who lived in a joint family. She had one son who was married, while *Chhota Pisa* had four sons and three daughters-in-law (one son was not yet of marriageable age). The moment I entered, their daughters-in-law, my *Bhabis* (Sisters in law), would take charge of me, preparing a delightful variety of dishes that I relished. Despite all the enjoyment, there was a downside for me. When we arrived, I would greet everyone but never said "Namaste" to anyone. In contrast, my elder brother was obedient, conventional, and respectful to our elders. Upon entering, he would bow his head and greet everyone. As a result, I was not very popular among the villagers. They perceived me as arrogant, but in reality, it was simply my overwhelming shyness when faced with elders and learned individuals. On some weekends, we would spend Saturday evenings there and return to Angul on Sundays. I vividly remember my father getting angry with me for my careless attitude and lack of respect for elders. He would often compare me to *Duryodhana* from the *Mahabharata*, saying that *Duryodhana* was arrogant like me and never bowed to anyone. He added that at least *Duryodhana* was an aggressive fighter, while I was not even that. I never reacted to his comparisons; I simply accepted the idea that perhaps I was indeed like that.

Whenever my mother visited Angul, we would go to the temple of *Budhi Thakurani*, a revered deity in the town. The temple is situated on one side of *Sunasagad* Hill, right in the heart of Angul. The *Bigraha* of the Goddess is made from black granite stone and resembles a pillar, standing tall and majestic.

CHAPTER – 6

Youth And Waywardness

I stayed at that school year after year and received promotions in each class. The senior Sanskrit teacher at the school was my maternal uncle, and we were linked to the junior Sanskrit teacher as well. Up till class VII, we had a Hindi teacher. My Hindi and Sanskrit skills were really lacking. Furthermore, the Hindi instructor used to beat me on the smallest pretest, which is why I never liked him. Up until Class VII, everything was good. I became disobedient and got into bad company while I was in Class VIII. I hardly showed up for class when I left home for school. I used to wander around drinking tea with friends and occasionally smoking a cigarette at the Angul bus stop. My dad was unaware of it, since every evening I used to study like a diligent boy.

A newspaper ad advertising an acting school in Bombay (now Mumbai) caught my attention. I had aspirations of attending such a school. My career as a movie actor would benefit from this. I sent a letter requesting admission to the acting school. I had provided the address of my father. My father received the call for admittance in his office. He read the letter after opening it, out of curiosity.

Presumably detecting my drift, he tore the letter but said nothing to me.

In those days, the monthly tuition fee cost was half a rupee. I once failed to pay the school fees that my father had given me to deposit with the school administration. I used it up. After learning of the non-payment, my maternal uncle—the Sanskrit teacher—paid it. When the Class VIII exam arrived, I took it and received dismal marks. I didn't show my father my marksheet. I stated that no mark sheet was provided. After asking my maternal uncle, my father eventually learned about my waywardness. British culture had an influence on my father. I stopped being a miscreant when he gave me good. He excelled in both English and maths. He personally looked after my education especially Mathematics.

CHAPTER – 7

Education and Erudition

I continued in Class IX, striving to make up for the time I had lost. Our Headmaster frequently made surprise visits to our class, keeping us on our toes and motivating us to be diligent in our studies. Gradually, I began performing well in my examinations. During that time, the student agitation in Odisha escalated significantly. In Angul, the movement was led by the President of the Students' Union of Angul College, the late Madhu Sudan Mishra, who was a final-year B.A. student. Students from Angul High School, including myself, also joined the agitation. I recall participating in the processions during the strike, which began in September 1964 and continued for some time. If memory serves me right, the agitation initially erupted from an altercation between a bus conductor and a group of students, leading to a series of events, including a storming of the State Assembly. The colleges closed for the Puja vacation, but when they reopened in October, the students continued their strike to protest against police excesses. At that time, late Mr. Biren Mitra, the only Bengali to have served as Chief Minister of Odisha, was in office. On November 5, a pact was finally signed between the students and the Chief Minister, though it was violated shortly thereafter. Initially, the protests targeted a state minister, but it ultimately succeeded in not only forcing the minister out of office but also toppling the local government entirely.

Although I excelled in mathematics and science, I struggled to secure even 40-45% in subjects like Sanskrit, Oriya, and Social Studies. Despite this, my father was pleased with my strong performance in mathematics. Towards the end of Class X, there was a change in leadership at our school. A new Headmaster, late Mr. C.C. Mallik, took charge. He was a fair-skinned man with a dignified presence, always seen in a suit and hat, carrying a stick. He was renowned for his strictness and commitment to discipline, unlike any Headmaster I had encountered before. Mr. Mallik introduced mandatory coaching classes for Class XI students, requiring us to start at 9 AM instead of the usual 10:30 AM. I attended these classes diligently, which brought me to his notice. One day, during the school assembly, he unexpectedly introduced me as a disciplined student. It was a moment of great happiness for me, especially since I had always thought of myself as undisciplined until that point.

At that time, there was a shortage of textbooks in the market, making it difficult for us to access the necessary study materials. Even when books were available, money was often a challenge, and we had to manage with limited resources. We frequently shared books among ourselves to overcome this problem. Just before the final school examination for Class XI, my elder brother, who was studying at the engineering school in Cuttack, brought home two books titled *"Possible Questions and Answers"*. One was for me, and the other was for a friend in the village. The book proved to be very helpful for our exam preparation.

The Class XI final examinations marked a crucial

stage in my schooling. At that time, school education concluded with Class XI, after which students would proceed to college for Pre-University (one year) and Pre-Professional (one year) studies, followed by graduation. Our examination centre was Angul College, where I appeared for the exams along with my peers. The results were announced in June 1967, and I passed successfully. I was particularly proud to achieve full marks in Mathematics. Additionally, I had chosen an optional Mathematics paper in Class IX, for which I also scored very high marks. Achieving such scores was a rare accomplishment in those days, making it especially gratifying. However, my marks in Sanskrit and Oriya were below average. Though I got good scores in Mathematics and Science, my child hood passed without any focus on science education.

When my father worked with the King of Hindol, he developed a passion for astrology. The Angul High School had an age-old library known as the 'Integrated Library,' which housed many ancient books. The librarian was familiar with my father, allowing me to borrow some of these rare texts on weekends and during vacations. In Class IX, I began learning astrology from my father, and by Class X, I was already casting horoscopes for newborns. I diligently studied numerous astrology books from the school library, immersing myself in the subject. After finishing school, I started making small predictions, and my interest in Indian astrology grew steadily, becoming a primary topic of discussion between my father and me. He was pleased that one of his children was taking up astrology, which he had pursued as a hobby. He advised me never to accept money or gifts for any astrological guidance I provided. I have honoured that promise to this day. Even during my time at Angul College, when people came to our house with sweets to celebrate successful predictions, we accepted the treats but chose not to consume them ourselves; instead, we distributed them among our neighbours. Astrology became a cherished pastime for me, and in my leisure time, I delved deeper into the subject, eventually completing nearly all the books on Indian astrology.

After completing my schooling, I enrolled in the Pre-University Science program at Angul College, the only government college in Angul at the time. During my year there, I encountered two principals, Dr S.R. Upadhayay and Dr P.N. Chatterjee, both of whom taught Zoology. By that time, my elder brother, a civil engineer, had secured a job in Bhubaneswar. After successfully passing the Pre-University examinations in 1968, I needed to enrol in a pre-Professional course. My brother took me to Bhubaneswar, but since admissions at BJB College were closed, I had to enrol in the pre-Professional course at the Basic Science College under the Orissa University of Agriculture and Technology, where Professor B.D. Samantaray served as Vice Chancellor. While studying in the pre-Professional program, my brother was transferred, prompting me to move into the college hostel. I actively participated in extracurricular activities, including the NCC, but I still longed for the familiar atmosphere of Angul. My memories of Angul lingered, and at that time, Bhubaneswar was still not fully developed.

While studying at Basic Science College, my elder brother, who came to Bhubaneswar, took me on a trip to Puri. We visited the Lord Jagannath temple, but my experience there was disappointing, particularly due to the attitude of the '*Pandas.*' Their demeanour left a sour impression on me, and I promised myself not to return to the temple. True to my word, I did not visit again for several years.

I completed my pre-professional course in 1969 and enrolled in the first year of B.Sc. (Honours) at *Buxi Jagabandhu Bidyadhar* (B.J.B.) College in Bhubaneswar. At that time, it was one of the most prestigious colleges in the region, and it remains so today. I chose to specialize in Zoology. The college had excellent faculty, and our principal, Dr S.R. Panda, a mathematician, was known for his strictness. The campus featured a Science Block and an Arts Block, separated by a road.

I stayed in the hostel on the ground floor, sharing my room with three other students. The warden, Dr R.K. Mohanty, was a lecturer in Zoology and had a soft spot for us. There were 14 students in the B.Sc. Honours program, most of whom lived in the hostel. We would often meet Dr Mohanty during his visits, and I quickly developed friendships with many of my fellow students. My friends would often relay their grievances through us to the warden. On weekends, our primary entertainment was watching Hindi movies, as there were only two cinema halls in Bhubaneswar at that time: Ravi Talkies and Kalpana Cinema. During my time, there were no computers, calculators, or television, so going to the movies was our only weekend pastime. The demand for tickets was high, and I often found myself breaking the queue with friends to secure tickets.

I had friends from both the science and humanities departments. Among them were a few very close friends from the History and English departments, as well as some notorious characters from other disciplines. I maintained good relationships with all of them. When I joined the B.Sc. program in 1969, Dr Harapriya Devi was the Head of the Department of Zoology. She had a great personality and was an excellent teacher. Later, she was succeeded by Mr.

U.C. Panda, who was like a father figure to all the students, including me. I was known as an obedient and innocent student, yet I occasionally found myself caught up in the mischiefs instigated by some of my more notorious friends. However, I was usually excused, thanks to the positive impression I had made on all the teachers, including the principal.

However, like in Class VIII, I found myself falling in with a bad crowd again. This time, though, my studies took priority, and the bad company became more of a pastime. In those days, before any final university examination, there were pre-tests and test examinations. Students who passed the test examination were allowed to appear for the final exams. During recreation time at college, I would sometimes join the other group of students. Oneday, while we were strolling around the college grounds just before the test examination, the principal happened to pass by. A group of students quickly gathered around him, suspecting that the small diary he carried in his pocket contained the question papers. One student urged me to sneakily retrieve the diary. Given my short stature, I managed to do so without the principal noticing. However, to everyone's disappointment, there were no questions inside.

CHAPTER – 8

Men of Honour and those Without...

There were 14 students in the B.Sc. Honours program, but many others were enrolled without honours as well. During my second year of B.Sc., one efficient teacher returned from Canada and joined the B.J.B. College as our modern biology lecturer. The classes were engaging, and we were making great progress. However, one day, there was a student agitation, and some notorious students came to our class, urging everyone to come outside. Without thinking much, I stood up and followed them, along with my classmates. He was clearly displeased with my decision at the time. Despite that initial incident, we later became quite close, and he turned out to be one of my well-wishers.

In our class, there were a few students who were not enrolled in the honours program, and their practical examination schedule differed from ours. During their practical exams, one student approached me for help in identifying biological samples. I leaned closer to the examination laboratory to assist my friend but was promptly caught by the external examiner. He asked me several questions, but I managed to wriggle out of the situation. A few days later, it was time for our Zoology Honours practical examination, which involved dissecting various animals, from cockroaches to rabbits. Although I was a Zoology Honours student, I had a fear of frogs. The practical exam consisted of a major dissection and a minor dissection, and I remember the major dissection involved a rabbit, while the minor dissection was, unfortunately, the hyoid apparatus of a frog. I felt extremely nervous. I knew the location of the hyoid apparatus and how to perform the dissection, but my fear completely overwhelmed me. One of my classmates, who was seated near me and was aware of my fear, came forward to help without the examiners noticing. She pinned the frog to my dissection tray, allowing me to proceed with the dissection. Although she assisted me, she likely didn't have enough time to complete her own dissection. This incident during my graduation haunted me psychologically. My adolescent years were even more challenging than my already difficult childhood. Teenage life was not a walk in the park for me.

Now, I realize that I have been somewhat unconventional since childhood. I never embraced a routine lifestyle; instead, I thrived on change. For me, life is about living independently, and I hold great respect for freedom and autonomy.

Our B.Sc. results were declared on time, and I returned to my native village during the summer vacation. A family discussion ensued regarding my future course of action. My father wanted me to pursue further studies. However, a relative visited our village and convinced my father and uncle that I should not continue my education. Instead, he suggested I take a job as a science teacher at a nearby high school, allowing me to stay in the village. Following my father's advice, I went to Rasol, about 10 kilometers from our village, to meet the headmaster of the school. I managed to secure the job, but my heart wasn't in it. A few days later, my elder brother visited us, and I expressed my lack of interest in the job, emphasizing my desire to continue my studies. He successfully convinced my father and uncle to support my ambitions, and soon after, I was sent to enrol in an M.Sc. program at a reputable university in Odisha.

CHAPTER -9

A New Dawn at Utkal University

At that time, there were three universities in Odisha. Utkal University in Bhubaneswar was the oldest, and its Zoology department was operating at the historic Ravenshaw College (now Ravenshaw University) in Cuttack, located 23 kilometers from Bhubaneswar. I enrolled in the first year of my M.Sc. in Zoology at Utkal University (Ravenshaw College).

Utkal University is the oldest university in Odisha, established in the pre independence period, and is the 17th oldest university in India, located in Bhubaneswar. The Post Graduate Department of Zoology began at Utkal University in 1960, with the late Professor B.K. Behura serving as the founding professor and head. The department later moved from the Ravenshaw College campus to the Utkal University campus in Bhubaneswar in July 1973. The late Professor M.K. Rout was the principal of Ravenshaw College. He was a short person, much like me, and was always dressed in white. Every day, he took morning rounds around the college premises and invariably noticed me as I entered the department, since I was the only student wearing a complete white outfit. Sometimes, he would call me over for a small chat. When he learned that I was studying for my M.Sc. in Zoology, he seemed pleased, presumably because our professor and head, Professor Behura, was a good friend of Professor Rout. We had several teachers in the Post Graduate Department of Zoology, all of whom were excellent. Professor Behura earned his M.Sc. from Calcutta University and completed his Ph.D. at Edinburgh University in the UK. During his Ph.D., he published two papers in the renowned science journal *Nature* in 1950, focusing on the European earwig. He was tall and fair-complexioned, with a commanding yet somewhat bossy personality. In the department, few dared to approach him. He would come to class, deliver his lecture, and then return to his office. No student would ask him questions during class. However, he had a remarkable clarity in his teaching; everything he explained remained etched in our minds and memories forever, eliminating the need for further reading.

While pursuing my M.Sc., the Orissa government awarded two merit scholarships to two students, each worth fifty rupees per month. I was fortunate enough to be one of the recipients of this scholarship. Additionally, my brother sent me Rs 120 every month. The state government also offered interest-free loans of Rs 900 per year for two years, which were to be repaid after a few years. Without informing my family, I decided to take advantage of this loan. Consequently, I was receiving a total of Rs 245 per month—a significant amount at the time. This financial support allowed me a more liberal lifestyle. Every early evening, I would go to "Cuttack Sweets Stall" with friends, and on weekends, we would watch movies together. During my M.Sc. studies, I stayed in the central hostel, which was conveniently located in the heart of the city, behind the Medical College. The rooms were spacious and comfortable. My younger brother also came to Cuttack for his studies and stayed with me for a few days. Later, my nephew, the eldest son of my eldest sister, joined us in Cuttack for his studies and stayed with me for a while. He is now a neurologist at Apollo Hospital.

We pursued our M.Sc. at Ravenshaw College from 1971 to 1973. Afterward, the department relocated to its original campus at Utkal University in Bhubaneswar, and we made the shift in July 1973. Once there, hostels were allocated to us on the university campus, and we began living in the hostel. In 1973, a local student agitation disrupted activities on campus, leading to the indefinite postponement of our examinations. Ultimately, the examinations were held in January/February 1974. By that time, our department had only five teaching staff members, who held the designations of Lecturer, Reader, and Professor. Prof. Behura continued as our Professor and Head, as the rotation system for headship had not yet been introduced. One of the lecturers, a female professor, was particularly effective in her teaching. A few of us would often visit her home in the early evening, where she lived with her parents, to clarify our doubts. I also had the liberty to enter her office in the department for further assistance, and she took special care to ensure I performed well in the examinations. As a result, I found myself paying less attention to the other lecturers. When the practical examinations arrived, we faced two dissections: one major and one minor. The internal examiner was from our department, while the external examiner came from other universities, often from different states. Typically, the external examiner selected the major dissections, while the internal examiner decided on the minor dissection. I had a fear of touching frogs, so before the practical examination,

I approached the internal examiner, a lecturer, and requested him to avoid assigning frogs for dissection. He assured me he would accommodate my request, but when the examination arrived, the minor dissection was again on frogs. It became evident to me that the internal examiner was not pleased with my request. Back then, scoring 60% to qualify for first class was quite difficult, as some examiners were very strict in their grading. The results were announced in June 1974, and I was delighted to find that most of my closest friends, including myself, had earned a first class. I remember achieving 65%, which made me quite happy.

When I returned to my native village, I received a warm welcome. My uncle came to the bus stop to greet me. I was the first person in my village, as well as in all the nearby villages, to earn a Master's degree, and I achieved it with first-class. Our house was located right in the middle of the village. I vividly remember the day I arrived home. My uncle sat with me on the tall verandah, and he called out to anyone passing by, proudly announcing that our son had passed his M.Sc. with first-class. However, my father seemed less enthusiastic. Perhaps he had higher expectations for me.

CHAPTER – 10

Research and Revival

After completing my Master's degree, the question arose: what next? Research was not a popular choice in Odisha at the time. Most of my classmates sought jobs. A couple of months later, I also began applying for various positions. In November 1974, a research fellowship was allotted to each department at the University, with a value of Rs 250 per month. The Zoology Department received one as well. My professor wrote to me, asking if I was interested in pursuing a Ph.D. After discussing with my father, who encouraged me, I decided to go for it.

    I travelled to Bhubaneswar to meet my professor and expressed my interest in conducting research under his guidance. He agreed and asked me to submit an application before returning home. I applied and went back to my village. A few days later, I received a letter to join as a Research Scholar in the Department of Zoology, Utkal University. I remember joining the department on 5th December 1974 and registering for my Ph.D. on 7th December 1974. I was the first Research Scholar in the Zoology Department at Utkal University on a regular basis. There were no provisions for hostel accommodation for research scholars, so I had to stay in a rented house in Bhubaneswar with two others. From 9 a.m. to 7 p.m. daily, I dedicated myself to my research on the biology of the maize aphid. Research was truly challenging in that environment. There were no computers, no internet, no calculators, not even an electronic typewriter. I frequently visited the libraries of Utkal University, the Agriculture University, and occasionally the Central Rice Research Institute in Cuttack. After six months, I was selected for a UGC research fellowship, which increased my fellowship to Rs 400 per month starting in July 1975. In August 1976, I was promoted to a UGC Senior Research Fellow with a fellowship of Rs 500 per month.

When I began my Ph.D., I had limited knowledge about my research area. One of my primary concerns was to quickly learn as much as possible. It seemed to me that there were two main ways to learn about science: reading related research papers and attending talks. As I mentioned earlier, there were no computers or emails at that time. We would purchase reprint request cards and use them to request various scientists to send us their publications. This was done solely via surface mail or airmail. Whenever new papers were published in my field, I would select a handful and request copies from the authors. Occasionally, I came across some very interesting papers, although, most of the time, the reading process was quite challenging. However, within a few months, I was able to pick up the subject quite well.

By 1976, the number of Research Scholars at the University had grown significantly, yet the University was still not providing hostel accommodation for us. Despite individual requests and representations, the administration did not seem to take any action. This led to the formation of the "Research Scholars' Association," and I was elected as the President, with Mr. D.C. Sahu (who later joined the Civil Service) from the Sociology Department serving as Vice President. We organized a meeting under the aegis of the Research Scholars' Association, inviting the Vice Chancellor and a few influential Professors, including my own. The Vice Chancellor inaugurated the association, and we presented our grievances in a composed and respectful manner. Fortunately, our requests were accepted. Within a week, a hostel was allotted to the Research Scholars, and we moved in. Each of us was provided with a single-occupancy room, allowing us to continue our research peacefully.

During the Emergency, declared in July 1975, Bhubaneswar remained peaceful, and we enjoyed a comfortable life at the University. Within a few months of joining as a research scholar, I had an interesting experience related to my hobby in astrology, which I have mentioned earlier. Although astrology was just a pastime for me, a few people at the University, including some officials, became aware of my interest. In the evenings, we would gather at the University canteen for a cup of tea, and during these informal meetings, people would often seek astrological advice from me.

Before the Emergency was declared, the Allahabad High Court delivered a historic judgment against the then Prime Minister. One evening, after the judgment, while we were at the canteen, people asked me what I thought would happen next. After some astrological analysis, I predicted, "The current Prime Minister will continue in power, regardless of the steps she may take." When the Emergency was subsequently declared, my popularity soared, and many more people became my admirers. A couple of years later, the Emergency was lifted, and elections were announced. Once again, people came to me for predictions about the election outcome. After some analysis, I told them that if the elections were held after August, the same government might return to power; otherwise, it would not. The elections took place around April, and the government changed. As a result, my fan base grew, and I became quite popular in Bhubaneswar, with many more people learning about me.

I was pursuing my research with great dedication. Aphids, also known as plant lice, are winged carriers of plant viruses. Since my research focused on the biology of the maize aphid, I planted maize and observed that the aphids would infest the plants after a certain period. I noticed a correlation between the timing of the infestations and the dates when the seeds were sown. Intriguingly, I also found a connection between the astronomical positions of the Sun and Moon and the aphid infestations. However, I chose not to pursue this line of study further, as astrology and science are traditionally viewed as contradictory fields. I didn't want to mix them, so I set aside my knowledge of astrology, keeping it as a hobby. While I never relied on astrology for myself, I would offer advice to anyone who approached me for astrological assistance, given my familiarity with the subject.

Ph.D. Student at Utkal university, 1976

When I joined as a research fellow at Utkal University, we had the same set of teachers: one Professor and four or five lecturers. During my Ph.D., the recruitment of Readers began in 1975, and Dr Priyambada Mohanty Hejmadi, who came from Michigan University, USA, joined as a Reader. Another candidate who was hoping for the position was not selected initially but was chosen in the next round. By 1976, the department had expanded to one Professor, two Readers, and four Lecturers, and research activities intensified, though most studies were still classical in nature. Modern biology had not yet become prominent in the department. Dr Hejmadi initiated some promising work in developmental biology, while the other Reader, who had completed his Ph.D. from BHU, led a group focused on classical endocrinology. Although I was a student of Prof. Behura, I maintained good relations with all the faculty members. Everyone was supportive, with Dr Hejmadi even helping me with the English editing of my research papers. However, the other Reader consistently criticized my activities, and to this day, I am unsure why. It could have been due to some unresolved issues with my supervisor.

During my Ph.D., I was unable to publish any research papers in international journals. However, I managed to publish around three to four papers in Indian and local journals. In fact, I didn't observe any significant publications from the department for a long time, except for one by Prof. Hejmadi in *Nature*.

In 1977, the Indian Science Congress was held in Bhubaneswar, with Dr H.N. Sethna serving as the General President. The Indian Science Congress Association, a scientific organization based in Kolkata, was established in 1914 and convenes annually in the first week of January. The 64th session of the Indian Science Congress took place at Utkal University, Bhubaneswar. Dr H.N. Sethna delivered his presidential address on "Survey, Conservation, and Utilization of Resources." As is customary, the Science Congress was inaugurated on January 3, 1977, by the then

Prime Minister. The Zoology Department was responsible for food and entertainment, and I was actively involved in organizing these activities. The entertainment programs were of very high quality, featuring a performance by Guru Kelu Charan Mohapatra in a dance drama about "Konark. " During this event, I had the opportunity to connect with many senior professors of Zoology from various universities. My guide, Professor Behura, was contesting in the election for the Sectional President of Zoology. The election results were announced on the last day of the conference, and I was pleased to learn that he won the election, securing the position of Sectional President of Zoology for the next Science Congress, scheduled to be held in Ahmedabad in January 1978.

The festive mood dissipated along with the conclusion of the Science Congress, and everyone returned to their regular work. During that time, Ph.D. scholars were permitted to teach post-graduate classes, and I was assigned courses in Evolution, Parasitology, and Entomology. I regularly conducted these classes and developed a friendly rapport with the students. I recall that we had a tea club in the department, where tea was prepared on a rotation basis, and everyone enjoyed taking breaks together. There was a particular M.Sc. student from 1975 to 1977 who stood out for her sincerity and meticulousness. Everyone admired her dedication. Each year, the department awarded a Memorial Prize to the student with the best seminar presentation, and she received this prize in 1976 or 1977 (I don't remember the exact year). I distinctly remember the day the award was presented and the sarcastic remark made by one faculty member in the presence of both the Professor and the student. In today's legal and societal standards, such a comment would be considered derogatory. I wondered how he could make such a comment and face no consequences. The faculty member's unhappiness toward the Professor was quite apparent to me at that time. I felt uncomfortable about the remark; perhaps I was a bit immature then. I glanced at my professor, who ignored the comment with a smile before returning to his office.

I accompanied my guide to Ahmedabad for the 65th Science Congress meeting, and we booked our tickets for the train. Many others from Odisha joined us, and we arrived in Ahmedabad on the morning of January 2, 1978. Accommodation was arranged for us, and we settled into our respective places of stay. We thoroughly enjoyed our time in Ahmedabad. At that time, the "Sunset Drive-In" cinema hall was a major attraction. This open-air theatre, established in 1973, was equipped with modern technical systems and featured the largest screen in Asia, capable of accommodating more than 600 cars and 6,000 people at a time. During our week-long stay, we dedicated one day to watching the movie *Parvarish*, which had just been released. We enjoyed both the film and the unique ambience of the open-air theater. That experience marked my first and last visit to such a venue. We left Ahmedabad for Bhubaneswar on January 8, 1978.

At the beginning of 1978, my Ph.D. work was nearing completion, but my thesis required some statistical analysis. Unfortunately, there was no statistician available in Bhubaneswar, so I was sent to the Central Rice Research Institute in Cuttack for assistance. There, I had to learn basic statistics, photomicrography, and Camera Lucida drawings for my research. I began writing my thesis and completed it by early 1978, but my guide wanted to review it only after it was typed. At that time, there were no computers or electronic typewriters. The cost for typing was half a rupee per page, which was quite significant back then. Affording the typing costs was challenging, especially since the thesis needed to be retyped after every correction until the final version was ready. As a result, I decided to learn typing on a manual typewriter. After typing my own thesis, I handed it over to my guide for correction. The heads of departments were typically very busy, so my guide took my thesis with him while traveling by train to Calcutta for Ph.D. examinations. After some time, he returned with corrections and asked me to make the final typescript for submission. I went to Cuttack to print all the photographs related to my work and purchased the appropriate bond paper for typing my thesis, along with new carbon paper to type four copies simultaneously. We were required to submit three copies to the university and keep one personal copy for ourselves. I completed all the necessary work and finally submitted three bound volumes to the university in June 1978, as per the rules at that time. I still had my fellowship for a few more months, so I continued working in the department. Later, I learned that one copy of my thesis was sent to the Director of the Forest Research Institute in Canada, and another was sent to the Professor and Head of Zoology at Bodhgaya University. Since there were no emails, faxes, or speed posts at that time, all correspondence with examiners was done by regular post, which could take around a year or sometimes even longer for the Viva Voce examination after the thesis submission.

Early disappointment and frustration

While pursuing my Ph.D. at Utkal University (1974-1978), other Ph.D. students joined, including a few under my guide. In 1977, there was an advertisement for a Research Assistant position in the Department of Zoology. At that time, we had no guidance, and securing a job was our top priority. I applied for the position, as did another Ph.D. student who was junior to me but under the same guide. Many believed, including myself, that my professor valued my hard work and sincerity. When the interview calls for the Research Assistant position came, I felt confident and performed well during the interview. Everyone at the university expected me to be selected, and I was sure of my chances. However, after a few days, the appointment letter arrived, and to my dismay, it was awarded to the other student from my department. I was crestfallen and very sad, feeling as though my world had collapsed. I left Bhubaneswar and returned to my village, where I shared everything with my father and uncle, a respected Sanskrit Pandit. My father reassured me, saying, "You have come to pursue your Ph.D. Your priority should be to complete it first. Who knows, something better may be in store for you." My uncle echoed this sentiment. Encouraged by their support, I returned to Bhubaneswar and continued my research. Shortly after, the other student who had been selected joined as a Research Assistant.

    Now I realize how right my father was and how powerful time can be. Time is indeed the best deciding factor and never betrays. The boy who joined as a Research Assistant ultimately retired in the same position.

CHAPTER – 11

The Keonjhar Project

In early 1978, the Indian Council of Medical Research (ICMR) launched extensive field operational research projects on malaria in several sensitive sites across India, including one in Andhra Pradesh, two in Gujarat, and one along the Orissa/Bihar border complex. The National Malaria Eradication Programme (NMEP) served as the executing agency, with the Regional Director of NMEP in Orissa overseeing the projects in Andhra Pradesh and Orissa/Bihar. They advertised two posts for Research Officers, requiring a first-class M.Sc. in Zoology, preferably with a Ph.D. By that time, I had already submitted my Ph.D. thesis, so I applied for the position. I received a call letter to appear for a written test in the first week of July 1978, where I performed exceptionally well, ranking first among all candidates. The two available positions were for Orissa and Andhra Pradesh. The individual who came second had political connections and was attempting to secure the posting in Orissa. I met the Regional Director, the late Dr A.K. Guha, and explained that I had submitted my thesis and was awaiting my Ph.D. viva examination, which could occur anytime. For my academic interests, I requested a posting in Orissa, and he agreed. We were asked to join on

August 16, 1978, and all of us reported for duty. Shortly after joining, we were sent to the National Institute of Communicable Diseases (NICD) in Delhi for three months of practical training. I received my train tickets and had to travel the next day. Since there was no direct train from Bhubaneswar to Delhi at that time, I travelled via Calcutta, taking a train from Bhubaneswar to Howrah, and then another train from Howrah to Delhi. I arrived at Delhi railway station on the night of August 20, 1978. This was my first visit to Delhi. From the railway station, I went to the NICD hostel, where my accommodation was arranged, and I found it comfortable. The next day, I reported for training, which was sponsored by the WHO, with the late Dr B.L. Wattal overseeing the program. There were around 20 candidates from all over India participating in the training. The training was rigorous, and the last few days included field training at the NICD field station in Alwar, Rajasthan. We travelled to Alwar by bus and stayed at a youth hostel there. Dr S.J. Rahman, one of the faculty members, prepared excellent biryani, which we all thoroughly enjoyed. We learned various techniques in the field. After returning to NICD from the field training, we faced an examination followed by a viva conducted by Dr Wattal. When he discovered that my Ph.D. thesis was on aphids, he asked me about the similarities between aphids and vectors. I responded, "Aphids are also vectors of plant viral diseases." He was pleased with my answer and revealed that he had also completed his Ph.D. on aphids. I was later informed that I had achieved the highest marks in the training.

Dr S. Pattanayak, the Director of the National Malaria Eradication Programme (NMEP) in Delhi, explained the origins and objectives of the project. India has a long history of being endemic to malaria, marked by both successes and failures. At the time of independence, the country faced approximately ten million malaria cases, resulting in around 800,000 deaths. The implementation of the National Malaria Control Programme, followed by the NMEP, led to significant successes, drastically reducing malaria cases by the 1960s and achieving zero deaths due to malaria. However, the program became complacent over time, leading to a dilution of control activities. This complacency resulted in a resurgence of malaria, which peaked in 1976 with six million cases and numerous fatalities. In response, the Government of India initiated the Modified Plan of Operation (MPO), focusing primarily on research. Despite a significant reduction in malaria, the disease persisted in six endemic pockets, which later contributed to its resurgence. These pockets were located in Gujarat, Andhra Pradesh, and the Orissa/Bihar border area. Consequently, the Government of India initiated field operational research projects to investigate the causes of persistent malaria transmission in these specific localities.

After completing our training, we returned to Bhubaneswar in November 1978. The project focused on the Orissa/Bihar border complex, with its office to be established in Keonjhar, Odisha. The following day, I was dispatched to Keonjhar. By that time, the National Malaria Eradication Programme (NMEP) had already recruited 80 staff members for the project, including Assistant Research Officers (AROs), laboratory technicians, and field assistants. Two vehicles were allocated for our use. Upon arriving in Keonjhar, I stayed in a government rest house arranged for me and rented a house to serve as the project office. The project commenced immediately, covering two blocks: *Jhumpura* and *Bhanda*, which together encompassed

316 villages and a population of approximately 135,000 in 1978. The project kicked off with full momentum, though studying mosquito behaviour in tribal areas presented significant challenges. I established two sub-offices—one in *Jhumpura* and another in *Champua*, the locality bordering Bihar—with the main project office located in Keonjhar.

Keonjhar was a princely state in Odisha, situated on an upland plateau and bordered to the west and south by low hills. The main river flowing through the region is the *Baitarani*, while the prominent mountain is *Gandhamardan*. Historically known as *Keonjhargarh* when it was a princely state, Keonjhar in 1978 was renowned for its natural beauty. After a few days of my arrival in Keonjhar, word spread about my hobby of astrology. Mr. Bhanj Deo, the younger brother of the king of Keonjhar Garh, who resided in a palace near the circuit house, became a friend. Despite being quite old at that time, we began to meet every alternate evening when I was in Keonjhar. He also possessed considerable knowledge of astrology, and our discussions over a cup of tea often revolved around this shared interest. I had the pleasure of enjoying royal dinners at his house. Frequently, he would travel to his in-laws' home in Dewas, Madhya Pradesh. Nearby Keonjhar town, there were scenic picnic spots such as *Sana Ghagara* and *Bada Ghagara*. *Sana Ghagara*, which means "small waterfall," is particularly enchanting. It stands out as one of the top places to visit in Odisha, allowing visitors to appreciate the resplendent side of nature.

I was a bachelor living alone in a rented house in Keonjhar. Within a few months, I made several friends in the area, despite the fact that I was busy with work. We typically worked from Monday to Saturday, and on Sundays, people would come to me for astrological assistance. I joined as a

Research Officer (now Scientist-B) in August 1978 and was promoted to Senior Research Officer (now Scientist-C) in September 1979.

In 1978-79, the Government of India received a significant grant from Sweden to combat *Plasmodium falciparum* malaria, leading to the launch of the *Plasmodium falciparum* containment programme (PfCP). A medical officer was assigned to each district in Odisha under this initiative. The World Health Organization (WHO) also sent a scientist from the USA, Mr. Collins, to Odisha for the PfCP. He was staying in Bhubaneswar. Prior to his arrival in Odisha, he had been working in the Philippines, where he married a Filipino woman. He and his wife lived in the *Bhimtangi* area of Bhubaneswar. Soon, we became friends, and he often invited me to his house for dinner. On several occasions, he visited Keonjhar and was impressed with our work. Dr Orlov and Dr Kondrashin from Russia also visited the Keonjhar project, which had gained significant popularity. As a result, any delegation coming to study malaria in India was directed to Keonjhar to observe our project. I was frequently invited to Delhi to present our work to various committees and delegations.

Keonjhar is situated within the *Singhbhum-Keonjhar-Banei* iron belt and is rich in mineral resources. The regions around Joda and Barbil in Keonjhar district boast some of the largest deposits of iron ore and manganese ore in the world. These areas serve as significant sources of revenue for both the central and state governments. In addition to their economic importance, Barbil is surrounded by breathtaking natural scenery. Despite these advantages, however, it was still regarded as a backward district, heavily affected by malaria.

As previously mentioned, our project area primarily

included the tribal population of Keonjhar district. During our fieldwork in the Champua area, we stayed in the Revenue Inspection Bungalow (IB) at Champua, which is located near the border with Bihar. The river separating Orissa and Bihar is situated close to Champua, and there is a bridge that connects the two states. The Orissa government maintains one half of the bridge, while the Bihar government is responsible for the other half. Occasionally, we would cross to the other side of the bridge to assess the malaria situation in Bihar. Among the tribals of Keonjhar, the Ho and Juang dances are particularly popular. The Ho Dance is performed by the Ho-speaking tribe, while the Juang Dance is performed by the Juang tribe of the district. We had the opportunity to witness these vibrant tribal dance forms.

After working hard for about a month, we decided to unwind by watching some movies. There was a primitive cinema hall in Keonjhar town, but for a better experience, we would travel to Jamshedpur, which was 180 km away. Once every month or two, we would go to Jamshedpur on a Saturday evening, stay in a hotel, and watch a movie at the famous Nataraj Cinema. Our first film at Nataraj Cinema was *Noorie* in 1979. We would then return to Keonjhar early Sunday morning.

CHAPTER – 12

The Wedlock

While I was working in Keonjhar, my parents and uncle began searching for a suitable girl for my marriage and were about to finalize a match. At that time, I wasn't serious about marriage and was trying to avoid it. By 1980, however, I found myself quite comfortable in the company of Vijaylakshmi, who had received the memorial prize in the Zoology Department (as mentioned in Chapter 10) and was five years younger than me. Our connection likely began in 1977, although I was very shy and socially awkward back then. I managed to exchange a few hellos that year. The next time I encountered her was in August 1978 while traveling to Delhi via Calcutta. To be honest, I don't remember much of our brief conversation. In early 1979, she received a fellowship at Utkal University and moved to Bhubaneswar to pursue her Ph.D. Interestingly, she registered under the same guide with whom I had completed my Ph.D. At that time, I was in Keonjhar but frequently visited my office in Bhubaneswar. During those visits, I would often stop by the Zoology department to catch up with some old friends, which allowed me to become friendlier with her. As we spent more time together, our bond grew stronger. I felt a connection with her that I couldn't explain, one that was different from my interactions with others in our friend group. Eventually, as our relationship progressed, we decided to marry. This led to complications, as I came from an orthodox Brahmin family in a remote area, while she belonged to a well-established Brahmin family; her father was the Director General of Police in Odisha. My parents and uncle continued to pressure me about marriage. Knowing my father was a progressive person, I decided to visit my village and express my desire to marry Vijaylakshmi, explaining her background. There was a deafening silence in the room. My uncle advised me to forget about her and go ahead with the proposal they had arranged. My father, however, remained silent on the matter. I returned to Bhubaneswar, then back to Keonjhar. Meanwhile, Vijaylakshmi's parents learned of my intentions. The Superintendent of Police in Keonjhar visited my office and spent an hour with me, trying to gather details about my background. Additionally, Vijaylakshmi's father reached out to Prof. Behura, my Ph.D. guide, seeking information about me. Although I had a good relationship with Prof. Behura and his family, I never understood why he spoke negatively about me. He acknowledged that I was a good person but claimed I was not a suitable match for Vijaylakshmi.

As I mentioned earlier, I always wore white attire since my graduation days. In late 1981, Vijaylakshmi gifted me a pair of pants and a pink shirt. When I hesitated to accept them, she assured me that they were purchased with her fellowship money. After that, I began to incorporate coloured clothing into my wardrobe.

A few days later, Vijaylakshmi called to inform me that her father wanted to meet with me. She arranged an appointment for my next visit to Bhubaneswar. Since the

Police Headquarters for Odisha was located in Cuttack, I travelled there to meet him. I don't recall the exact date or day, but I went straight to the headquarters and had a brief discussion with him. Ultimately, he advised me to forget about his daughter and wished me well. I didn't react and simply returned home. After informing Vijaylakshmi about the outcome of my meeting, I went back to Keonjhar. I remained silent for some time, focusing on the work for the Keonjhar project, which was at a crucial stage as we were gathering very important scientific data.

Time passed, and after a couple of months, I received a call from an IPS officer in Cuttack whom I knew. During my next visit to Bhubaneswar, I went to meet him in his office. He suggested that I meet Vijaylakshmi's mother and offered me his car for the visit. I went to Vijaylakshmi's house on Cantonment Road in Cuttack, where I met her mother. She primarily inquired about my family. They had learned about Dr Sudhakar Acharya, a practicing doctor from our village who was active in politics at that time. Vijaylakshmi's father also contacted late Dr Acharya to ask about me, but I'm unaware of what he said. My horoscope was examined and shown to several pandits in Puri, who strongly recommended the marriage. After a few days, her parents agreed to this. According to our traditions at that time, the boy's family was required to send a proposal to the girl's family to proceed further. Thus, they insisted that my parents should send the proposal first. I returned to my village and spoke to my parents and uncle about it. My elder brother, who was working in western Odisha at that time, was not available in the village. Although my uncle continued to discourage me from pursuing this marriage, my father wrote a letter to Vijaylakshmi's father and sent it through a friend of mine, the late Pitambar Mohanty, who lived in Cuttack. Vijaylakshmi's parents then invited my family to visit their home. My elder brother was called back and came home on leave. One evening in February 1982, my father, uncle, and elder brother visited their house, and everything was finalized. An engagement ceremony was necessary before the marriage. My father was born on *Akshaya Tritiya,* so the engagement took place on *Akshaya Tritiya,* April 25, 1982, in a temple in Bhubaneswar. Our marriage was held on May 31, 1982.

May was typically the hottest month in Odisha. Fortunately, the auspicious time for our wedding was set for the morning. The *Baraat* arrived early, and the ceremony concluded by lunchtime. The reception in the evening was quite crowded, with Justice G.K. Mishra, the retired Chief Justice of Odisha and many Ministers, in attendance. Justice Mishra was a classmate of my father, and they had not seen each other in a long time. Justice Mishra took my father and introduced him to his family members. Although many guests attended the reception, Professor Behura was notably absent; perhaps he and his family chose to avoid it. After the wedding, we moved to Dhenkanal for a few days before relocating to Keonjhar, where I was working. At that time, my salary was Rs 2,000, which I handed over entirely to my wife, as I was not a good manager of money. This amount was sufficient for both of us, especially since everything was quite affordable in Keonjhar. My family from the village sent a boy to work for us at home. We paid him only Rs 50 per month, including food, and he was very happy with this arrangement. In August 1982, I took a few days of leave, and we travelled to Delhi, where I booked a room at the NICD guesthouse. However, my wife was not pleased with the accommodations. The next day, we moved to Jaipur and then to Agra before returning to Keonjhar via

Bhubaneswar. During our time in Delhi, there was a dengue outbreak in 1982. Upon our return, my wife contracted dengue and had to stay in Cuttack for treatment. I went back to Keonjhar, and a few days later, I also fell ill with fever, most likely due to dengue as well. Unfortunately, there was no way to diagnose dengue in Keonjhar at that time. The Superintendent of Police in Keonjhar was kind enough to take care of me during my recovery, which took some time.

Marriage on 31st May 1982 at Cuttack. With wife and in-laws after marriage

My son was born in April 1983. My father-in-law named him "Anjan," and my mother-in-law affectionately called him "Raja." Over the next few years, we experienced a mix of ups and downs, but we faced everything together. At the time of his birth, our son had a colon problem, which necessitated treatment at the All India Institute of Medical Sciences (AIIMS) in New Delhi. My younger brother-in-law, who was pursuing his Master's in Surgery, accompanied us, along with my nephew, who was doing his MD in paediatrics. Dr Upadhyay, the Professor and Head of Paediatric Surgery, performed the surgery. We were informed that the entire procedure would require three surgeries since our son was only three months old. Both my wife and I were in psychological turmoil, but my wife lost her happiness and smile the most. Each day was spent in agony. After the first operation, we returned home, but a few months later, we had to go back to AIIMS, Delhi for the second operation, which was successfully completed. During that time, we faced considerable expenses, and I had to borrow money from friends. That was still not enough. When my wife was pursuing her Ph.D., she saved her entire fellowship to book a small house in Bhubaneswar. After our marriage, the house was ready and handed over to us. It was a modest dwelling on a comparatively larger piece of land. However, due to our financial situation, we had to sell the house for a marginal amount of twenty or thirty thousand rupees. Now, when I visit that place, I see a grand palatial building in its place.

Marriage marks a new beginning in one's life, a fresh start filled with special moments and new experiences. Couples enter this phase with many expectations and dreams for a happy future together. Typically, after marriage, couples save to acquire a home. However, our situation was different. My elder brother also supported me financially during this time. We were advised by AIIMS that the third operation could be performed in Cuttack by Dr Saifullah, a competent surgeon. We followed this recommendation and successfully completed the operation in Cuttack. Gradually, our son began to recover.

The Keonjhar project concluded on 31st August 1983. By that time, the Regional Medical Research Centre (RMRC) had been established in Bhubaneswar, and I joined RMRC on 1st September 1983. Before the project ended, two of the project staff joined the Malaria Research Centre's field unit in Gujarat, while the rest took various positions with the State Government. I arrived in Bhubaneswar on the night of

31st August and started my tenure at RMRC the next day. The foundation stone of RMRC, Bhubaneswar, was laid in 1981 by the late Mrs. Indira Gandhi, then Prime Minister of India. The Government of Orissa initially offered 100 acres of land for RMRC, but the management opted for only ten acres. When I joined RMRC, two other scientists had already come on board: Dr Santosh Kar, who arrived from JNU, New Delhi, and Dr Shantanu K. Kar, who transferred from an ICMR institute in Ahmedabad. At that time, RMRC operated from a rented house in Acharya Vihar, with three scientists, including myself. We later moved to the State's Drugs Controller's office building temporarily before relocating to our own RMRC campus in Chandrasekharpur. After joining RMRC, we approached the Government of Orissa in 1983 to request additional land for the Research Centre. Unfortunately, the initial land proposed for RMRC had been allotted to another organization, but after much effort, we secured an additional ten acres, bringing the total to 20 acres. Dr S.P. Tripathy, Director of the Tuberculosis Research Centre (now the National Institute for Research in Tuberculosis) in Chennai, served as the Director in charge of RMRC, Bhubaneswar. He later became Deputy Director General, Additional Director General, and eventually Director General of the Indian Council of Medical Research (ICMR) in 1991. He continued as the Director in charge of RMRC, Bhubaneswar, until February 1985, when Late Prof. L.N. Mohapatra, then Professor of Microbiology and Dean at the All India Institute of Medical Sciences (AIIMS), New Delhi, took over as Director of RMRC. At that time, late Prof. V. Ramalingaswamy was the Director General of ICMR.

My wife stayed with her parents in Cuttack with our small child, while I was living in the Utkal University guest house and occasionally in Cuttack. A couple of months later, my in-laws moved to their house in Bhubaneswar, and I began staying there for a while. My wife's elder brother, who had been in Hong Kong, returned around 1984. In the meantime, I arranged for a rented house near Utkal University, and we moved there in early 1984. My younger brother stayed with us for some time, and my father frequently visited. The house was often crowded, and we were not financially well off. We always had a boy helping us around the house. At that time, I had a scooter. Since my wife was expecting, my father-in-law would come every afternoon to take my son to their house. We would ride the scooter in the evening to bring him back.

My daughter was born in November 1984 at Cuttack Medical College. By 1985, managing two small children became really challenging for us. I was busy in my laboratory and office, often going out for fieldwork. From the beginning, I was a workaholic. Additionally, I had little understanding of how to care for young children. I'm not sure if I was avoiding responsibility or simply not ready for it. My wife suffered the most - she had left her job long ago to take care for the children. As I mentioned, my wife was pursuing her Ph.D. at Utkal University under the same guide, Prof. Behura, who had not recommended our marriage and did not attend our wedding. After our marriage, he became hostile towards her, which hindered her progress in obtaining her Ph.D. After a couple of years, we approached him for assistance with her thesis. Eventually, she submitted her thesis and earned her Ph.D. degree in 1985.

The residential quarters on the RMRC campus were completed by 1986, and we moved into our official residence in October of that year. However, the construction of the RMRC office and laboratories faced delays, as the buildings were being constructed by the State Public Works Department. At that time, Late Mr J.B. Pattanayak was the Chief Minister, and Mr Niranjan Pattanayak, a known acquaintance from my time in Keonjhar, was the Health Minister. The Director of RMRC and I discussed how to expedite the construction process. Together, we met with the Health Minister, who promptly called a meeting with high-ranking officials. Following this meeting, construction resumed at full speed, and the buildings were completed. We officially began working from the campus in 1988 or 1989.

CHAPTER – 13

The Field Days

For anyone considering a career as a research scientist, it's essential to understand the personal qualities and professional qualifications that will contribute to success. While strong research and analytical skills are crucial, excellent communication and presentation abilities are equally important. Additionally, a capacity for teaching can be beneficial. Pursuing a career as a research scientist can be one of the most fulfilling and life-affirming experiences. However, I struggled with communication skills, and my research area required collecting biological samples from the field. I focused on parasitic and vector-borne diseases, particularly because Odisha has been endemic for significant vector-borne diseases such as malaria, lymphatic filariasis, and dengue. To address these challenges, I established the Department of Medical Entomology and Parasitology at RMRC Bhubaneswar. Shortly thereafter, technical staff were sanctioned and recruited to support our efforts. During this time, late Prof. L.N. Mohapatra served as the Director of RMRC, and Dr S.P. Tripathy was the Senior Deputy Director General of ICMR. By then, Prof. Ramalingaswamy had retired, and Late Prof. A.S. Paintal had taken over as the Director General of ICMR.

I worked as a scientist at the Regional Medical Research Centre (RMRC) in Bhubaneswar, where I established the Department of Medical Entomology and Parasitology from the ground up. The institute was headed by a director, primarily a medical professional who had limited understanding of basic biology and field biology. At that time, there were five RMRCs under the Indian Council of Medical Research (ICMR), and all their directors held medical degrees. This was a longstanding convention within the ICMR. While I had supportive colleagues who were basic scientists, I often found myself in uncomfortable situations. I was actively seeking an opportunity that would define my career and life. Eventually, I discovered a place where I could move forward and reshape myself into the person I aspired to be.

CHAPTER – 14

Shaping the Scientist

No, it was not some outstanding position which was to redefine my life, it was a shaping phase, and I am what and who I am are based on these experiences. I was "happily" married, or so I think. Everyone knows the ultimate family dream, a loving wife, two children, a decent house and a secure job.

I was sending my technical staff to field for collection of mosquitoes. At that time suction tubes were used and one had to use the mouth to collect the mosquitoes. I procured some mechanical aspirators from USA which were used by batteries. Another scientist who was very forceful in nature demanded mechanical aspirators and the Director diverted some of my mechanical aspirator to him. I objected. But the Director was helpless. I felt lost and frustrated a lot of times while working in lab especially at the start of my research studentship. Later I accepted these realities because I realized that these feelings are normal in a research environment. I continued my work with my team.

In early 1988, the RMRC advertised a position for a research officer, specifically created for my department. At the time, I didn't realize that a senior official at headquarters had established this post to accommodate someone from his hometown. In those days, creating new positions was relatively easy, as the Director General of ICMR had the authority to do so until around 1988. My wife, who was more than qualified for this role, expressed her desire to apply. However, I discouraged her, believing that the research environment within the ICMR was not favourable at that time. Eventually, her father convinced me of her potential, and she decided to apply.

The Director appointed me as a member of the shortlisting committee alongside two other scientists. I approached the Director personally, requesting to be removed from the committee since my wife was an applicant. He reassured me, saying, "It's just to check eligibility, and you can be there." Despite my request, he did not remove me. However, during the shortlisting process, I recused myself, citing my wife's candidacy. Those records should still be available at RMRC. The interview took place in mid-June 1988, and I later learned that my wife had been selected. The high official from ICMR who had created this position for someone from his hometown also chaired the selection committee, representing the DG of ICMR. The news of my wife's selection quickly circulated among my colleagues. Until that point, I was unaware of the concept of professional jealousy. Some colleagues, who I considered close friends, began to express jealousy over her selection, discussing among themselves, "We should ask our wives to apply for jobs here too." When professional jealousy exists in the workplace, gossip often follows, creating a toxic environment. It felt like I was caught in a battlefield of negative emotions and animosity. This jealousy crept in slowly, sitting beside me silently until I returned home, puzzled by the sense of dissatisfaction that lingered within me.

Soon, an anonymous letter reached the ICMR headquarters, prompting a swift response from a few officials. An inquiry was initiated, with a Senior DDG (Admn.) overseeing it; she was an IAS officer. After the investigation, she recommended my wife's appointment. However, her recommendation was rejected by senior management, at the instance of one senior officer, who was a member of the selection committee. In response, we approached the High Court of Orissa. During this tumultuous period, ICMR became increasingly hostile toward me. The case progressed through multiple hearings, with late Prof. Mohapatra serving as the Director of RMRC. My colleagues advised him to hire a powerful advocate. Consequently, ICMR appointed a costly attorney, disregarding all government norms under the guise of being an autonomous body. The case was heard by a Division Bench of two judges. One of the judges appeared to be particularly biased against us. To make matters worse, the main accused in the case was removed from the list of defendants without our knowledge. It seemed that our advocate might have been influenced by the opposing counsel, as several crucial documents were not presented before the Bench. The case dragged on for a year, and we incurred significant expenses. Finally, in May 1989, the judgment was delivered, and we lost the case. The verdict was unsatisfactory, leading me to lose faith in the judiciary. We felt utterly defeated—not solely due to my wife's job loss, but because of the overt injustice we faced. The root of the problem lay in our outdated and dogmatic system, which was exacerbated by conservative technocrats within scientific organizations.

We decided to approach the Supreme Court and sought the assistance of a Supreme Court advocate from Orissa. We met him at his residence in Cuttack during one of his visits from Delhi. After reviewing our case, he expressed that it was strong and encouraged us to proceed. We engaged him, providing all necessary documents and the required fees. The case was officially filed, with an initial hearing scheduled for November 16, 1990. Once again, the case was presented before a Division Bench, and ICMR retained a formidable senior advocate for the proceedings. I recall that a group of administrative officers from ICMR was present in the courtroom that day. Accompanied by a friend who offered moral support, I attended the hearing. The case was disposed of with a speaking order, stipulating that the post needed to be re-advertised and that my wife, as the petitioner, should be given an opportunity to interview for any future vacancies. However, ICMR was adept at manipulating court judgments. In the meantime, my father-in-law recognized the toxic environment at ICMR and advised my wife to seek opportunities elsewhere. He also encouraged me to leave that unpleasant atmosphere and join a different organization. Eventually, my wife secured a position as a Lecturer in Zoology at Kamla Nehru Women's College in Bhubaneswar. Gradually, she moved on from her aspirations regarding ICMR, content to know that her husband was still working there. Despite the Supreme Court's ruling, ICMR did not consider my wife for any future vacancies. However, we chose not to raise any complaints, as my wife was happy in her teaching role.

It is important to highlight how ICMR managed the Supreme Court judgment during that period. My first Ph.D. student, a young woman, applied for a job at RMRC, Jodhpur, and requested my assistance. Given the challenging atmosphere at ICMR, I expressed my inability to help her directly but advised her to meet with a high official from Orissa, who was the Additional Director General of ICMR at that time, in Delhi. After meeting the official, she travelled to Jodhpur and was selected as a Research Officer at Desert Medicine Research Centre (DMRC), Jodhpur. A few months later, she married another scientist who was already working there and also hailed from the same hometown as the Additional DG. Both of them then approached the Additional DG for a transfer to their home institute, RMRC, Bhubaneswar. At that time, ICMR institutes in various states were regarded as "kitchen gardens" by some high officials in Delhi, and transfers resembled a game of chess. I happened to be in Delhi for official work when I was summoned by the Additional DG and was informed that the Research Officer from Jodhpur is transferred to Bhubaneswar against the vacant position in RMRC, Bhubaneswar. Within a couple of days, both the husband and wife were transferred to RMRC, Bhubaneswar, effectively sealing the position. Despite my wife's lack of interest in ICMR, I couldn't help but reflect on what kind of *"Guru Dakshina"* I received from my Ph.D. student. This was against the order of Hon'ble Supreme Court, which had directed the post to be advertised and my wife to be considered. However, the post was instead filled through lateral entry.

In those days, there was no concrete promotion policy in the ICMR, unlike the CSIR. Promotions were assessed irregularly. Although the rule stipulated that each scientist would be assessed for the next position every five years, some assessments were delayed by seven or eight years, depending on when the ICMR decided to conduct evaluations. I joined RMRC, Bhubaneswar, in 1983 but had to wait seven years for my assessment to Assistant Director. From 1991 onwards, the assessment process was streamlined, and I received my next promotion to Deputy Director exactly five years later.

CHAPTER – 15

Surge of the Scientist

The ICMR's Malaria Research Centre (MRC) in Delhi was gaining prominence under the leadership of Dr V.P. Sharma. In 1984, while I was serving as the Senior Research Officer at RMRC, Bhubaneswar, MRC advertised two Assistant Director positions. I applied and was shortlisted for the interview. However, I learned that there were two internal candidates, Dr Sarla Subbarao and Dr Ansari, for whom the positions seemed to be intended. Consequently, I chose not to attend the interview. Later, late Dr Sriramachari, the Chairman of the selection committee, who was confident of my selection, expressed his disappointment and anger at my decision. I felt regretful at the time, but in hindsight, it seems that someone up there had already scripted my life's path.

In 1991, Dr. S.P. Tripathy, who hailed from Odisha, became the Director-General of ICMR. Up until 1993, I remained largely unsatisfied with my experience at ICMR. Despite this, I am inherently optimistic—my sorrows and disappointments never linger because I always look forward to the next great moment. I also forgive easily. During this time, I received the Dr T.R. Rao Award from ICMR for outstanding contributions to vector-borne diseases, which recognized young scientists below 40 years. In 1993, I applied for a WHO grant and was awarded substantial funding for a major project. This initiative involved two vehicles and approximately 80 staff members, focusing on field operational research to assess the efficacy of *Bacillus sphaericus* against lymphatic filariasis and its vectors. The project took place in the Khurda and Pipili areas, with daily data collection and sample transfers to the RMRC laboratory for further analysis. Despite facing extreme jealousy from some colleagues, I pressed on, and the project ran smoothly, attracting many visitors, including international experts from WHO. One of the notable visits was from Dr. Utton Raffaie, the Regional Director of the WHO South-East Asia Region, who was highly impressed by our work. He was accompanied by Dr Palitha Abeykoon, Director of Family and Health Research at WHO (SEARO). I invited them both to my home for a simple dinner, where Dr Raffaie even played with my children. Back then, appreciation for good work in India was rare unless it came from foreigners, so their positive feedback helped me build connections with many national and international scientists. Dr V.P. Sharma, Director of the Malaria Research Centre (MRC), also took an interest in my work. Whenever I was in Delhi, I would visit MRC, and gradually, I got to know the then adviser in the Department of Biotechnology. I was invited to their home for dinner on several occasions. Since *Bacillus sphaericus* was effective against mosquitoes, especially *Culex*, I would often discuss my data with Dr Sharma. Our good relationship dated back to 1980s. On one occasion, he was sent from Delhi to persuade my wife and me to withdraw a court case, which my wife filed.

In the early 1990s, then Adviser, Department of Biotechnology faced significant harassment from a Joint Secretary named Mr. Kapoor during the Congress Government's tenure. Her family asked me, since I was very close to them and I intervened through a minister I knew in Odisha, who was close to the then Minister of Science & Technology, Mr. Bhubanesh Chaturvedi. The matter was resolved, though my role in the process went unacknowledged. It did not bother me. In 1996, BJP briefly came to power for few days with late Mr. A.B. Vajpayee as Prime Minister, during which time the same adviser was appointed Secretary of DBT. At the time, the retirement age for government servants was 58, and she was due to retire in February 1998. However, she received a two-year extension, and when the government increased the retirement age to 60 in April 2000 (and to 62 for scientific secretaries), her tenure was extended until February 2002, followed by another extension until February 2004. I continued to maintain a close relationship with them and enjoyed meeting the family whenever I was in Delhi. Further details will be covered in the following pages.

A new DG (hailed from Odisha) served ICMR from September 1991 to March 1994. Despite some initial tension due to the court case my wife filed, he gradually returned to normal interactions with me. Soon after becoming DG, he expressed an interest in sending me abroad on a fellowship, though this plan did not come to fruition. During this period, RMRC underwent several leadership changes. Prof. L.N. Mohapatra retired in 1985, and Dr M.S. Dash took over as Emeritus Medical Scientist and Officer-in-Charge for more than a year. Following him, Dr Krishnamachari, who was previously Officer-in-Charge at the Desert Medicine Research Centre, Jodhpur, was appointed as Director of RMRC, Bhubaneswar. His wife, Dr Rajalaxmi, also a scientist, transferred to Bhubaneswar from Jodhpur. Dr

Krishnamachari took a keen interest in my work and often visited my lab for discussions, showing appreciation for my research and Ph.D. students. However, he faced issues with ICMR by 1992; his wife resigned to join the British Council office in Bhubaneswar, and shortly thereafter, Dr Krishnamachari himself resigned to join the British Council in Hyderabad. Following his resignation, a colleague senior to me was appointed as Officer-in-Charge of RMRC. Around that time, then Director of RMRC in Dibrugarh, sought a transfer to Bhubaneswar due to unresolved problems at his former location. His transfer happened rapidly. He had a distinct personality, and soon after his arrival, he noticed the two new vehicles associated with my WHO project. This drew his attention, and my envious colleagues quickly formed an alliance with him, leading to challenges for me and my project. The new Director's attempts to undermine my work were unexpected, as I had not anticipated that professional jealousy could escalate to the level of a director. He tried various tactics but did not succeed. At one point, he halted my salary increment, prompting me to directly address the issue with the DG, ICMR, in his presence. The DG intervened, advising him against taking such unauthorized actions. Subsequently, this director and I developed a friendship. Meanwhile, a colleague alleged to be close to the DG received a significant promotion to Director of another ICMR Research Institute. This career advancement was surprising to many, given its magnitude.

During the court case, while we were enduring a traumatic period, my wife encouraged me to pursue a D.Sc. degree. I was torn about the decision, as we were not financially strong and were already overwhelmed by the court case and our son's medical issues. However, I didn't want to reach a point where I felt incompetent. I needed motivation, and there was no one to provide it except my wife. Her encouragement was crucial at that time. I had to grow and learn simultaneously, so I began to assess my strengths and weaknesses. I realized that motivation is the driving force in life. It represents the inner urge to act, the will to achieve, and a passion for success—traits that distinguish a winner. For those lacking motivation, life becomes a burden. I found that one can inspire oneself through self-awareness, setting meaningful goals, understanding life's purpose, embracing a love for work and life, maintaining positive thinking, and developing an optimistic outlook. If life is a vehicle, motivation serves as the fuel that powers it, and in my life, my wife was that fuel. With her support, I reshaped my lifestyle. I decided to pursue my D.Sc. while engaging in various official activities. At that point, I viewed activity as life itself, and inactivity as a kind of death.

I registered for a D.Sc. degree in Zoology at Utkal University, focusing on the transmission biology of vector-borne diseases in Orissa. My wife played a significant role in supporting my studies; she bought a chair and table and set up a study room in our official residence at RMRC, Bhubaneswar. The work progressed well, except for a turbulent period in 1990, when I had to pause my efforts from May to November. Fortunately, in September 1990, just before the Supreme Court's judgment, my wife secured a job as a Lecturer in Zoology at Kamla Nehru Women's College in Bhubaneswar. From January 1991, I began to gather myself and resumed work on my D.Sc. thesis. By the end of 1992, I had submitted it for examination. The D.Sc. thesis followed a rigorous evaluation process, similar to that for a Ph.D., with the thesis being sent to foreign examiners. Given the time, everything was conducted via surface mail and sometimes by airmail. The report came back in late 1993, and my viva voce examination was scheduled for early 1994. The Plant Protection Adviser to the Government of India, late Dr Banerjee, served as the examiner for the viva voce. My viva voce was completed, and I was awarded the D.Sc. degree in Parasitology—a true testament to the rewards of hard work.

Until 1995, I was still an Assistant Director at RMRC. In early 1994, there was an advertisement for the position of Deputy Director and Officer in Charge at DMRC, Jodhpur, and I decided to apply. The Director at RMRC, Bhubaneswar, was quite pleased with my decision to seek opportunities elsewhere, as many were eyeing my research project, which included two vehicles. I was called for the interview, attended, and was subsequently selected for the position. After a few weeks, I received the appointment order and prepared to move. At that time, I did not know how to cook; the only thing I could make was 'tea". Although I am a non-vegetarian and enjoy simple food, I have a discerning palate for gourmet dishes. Knowing I was about to move to Jodhpur, I asked my wife to teach me how to cook chicken, mutton, and some traditional Oriya dishes like *"Dalma" and "Shantula."* It took some time, but I eventually learned the basics of cooking.

There was no issue getting relieved, as the Director at that time was eager for me to leave. I handed over my responsibilities at Bhubaneswar and proceeded to ICMR Headquarters to formally take charge, as one Deputy Director General, late Dr. R. Ramachandran, was serving as the Director in charge of DMRC, Jodhpur. The next day, I took over from him and went to meet the DG of ICMR, to inform him that I was flying to Jodhpur the following day to assume my new role. That evening, I visited his residence in

Delhi on invitation, where he suddenly began discouraging me from going to Jodhpur, advising me instead to return to RMRC, Bhubaneswar. I was puzzled, as I had already completed my farewells, handed over my duties, taken ver charge of DMRC Jodhpur in Delhi and booked my flight to Jodhpur. Despite my explanations, he assured me that everything could be managed. The next day, I returned to ICMR Headquarters, where the Administrative Officer, late Mr. V.K. Kapur, was instructed to cancel my flight ticket. My appointment at DMRC, Jodhpur was reversed, and the Director of RMRC, Bhubaneswar was asked to reinstate me without any issues. The very next day, I returned to Bhubaneswar. Everyone was surprised, but my students and department staff at RMRC, Bhubaneswar were delighted to have me back. As for others, I can't say for sure how they felt. Later, I learned that the person on the waiting list for the Jodhpur position, one Dr Choudhury, a professor of medicine at Jodhpur Medical College, was subsequently offered the appointment and joined RMRC, Jodhpur in 1994. Since there was no Director's post at RMRC, Jodhpur at that time, the Deputy Director acted as Director in charge, wielding full powers. I was angry internally, feeling frustrated and deceived, sensing some underlying motive behind ICMR's decision to appoint Dr Choudhury over me. It seemed that they wanted me to be offered the position first, only to persuade not to join so Dr Choudhury could be appointed from the waiting list. Nevertheless, I resumed my work at RMRC, Bhubaneswar, continuing my project efforts.

CHAPTER – 16

Flight to Maroua

In 1993, a review meeting cum workshop for all WHO projects on biological control were held in Cameroon, West Africa. At that time, there were five such projects worldwide: one in India under my leadership, one in Sri Lanka led by Dr Indira, one in Africa headed by late Dr Philip Barbazone from the Pasteur Institute, France, one in Germany under Dr Norbert Becker, and another in Brazil managed by Dr Leda. Dr Boris Dobrokotov served as the Nodal Officer from the World Health Organization in Geneva, coordinating these projects.

Dr Philip Barbazon was organizing the meeting and was residing in Cameroon with his family. My tickets were sent to me, but there was no direct flight from India; I had to travel via Mumbai, Paris, Douala, and finally to Maroua, where the workshop was held. I went to Mumbai and stayed there overnight. With no work to do, I took the opportunity to watch the movie "Mohra," which had just been released. The next day, I packed my bags to catch the Air France flight to Paris. At the Mumbai airport, I met Dr Indira from Sri Lanka, who was also attending the same workshop. We boarded the flight together and landed at Charles de Gaulle Airport in Paris. Our ticket from Paris to Douala was with Cameroon Airlines, which operated from a different airport—like Paris Sud. Indira was met by her uncle, who lived in Paris, while I took a bus to the other airport. After a brief breakfast at the airport, I boarded the flight to Douala, Cameroon. I had requested a vegetarian meal on the flight, unaware of their definition of vegetarianism. At that time, their vegetarian meals often included only basic vegetables, like cabbage, and did not include eggs or milk, which were considered non-vegetarian. Nevertheless, I managed and arrived at Douala Airport. Upon arrival, we were received by Philip, who took us to a hotel in Douala. By then, it was evening, and we were all invited to dinner at Philip's home. After freshening up, we headed to his house, where we had a brief interaction and introductions over dinner. The next day, we departed Douala for Maroua on a local flight and arrived by noon.

Maroua is the capital of the Far North Region of Cameroon, situated along the banks of the Ferngo and Kaliao Rivers, in the foothills of the Mandara Mountains. It borders Chad and Nigeria. At that time, Maroua was endemic for lymphatic filariasis, which is why the project was operating there. Consequently, Philip organized the workshop in Maroua. We stayed in a beautiful hotel near the river, although I don't recall its name. Since Philip was working in Maroua with his team, he was quite popular in the area. The workshop commenced, and I was scheduled to make a detailed presentation of our project after Dr Boris and Dr Norbert. Our work was highly appreciated, and everyone gained valuable insights from our project in India. The workshop also included field visits, allowing us to familiarize ourselves with the working style and project conditions in Cameroon. Philip's group was doing an excellent job. One evening, Philip took us to the local market, which was quite fascinating. It resembled our local weekly *"hat"* (market) in rural India.

Every day, we were busy with the official workshop and field visits, and lunch was arranged at the hotel where we were staying. Initially, I faced difficulties with the food, as I was the only person who did not eat beef. Boris, knowing that I was a rice eater, found a French cook at the hotel through Philip and asked him to prepare some plain rice in Indian style. This made my meals more manageable. On a few occasions, we visited the river in Maroua, which we thoroughly enjoyed. Since Philip was quite popular in the area, local village leaders invited us for dinner at their homes on three occasions. This was the first time we tasted local Cameroonian food. The village leaders were very fond of us and organized the dinners with great love and affection. From the appearance of the meat dishes, I couldn't determine what type of meat it was, so I chose to avoid it. However, there was a delightful dish made with local freshwater fish, similar to *Rohu*. The preparation was unique; the fish was served whole, not cut into pieces. They cleaned out the insides, filled it with something, and then cooked it. It was very tasty, and we enjoyed these wonderful dinners for three consecutive days.

When I went to Cameroon, I brought a small *Pipili* wall hanging as a token from Odisha for Philip, which I handed to him during dinner at his home in Douala. On the last day of the workshop, we held a valedictory meeting before departing for Yaoundé, the capital of Cameroon, the following day. The final meeting was quite emotional after spending two weeks together. In the presence of everyone, Philip presented a beautiful necklace and earrings made of Malachite stones for my wife. I graciously accepted the gift to applause from all attendees. Cameroon is renowned for its Malachite stones, and this gift was a thoughtful reminder of the country's unique charm.

The next day, we left Maroua and reached Yaoundé, the capital of Cameroon, by the afternoon. We stayed overnight in Yaoundé and the following day travelled to Paris via Rome, Italy. We spent some time in Rome before arriving in Paris that night. Philip, being French, had booked a comfortable hotel for me in Paris, where I stayed for two days before my flight to Mumbai. During my time in Paris, I visited the museum and a beautiful church, mostly exploring the city on foot. On my last day, I planned to go shopping. While walking, I encountered an Indian man and asked him for directions, but he did not respond. A short while later, I met another man who resembled an Indian and asked him for guidance. To my surprise, he not only provided directions but also accompanied me almost all the way to my destination. I was pleased and inquired about his background, only to find out that he was from Pakistan. I thanked him and continued on my way to shop. The next day, I returned to India. At that time, there were no mobile phones, so I couldn't contact home for a long period. I managed to reach out once from Cameroon and once from Paris. Upon returning home, I went to the office and discussed my experiences in Cameroon with the project staff, outlining what we had learned and how to proceed with the next phase of the project. We continued our work on the project with renewed energy and insights.

Each national research institute in India has a Scientific Advisory Committee (SAC), which meets at least once a year to review all research work undertaken by the scientists. Eminent individuals in their respective fields are generally nominated as SAC members. The SAC has been in place since around 1985, and the chairman during that time was late Dr R.G. Roy, with whom I had previously worked. Dr Roy held a favourable opinion of my work, and my projects progressed well. When I initially joined RMRC in Bhubaneswar, I encountered some challenges with a senior officer. However, Dr Roy always supported me. After three years, he was replaced, and Dr M.R. Das from NICD, Delhi was nominated as a member from my field. Unbeknownst to many, I had also worked with Dr. Das during my time in Keonjhar, and he too had an excellent opinion of me. A couple of years later, he was replaced by his opponent, Dr V.P. Sharma, who was then the Director of MRC. Again, Dr Sharma had a good opinion of my work and this change did not stop the senior officer at the headquarters from undermining my work. Eventually, a wily manoeuvre was orchestrated against me by a scientist at MRC, who was initially close to it's Director but later became his adversary. Their Director approached ICMR to have him transferred immediately. At that time, he was just a few days senior to me in the ICMR cadre. The ICMR transferred him to RMRC in Bhubaneswar with the intent that he would oversee my work since he was from my area. He joined the institute, and there were numerous attempts to take away my project. However, the WHO rules dictated otherwise. I had secured the project from WHO as the Principal Investigator, making it impossible for anyone else to take it over. I continued my work as usual. By that time, I had not only built a substantial team of staff members but also had several Ph.D. students, which was uncommon for other scientists at RMRC. The scientist who had been transferred from Delhi eventually faced difficulties with the RMRC Director and was subsequently transferred to the RMRC-VCRC field station in Koraput.

Many scientists from abroad frequently visited our

project sites. At our request, the World Health Organization deputed Dr Edwin Michael from London to assist us in analysing our data from a mathematical perspective. He stayed with us for two weeks, thoroughly examining the extensive data we had generated. Our interactions with him were excellent, and after his analysis, he submitted a report to the WHO, praising our work highly. However, this recognition sparked jealousy among a few of my colleagues, particularly the scientist who had transferred from Delhi. This led to the issuance of several unanimous letters against me. Unfortunately, at that time, the ICMR prioritized these unanimous letters over genuine, signed representations from its scientists. In our professional environment, jealousy often arises over promotions, selections, attention, and international projects. It's easier to focus our envy on a person than to confront our own desires or acknowledge what we feel is lacking in our lives. Despite these challenges, the project continued to progress.

CHAPTER – 17

From Pondy to Trivandrum

In the late 1980s, I attended a conference on Vectors and Vector-Borne Diseases in Trivandrum, organized by Prof. Varma, then Professor and Head of Zoology at the University of Kerala. The late Dr P.K. Rajagopalan, Director of the Vector Control Research Centre (VCRC) in Pondicherry, was scheduled to deliver a plenary lecture. He invited me to join him in Pondicherry, and from there, we would travel together to Trivandrum. Accordingly, I travelled to Pondicherry and stayed overnight. Another professor from the London School was also there to join us. The next day, the three of us set off by road to Trivandrum. It was a unique opportunity for me to travel with the Director of VCRC and Professor Raja Varma from the London School. During our journey, I engaged in extensive discussions and learned many things. Prof. Raja Varma was a British citizen by marriage; his wife was from London, and they had established their life there. As far as I know, he continued to serve as an emeritus professor at the London School of Tropical Medicine until at least 2017.

The conference itself was enriching, and I returned to Bhubaneswar afterward. In the early 1990s, I attended another conference organized by the National

Environmental Science Academy (NESA) in Vellore, accompanied by my family and two of my Ph.D. students, Dr Ranjit and Dr Hazra. After returning to Bhubaneswar, Dr Ranjit and Dr Hazra encouraged me to start the Orissa chapter of NESA. At that time, NESA was managed by two professors from Bihar, whose efforts were not satisfactory to me, as the organization lacked reputation. However, we successfully established the Orissa chapter. The inaugural meeting of the Orissa chapter took place around 1993, with Mr. Biswa Bhusan Harichandran, then Minister in the Orissa Cabinet and now Governor of Chhattisgarh, serving as the chief guest. In the second meeting, Mr. Niranjan Pattanayak, another minister in the Orissa government, graced us as the chief guest. At that time, Dr. Krishnamachari was the Director of RMRC, Bhubaneswar, and he provided full support for the conference, unlike the previous director. Dr. Krishnamachari resigned from his ICMR position (from RMRC) in late 1993 and returned to Hyderabad, where he joined the British Council. The following year, in 1994, Dr. Krishnamachari organized the national NESA conference in Hyderabad. My family and I travelled there for the event. Immediately upon our arrival, Dr. Krishnamachari invited all twelve of us to his house. Although we were tired, we could not refuse his invitation. After enjoying a cup of tea, we were unexpectedly asked to leave for our respective accommodations. Fortunately, we had good accommodations. One of my students, along with her mother-in-law, stayed at Dr Krishnamachari's house until the conference concluded. We attended the conference and later returned to Bhubaneswar. However, the poor quality of the conference and NESA's overall management troubled me, leading me to lose interest in the Orissa chapter of NESA.

During Dr Krishnamachari's tenure as the Director of RMRC, Bhubaneswar, he maintained a friendly relationship with me and my colleague, Dr Ravindran. He had a daughter studying in the USA and a son named Shyam, who was also a friend of my children. Dr Krishnamachari frequently suffered from headaches and often took Novalgin several times a day. I recall him mentioning, while swallowing a tablet, that his reliance on medication would eventually lead to kidney failure—and unfortunately, that became a reality. After a couple of years at the British Council, he resigned and settled in Hyderabad, living on his and his wife's pensions. Over time, he developed kidney problems and required dialysis. To fund his daughter's education in the USA, he had to sell his house and moved to Visakhapatnam, his hometown, where his brothers lived. A few years later, we received the sad news that he had collapsed at home while preparing to go to the hospital for dialysis. Eventually, we learned that his wife had joined a private medical college in Visakhapatnam.

In the late 1980s, the VCRC in Pondicherry began offering an M.Sc. in Medical Entomology, affiliated with Pondicherry University. I frequently travelled to VCRC until 1990 to teach some classes, and I also served as a question setter and examiner for the course. Additionally, I was often selected as a Ph.D. examiner and conducted Ph.D. viva. On one occasion, the viva was scheduled in Alleppey (now Alappuzha), Kerala. A WHO project on filariasis was being run by VCRC, and we travelled there along with the late Dr C.P. Ramachandran from WHO, Geneva, who served as the foreign examiner for the student. Since he was in India, he was invited to Alleppey as well. After the viva, we visited the project area to see the work being done, and we thoroughly enjoyed a boat ride in the picturesque surroundings.

As I mentioned earlier, after Dr Krishnamachari resigned from RMRC, Bhubaneswar, Dr Satyanarayana was transferred from Dibrugarh to serve as the new Director. By early 1994, I had lost interest in NESA, but I still wanted to create a platform for scientists in my area. I believed that a man who wants to do something will find a way, while a man who does not will find an excuse. I remembered the high-quality conference on Vector Borne Diseases organized by Prof. Varma in Trivandrum. By that time, Prof. Varma had retired. I discussed the idea with my staff and students, and we decided to organize a conference on vectors and vector-borne diseases at RMRC, Bhubaneswar, in November, 1994. Everyone was enthusiastic and agreed to the proposal. We met with the Director, who expressed doubt about funding but encouraged us to proceed as long as we could raise the necessary funds. Faced with this challenge, I began to think about how to generate funds. We wrote to ICMR for support but received no response. Then, I remembered that Dr Kedar had joined Bayer, India. Having served as his Ph.D. examiner, I decided to reach out to him without much hope. To my surprise, he replied almost immediately, asking how much funding we needed. With a conservative mindset, I requested fifty thousand rupees. When I didn't receive an immediate response, I thought I might have asked for too much. However, a few days later, a team of three members from Bayer, India, arrived at RMRC, Bhubaneswar. They discussed the conference with me and my team and decided to sponsor all expenses from "A to Z," with the condition that we should not accept sponsorship from any other source. We agreed to their terms. Although we did not receive any direct funding, Bayer arranged all expenses, including food, dinner, and hotel accommodations for our guests.

By that time, the DG, ICMR had retired, and Dr Satyavati had become the Director General of ICMR. Dr C. Silvera was serving as the Minister of Health. Born in Mizoram, Dr Silvera studied medicine at Christian Medical College (CMC), Vellore, where he earned his MBBS. We aimed to invite him as the Chief Guest for the conference. I travelled to Delhi and met his Secretary, Mr. R. K. Mishra, IAS, who took me to Dr Silvera. He was pleased that I had come from Orissa to extend the invitation and shared that he had worked for some time at a Missionary Hospital in *Bisam* Cuttack, Orissa. He graciously accepted the invitation and came to inaugurate the conference. The inaugural function was held at "Soochana Bhawan," Bhubaneswar, while the scientific sessions took place at RMRC. At that time, three institutes in India were focused solely on vector-borne diseases: the Malaria Research Centre led by Dr V.P. Sharma, the Vector Control Research Centre in Pondicherry under Dr Dhanda (who had succeeded its founding Director, Dr Rajagopalan), and the Centre for Research on Medical Entomology in Madurai with Dr Rachael Reuben as the Director. There was a notable lack of collaboration between these centres. I made it a point to bring all three together for the conference in Bhubaneswar. Dr Reuben expressed her fondness for Orissa, sharing that her father, Mr. Reuben, had been a Magistrate in Puri when she was a child, and she had attended primary school there. My late father-in-law confirmed that there was indeed a Magistrate named Mr. Reuben in Puri when he was a student. The conference was a great success, with around 120 scientists attending, including many from abroad, making it a truly international event of high quality. We also published the proceedings of the conference. Prof. Varma from Trivandrum, who had previously organized a similar conference there, attended as well. He encouraged me to organize the conference on a regular basis, as he had been unable to continue after his retirement.

In those days, vector-borne diseases posed a significant threat, impacting large populations and causing numerous deaths. Conferences like this one were crucial, as they provided a platform to discuss the status of these diseases, their transmission biology, control strategies, and emerging methods for containment. The deliberations contributed substantially to the development of effective measures to manage and reduce the impact of vector-borne diseases, ultimately serving human wellbeing. In essence, everyone involved was working towards human wellbeing, although the scale varied. For some, it meant addressing the health of individuals or their families, while for others, it encompassed the wellbeing of entire communities or even all of humanity. This collective effort, regardless of its scope, played a role in enhancing public health and reducing the burden of these diseases.

CHAPTER – 18

Birth of NAVBD

We decided to establish a registered scientific society under which we could organize conferences on vector-borne diseases. I began drafting the Memorandum of Association and the Bye-Laws for the new society. We named it the "National Academy of Vector Borne Diseases (NAVBD)." In December 1994, the NAVBD was officially registered under the Society Registration Act of 1860 at the Orissa Registration Office in Cuttack, with 12 founding members. Dr V.P. Sharma was appointed as the President, and I took on the role of Secretary General. Other founding members included Dr B.K. Das from SCB Medical College, Cuttack, the late Dr Namita Mahapatra, Dr M.R. Ranjit, and Dr R.K. Hazra from RMRC, Bhubaneswar. Dr Namita Mahapatra also served as Treasurer. The Director of RMRC granted us the necessary permission to operate the society from RMRC, Bhubaneswar. We decided to hold the conference every two years at different locations across India, with the next event planned for 1996 in Goa. By then, I was experiencing a particularly fulfilling and happy period in my life.

In May 1995, when my son was around 10 years old, we decided to hold his thread ceremony. We planned to have the event at the RMRC campus, for which I secured the necessary permission from the Director. The RMRC guest house, located in one of the quarters on the campus, was also booked for the occasion. The arrangements were made for an open-air ceremony, with all the decorations in place for both the ritual and the dinner. However, much to our surprise, unexpected heavy rain arrived and persisted for seven days. This left us in a difficult situation, unsure of how to proceed. Ultimately, we decided to conduct the thread ceremony rituals inside one of the rooms in our house during the daytime. The dinner had to be relocated to the entrance and corridors of the RMRC office. The rain was so intense that even the fish markets in Bhubaneswar were closed. I recall sending people to *Paradeep* and other nearby places to procure fish and prawns. Despite the challenging circumstances, we were happy that all our guests attended and made the event memorable.

We were staying in the RMRC campus and every evening after office, we used to go to my in-law's place in Saheed Nagar to spend some time with them. After an hour or so we used to come back to RMRC campus. At Saheed Nagar, my father-in-law used to spend time with me sharing some of his important experiences. He passed away after a prolonged illness in *Ispat* General Hospital, Rourkela in 1995. After all the rituals were over, the near and dear ones left Bhubaneswar and went to their respective workplaces. Our mother-in-law was alone. The servant also went away for some time. For few days, I was working in RMRC and after dinner I had to go to Saheed Nagar and stay the night there to guard the house. I contacted malaria there. After few days I developed high fever and it was found that I was infected with *P. vivax*. I took medicines, but it relapsed several times. I had to take a very long course of Primaquine. That was the time when I started losing hairs on my head.

The next conference was planned in Goa in May 1996. This time also I wrote to Bayer Germany and they sponsored the entire conference. Dr V.P. Sharma was also planning a global meet on parasitology in Hyderabad in 1997. He fixed an event manager company for that. Dr Sharma called me and wanted me to engage the same person for organizing the conference in 1996 at Goa and we agreed. The conference was organised. there were 300 participants from India and abroad. Full sponsorship came from Bayer, but the service of the event manager was far from satisfactory. We understood that the same person cheated Dr Sharma while organising the global meet on parasitology in Hyderabad in 1997. However, the conference was by and large successful. The representative from Bayer (Germany), Dr Hesse congratulated me and assured of further sponsorship of the next conference. We came back to Bhubaneswar after the conference and started our work in the laboratory as well as in the field.

Our WHO project on lymphatic filariasis was extended for an additional two years, which brought a lot of satisfaction to the team. We had gathered a substantial amount of data on the disease and thoroughly analysed all transmission parameters. However, it wasn't long before we observed that the filariasis vectors were developing resistance to *Bacillus sphaericus*, the bacterium provided by WHO for our project. We promptly reported this issue to WHO, and as a result, the use of *B. sphaericus* was eventually not recommended for filariasis vector control. Despite the development of resistance in later stages, the initial years of the project had demonstrated significant achievements in controlling transmission parameters, showcasing the potential effectiveness of the approach before resistance became a barrier.

By that time, the Government of Orissa had established the "Institute of Life Sciences" (ILS) in Bhubaneswar as an autonomous institute in 1989, under the administrative control of the state government. The initiative was driven by the then Chief Minister, Late Shri J.B. Patnaik, and Mr. Niranjan Patnaik, who was the Minister for Science & Technology, among other portfolios. Late Prof. M.S. Kanungo from Banaras Hindu University (BHU) was appointed as the part-time Honorary Director of ILS, traveling from Varanasi to Bhubaneswar once a month to oversee the institute's activities. By 1997, the institute faced significant internal problems. There were only a few faculty members, and most of them were dissatisfied with Prof. Kanungo's continued leadership, ultimately leading to his resignation. In response, the Minister for Science & Technology, Mr. Niranjan Patnaik, instructed the Governing Body (GB) to appoint a regular Director for ILS. The GB was convened and constituted a search committee to select a regular director for the ILS. The search committee consisted of Prof. G. Padmanaban, Director of I.I.Sc. Bangalore, Prof. Asis Dutta, Vice Chancellor of JNU, and Prof. Das, Vice Chancellor of Utkal University. The initial committee did not fully comply with the ILS Bylaws, which stipulated that at least three eminent life scientists should be included. The inclusion of a member from the English department instead of a life scientist led to the committee's expansion for a broader selection process. Eventually, the committee recommended three candidates: myself, a professor from JNU who had previously worked with ICMR, and another scientist from ICMR. This list was forwarded to the government for approval.

At that time, ILS was under state government administration, with Late Mr. J.B. Patnaik as the Chief Minister and Late Sri S.B. Mishra as the Chief Secretary. Given the challenges at ILS and the importance of appointing the first full-time Director, the government took an extra cautious approach. Since all the shortlisted candidates were from ICMR, the Director General (DG) of ICMR, who was also a GB member of ILS, was consulted for his remarks on each candidate based on their work and attitude in ICMR. The DG carried out an unbiased evaluation, ultimately leading to the decision in my favour. The Chief Minister approved my appointment in November 1997. Upon receiving the appointment letter, I applied to ICMR for permission to join ILS on deputation while retaining my laboratory at RMRC, located just opposite ILS. The Director of RMRC was quite eager to relieve me but insisted that I hand over the responsibilities of all projects and tasks under my purview before departing. Although some colleagues showed jealousy, and certain staff members, influenced by others, questioned my selection as Director, I remained unfazed.

Once all formalities were completed, I was officially relieved from RMRC on the morning of 2nd March 1998, at 10 AM. At that time, ILS was operating from two rented buildings in Saheed Nagar. After handing over the charge at RMRC, I proceeded to the Science and Technology Department at the Orissa Secretariat, where I submitted my joining report to Mr. Chahar, IAS, the Secretary. He accompanied me to ILS, where I officially joined as the first regular Director on the forenoon of 2nd March 1998. I continued to stay in my official accommodation within the RMRC campus.

CHAPTER – 19

A Challenging Life at Institute of Life Sciences

There were about half a dozen scientists at ILS when I joined, along with a few administrative staff. The Administrative Officer, who was on deputation from the State Administrative Service, handled most of the administrative tasks. On my first day, I spent time meeting with both the scientists and administrative staff to get a better understanding of the institute and its operations. At that point, a piece of land had already been allocated to ILS in Chandrasekharpur, near Kalinga Hospital. Although the size of the land was not sufficient for the long-term growth of the institute, I decided to retain it because of its strategic location, which was ideal for health-related research. I figured that we could secure additional land nearby in the future if the need arose. For a burgeoning institute like ILS, a substantial budget and robust infrastructure were crucial to driving progress. When I reviewed the budget, I found it extremely disappointing—around INR 32 lakhs for the 1998-99 fiscal year, which included the rent for the two rented buildings in Saheed Nagar. Some funds had been deposited with the Industrial Development Corporation of Orissa (IDCO) for constructing the ILS building on the allotted land. An architect from Mumbai had already been appointed, and the design had been approved, but construction had faced delays.

During this period, the Secretary of the Science & Technology Department changed, and late Mr A.K. Samantray took over the position. I reached out to him, requesting additional funding and seeking his help in expediting the construction of the ILS building. While he was unable to significantly increase the budget, he did facilitate the acceleration of the construction process. We held several meetings with IDCO, and soon, the construction began in full swing.

In the meantime, there was yet another change in the Secretary of Science and Technology, with Mr S.P. Nanda assuming the role. People warned me about him, describing him as someone from whom it would be difficult to get support or assistance. I was initially apprehensive. However, I knew the then Chief Secretary of Orissa, late Mr. S.B. Mishra, who reassured me. He told me that Mr. Nanda was an exceptionally honest person, as straight and firm as an iron pillar. This reassurance gave me the confidence to approach Mr. Nanda. Shortly after Mr. Nanda's appointment, he invited me to visit the construction site together. We went to the site, where he demonstrated his understanding of the construction process, having previously served as Managing Director of IDCO. When we returned to his office, I explained the challenging situation at ILS, including the severe lack of funding and infrastructure. He assured me that he would support the institute. True to his word, we soon received some additional funds, including the full amount needed to complete the building as initially planned. By October

1999, the building was finally ready. However, running the institute during this time was a tough challenge. The demands of establishing a new and ambitious institution like ILS, coupled with the lack of sufficient resources, left me with little time to focus on my family. The job required constant attention and effort, which made it difficult for me to devote enough time to my wife and children.

I aspired not only to be a loving human being but to embody the qualities of a respected academic and scientific leader: committed to ideology, a skilled strategist, an effective manager of people and events, and someone with a clear vision and development goals. While personal ambition may simply amplify what already exists within oneself, vision is about imagining new possibilities.

Upon joining ILS, Bhubaneswar, I discovered that a couple of scientists were not contributing to the work at all. It was evident and difficult to overlook. In 1998, I took the step of forming a committee to review the performance of the scientists. The committee, comprising experts from various parts of the country, came to Bhubaneswar to evaluate both the overall work of the institute and the contributions of each individual scientist. At that time, the scientific designations at ILS included Professor, Reader, and Lecturer. There was one Professor, two Readers, and three Lecturers, with all but one having received training abroad. The review revealed significant issues with one Lecturer's performance. The findings were unfavourable, and ultimately, the Lecturer chose to resign before any formal action was taken.

As I mentioned earlier, the second Conference on Vectors & Vector-Borne Diseases was held in Goa in 1996. The third conference was scheduled for 1998, and it was decided during the Goa meeting to host it in Orissa. We selected Hotel Toshali Sands in Puri as the venue for May 1998. After joining ILS on March 2, 1998, I found myself busy organizing the third conference. The weather was quite hot during that time. Once again, Bayer stepped in to sponsor the event, but this time we were also approached by AGREVO Environment, another international company. They expressed concern that NAVBD was only supporting Bayer. In response, we decided to split the sponsorship, with 50% coming from Bayer and 50% from AGREVO, and both companies agreed to this arrangement. The conference attracted around 350 delegates from India and abroad. Despite the sweltering summer heat, it was a successful event. I stayed in Puri for five days until the conference concluded. After the event, we all returned to Bhubaneswar and resumed our respective work.

The professor at ILS was recruited from the USA. He was a molecular biologist working for a reputable company there. We did not know that, he was planning to return to the USA and rejoin his original company. In 1999, without any prior notice, he left Orissa with his family and travelled to Delhi to catch a flight. Upon learning about his departure, we managed to reach out to him, and he eventually returned from the Delhi airport to Bhubaneswar and resumed his work at ILS. I had a long discussion with him during which I promised to provide all the necessary support for his research. Fortunately, he decided to continue with us.

In late 1999, we successfully shifted to the new ILS building in its campus after giving notice to the landlords of the previous locations. The owner of one building was a senior IAS officer, and the owner of the second building was a senior IPS officer. While we had no issues with the IAS officer, we faced challenges with the IPS officer. After extensive discussions, we managed to settle the matter, and we moved into our own campus in Chandrasekharpur, near Kalinga Hospital, in early October 1999. However, just a few weeks later, on October 29, 1999, Orissa was struck by a Super Cyclonic Storm that made landfall near Paradip. The storm brought maximum wind speeds of 260-270 km/h and created a storm surge that elevated sea levels by over 20 feet, resulting in the tragic loss of nearly 10,000 lives according to official reports. The estimated death toll was much higher, with around 30,000 lives lost, alongside devastating property damage. In Bhubaneswar, all the roads were blocked by fallen trees, and the city was ill-equipped to handle such a massive calamity. We were staying in the RMRC campus at the time, and the storm was so powerful that our beds trembled, leaving all of us terrified and uncertain about what would happen next.

During this challenging period, Mr. Giridhari Gomango was the Chief Minister of Orissa. The devastation caused by the cyclone left the region without electricity for many days, making it extremely difficult to maintain the laboratory equipment and costly chemicals at ILS. To address this issue, I had to meet with the then Energy Minister of Orissa, Mr. Niranjan Patnaik. I explained the importance of maintaining high-end equipment and sensitive chemicals in our laboratories for ongoing research. After our discussion, he agreed to provide ILS with a special electrical connection solely for the purpose of maintaining these essential resources. This support allowed ILS to resume functioning despite the widespread power outages, ensuring that our critical research could continue without significant interruption.

During this tumultuous time following the cyclone, the WHO sent an officer from its regional office to assess the situation in Bhubaneswar. Given the challenging circumstances, the officer reached out to me for assistance. I arranged for his accommodation and meals at a local guest house. However, after his stay, he left without settling his room rent and food charges, which unfortunately fell on my shoulders to clear. Fast forward ten years later, when I joined WHO, I encountered this gentleman again. Despite our previous interactions, he seemed to act as if he did not recognize me, yet he was very friendly during our meeting. It was an interesting reminder of how situations and relationships can evolve over time, especially in the professional world.

After the devastating cyclone, the Government of India dispatched a special team to Orissa to assess the health situation and coordinate relief efforts. This team included Dr Atri (Additional Director General of Health Services), Dr Shiv Lal (Director), and Dr Ichhpujani (Deputy Director) from the National Institute of Communicable Diseases (now known as the National Centre for Disease Control). I was designated as the contact person by the Government of Orissa to facilitate their stay and work. At that time, the Bhubaneswar Club was operational, and the team chose to stay there. Additionally, I arranged dinner for them on a couple of occasions at the Regional Plant Resource Centre (RPRC), where Dr Premanand Das was the director. The RPRC had a guest house and a skilled cook, making it an ideal venue. However, my relationship with Dr Atri became strained after an argument one day. Following that incident, I decided to keep my distance from him. Despite the challenges the team faced, Dr Shiv Lal, who was familiar with my work, blamed Dr Atri for the issues. The next day, Dr Atri approached me and apologized for his earlier behaviour, which allowed me to resume my role in coordinating their activities effectively. It was a reminder of the importance of maintaining professional relationships, even in challenging situations.

Following the devastating cyclone, I immediately recognized the need to assess the damage to the ILS campus, despite it being a newly constructed building. I constituted a committee within ILS to estimate the extent of the losses. The committee meticulously evaluated the damage and prepared a report, which I forwarded to the Secretary of Science and Technology. This report eventually made its way to the government in 2000. By that time, there had been a change in leadership, and Mr. Naveen Patnaik had become the Chief Minister of Orissa. Mr. Srinibas Rath, IAS; who was serving as the Development Commissioner, was assigned to visit ILS to assess the situation further. I guided him around the campus, highlighting the damage we had incurred. Following his assessment, he likely submitted his recommendations to the government. Thankfully, the government sanctioned several crores for ILS, which proved to be immensely beneficial. With the allocated funds, we were able to repair our equipment and restore the facilities. Gradually, the campus regained its vibrant look, and operations resumed as usual, allowing us to continue our important work in research and development.

Recognizing the need for more academic leadership at ILS, I promptly advertised for the position of another professor. Among the applicants were two readers from our existing staff. After conducting interviews, one of the readers was selected for the position. Initially, the other reader was unhappy with the outcome, but over time, he reconciled with the decision. While there were several other vacant positions, I refrained from advertising them due to the ongoing lack of adequate funding. During this period, I had the opportunity to work closely with Mr. S.P.

Nanda, the then Secretary of Science and Technology, who was providing unconditional support to ILS. At one point, we approached the Chief Minister to discuss the pressing need for increased funding for ILS. Our main goal was to request a substantial increase in the budget—ideally thirty-fold—to meet the genuine requirements of our ambitious institute. Unfortunately, we did not secure any commitment during that meeting, which left us in a challenging position. Managing the institute with such a meagre budget was indeed difficult. However, the scientists at ILS were proactive in generating extramural projects, which helped us maintain a level of good science despite the financial constraints. Their dedication and hard work ensured that we continued to make progress in our research initiatives.

The next conference on Vector-Borne Diseases was set to take place in Patiala, organized by Punjabi University. As we prepared for the fourth conference in the series, our team was quite busy managing the logistics and details. Approximately 350 participants from both India and abroad attended the meeting, making it a resounding success. Dr Jagbir Singh, a Professor of Zoology at Punjabi University, took the lead in organizing the event. He meticulously handled all aspects of the conference, ensuring that everything ran smoothly. While the days were filled with discussions on scientific papers and presentations, Dr Singh also arranged for a special colourful entertainment program each evening, providing a delightful break from the rigorous scientific agenda. After the conference concluded, we returned to Bhubaneswar, where I found myself extremely busy with various affairs at ILS. The momentum of our activities was essential for maintaining the institute's progress and focus on research and development. Balancing the demands of the conference with the ongoing responsibilities at ILS was challenging, but it was also an opportunity to further strengthen our commitment to the field of vector-borne diseases.

It was late 2000. ILS was still facing the financial crunch. Mr Ayyar, from the State Administrative Service, was the Administrative Officer of ILS when I joined. In 2000, he was transferred and another Officer, Mrs Rajashree Singh was posted. Both of them were excellent officers with high integrity and optimal honesty. At that time Mr Rajendran from Tamil Nadu was the Governor and Mr D.P. Bagchi was the Chief Secretary of Orissa. Once the Governor visited ILS in late 2000. He addressed the scientists and staff of ILS. I appraised him about the critical financial condition of ILS and requested him if he could see the Minister Science & Technology, Govt. of India; during his next visit to Delhi and put a word to consider taking over of ILS. He kindly agreed to this proposal.

With Mr Rajendran, Governor of Orissa.   With Padmashri P. Mohanty-Hejmadi and Padmashri G.C. Mishra at ILS

Mr. Bagchi, who previously served as the Secretary of Textiles in the Government of India, was now the Chief Secretary of Orissa. Recognizing the importance of securing adequate funding for the Institute of Life Sciences (ILS), I sought an appointment with Mr. Bagchi to discuss our dire financial situation. During our meeting, I expressed my concerns about the unsustainable operation of ILS without proper funding, stating that it might be better to close the institute than to allow it to remain underfunded. Mr. Bagchi was understanding of our plight, especially given the state's challenging financial conditions. He suggested writing to the Secretary of the Department of Biotechnology (DBT) to request special funding. However, I proposed inviting the Secretary of DBT, for a direct discussion at our institute, knowing her well. Mr. Bagchi agreed to my suggestion, and we organized the DBT Secretary's visit in June 2001. During her visit, we held a meeting at the Secretariat, where the Chief Secretary arranged for a gathering of all state secretaries. The DBT Secretary addressed the assembly, discussing the potential for establishing a State Biotechnology Board. This initiative aimed to create a Vision document for the development of Biotechnology in Orissa. I was honoured to be appointed as the Chairman of the newly formed State Biotechnology Board, marking a significant step towards enhancing the biotechnology landscape in the state.

With Secretary, DBT in ILS campus (2001). Secretary discussing with students

After our meeting with the Secretaries, I had the opportunity to take the DBT Secretary to meet the Chief Secretary, Mr. Bagchi. Prior to our meeting, I briefed the Chief Secretary on the possibility of requesting DBT to consider taking over the Institute of Life Sciences (ILS) under the Department of Biotechnology (DBT), Government of India. In our meeting, which was just the three of us over a cup of tea, the discussion flowed naturally until Mr. Bagchi suddenly suggested to DBT Secretary that she consider taking over ILS. She was taken aback and seemed momentarily speechless. We then returned to the State Guest House, where the gravity of the situation seemed to linger. The following day, I was scheduled to take the DBT Secretary to meet the Governor for a brief discussion. Before the meeting, I made sure to inform the Governor about the previous day's discussion with Mr. Bagchi, including the suggestion he had made regarding ILS. The Governor, already aware of ILS's situation, was pleased to hear about the Chief Secretary's request and expressed his support for our cause. During our meeting at the Governor's house, he reiterated the importance of considering the takeover of ILS by the DBT. He even mentioned his intention to discuss this further with then Minister of science & Technology, Govt. of India, during his next visit to Delhi. Afterward, when we returned to the State Guest House, I could sense a shift in her demeanour. She appeared more serious, perhaps realizing my role in facilitating the requests from both the Chief Secretary and the Governor. I had refrained from discussing the potential takeover with her beforehand, primarily because I was uncertain of her stance. At the time, then Chief Minister of Madhya Pradesh was actively pursuing the establishment of a new institute under the DBT. Hearing that the Government of Madhya Pradesh had even presented an award to her, I felt it prudent to avoid making assumptions about her openness to discussing the future of ILS.

Finally, the DBT Secretary broke the silence and asked me what steps to take next. By then, we had developed a rapport, and she had grown fond of me. I suggested that, given the government's request, we should make an earnest attempt to have ILS taken over by the DBT, and she agreed. She mentioned that as a first step, the Chief Minister—who was a coalition partner with then NDA government in Delhi—should write a letter to the Prime Minister, requesting the takeover. We drafted the letter, and she departed for Delhi on the noon flight. Before her departure, I went back to meet with the Chief Secretary (Mr Bagchi) to express my gratitude for his support and to suggest that the Chief Minister should send this letter to the Prime Minister. The Principal Secretary to the Chief Minister (Mr J.K. Mohapatra, who became the Chief Secretary later), took up this issue with the Chief Minister and convinced him to send the letter to the Prime Minister. I must emphasize that Mr. S.P. Nanda, the then Secretary of Science & Technology, played a pivotal role in this process. Without his support, I wouldn't have been able to make any progress. He acted as a vital link between me and the Chief Minister through Mr. Mohapatra and even discussed the proposal with the Chief Minister in favour of the takeover. Once the letter was sent, I took a copy of it to the Minister of Science and Technology, requesting him to follow up. By that time, the Governor of Orissa had also met with the Minister and briefed him on the ILS takeover proposal. The Prime Minister forwarded the letter to the Ministry of Science and Technology for necessary action, which eventually made its way to the DBT. The Chief

Secretary, Mr. Bagchi, also followed up with the Secretary of DBT regarding this matter.

Soon after, the Secretary of DBT wrote to me, asking for a detailed proposal outlining the future plans for ILS over the next 25 years. We collaborated on drafting the scientific portion of the proposal with input from Dr Supakar and Dr Sabat. The budgeting and financial aspects were equally important. I recalled an efficient Administrative Officer, Mr. Nityanand Rout, who had retired from the Institute of Physics, Bhubaneswar. We hired him for a couple of months to assist us with the proposal, and he did an outstanding job.

I was subsequently invited by the DBT to present our proposal for ILS at the Biotechnology Board. I prepared all the necessary documents and brought late Prof. Supakar along with me. The Chairman of the Board, Prof. G. Padmanaban, and other esteemed members, including Prof. Balaram from the Indian Institute of Sciences and Prof. P.N. Tandon, former Director of AIIMS, were in attendance. The presentation went well overall; however, Prof. Tandon was unduly critical, suggesting that our objectives were too ambitious to achieve within 25 years. I tend to speak my mind and don't overly concern myself with the consequences, which sometimes gives me peace of mind. I felt a bit upset by Prof. Tandon's remarks and engaged in a debate with him. Prof. Supakar, seated nearby, subtly urged me to cool down, while Prof. Padmanaban effectively managed the situation. Fortunately, the Secretary of DBT, who had been in a meeting with the Minister, arrived just in time to say, "We will recommend this proposal." Prof. Tandon had no choice but to remain silent after that. Following the presentation, we returned to Bhubaneswar.

Later, I learned that the Biotechnology Board

recommended the takeover of ILS by the Government of India under the DBT and suggested that a team visit ILS before sending the proposal to the cabinet. The DBT constituted a committee, led by Prof. Padmanaban and including Prof. Asis Dutta (then VC of JNU), Dr Sandeep Basu (then Director of the National Institute of Immunology), and Dr Sinha from DBT. This team visited ILS for three days, during which we had many fruitful discussions. Ultimately, the committee gave a favourable recommendation to the DBT. However, handing over the institute required formalities. By this time, Mr. Nanda had been transferred to another department, and late Dr Ajay Rastogi, IAS; had taken over as the new Secretary. He struggled to grasp the concept of the takeover, making it challenging for me to explain and convince him. Eventually, I had to seek intervention from Chief Secretary Mr. Bagchi, who successfully facilitated the process.

Unfortunately, no one in Orissa could tell us the procedure for the handover. We consulted the law department, and I also asked the DBT to consult their legal advisor for guidance. Ultimately, I reached out to a respected legal luminary I knew personally (a former Chief Justice of India), who provided clear guidelines for completing the legal handover. At that time, ILS had a minimal staff presence. Mr. Samal, the Stores Officer, was a bright, sincere, and hardworking individual. I involved him in the process, and his assistance was invaluable. According to the legal advice I received, the governing body of ILS needed to recommend the handover, and the original society that formed ILS had to pass a resolution agreeing to the transfer. We successfully managed to secure the governing body resolution, but obtaining a resolution from the original society proved challenging, as the members had retired long ago and were scattered across various locations. The members included Mr. Niranjan Patnaik (then Minister), late Mr. P.M. Mohapatra (IAS), late Mr. B.R. Patel (IAS), late Dr S. Torasia, and late Prof. L.N. Mohapatra. I drafted a resolution and sought signatures from the members, successfully obtaining all but Mr. P.M. Mohapatra and Mr. Patel. It was during a heavy downpour that we had to complete this task. Accompanied by Dr Sabat, I visited Mr. Mohapatra's house in Saheed Nagar, where we got his signature after braving the rain. After a quick cup of coffee, we hurried to Mr. Patel's house in Forest Park, where we also secured his signature before returning. With the resolution finalized, we sent the necessary documents to the DBT to complete the handover procedure.

For such steps, Union Cabinet approval was necessary. Soon, a Cabinet note was drafted. Dr Renu Swarup, who later became the Secretary of DBT, was a senior scientist in DBT at that time, and Mr. Sharma was the Financial Adviser of DBT. Dr Renu Swarup was appointed as the nodal officer from DBT to handle the issue of taking over ILS. The Cabinet note was circulated among all ministries, and all ministries gave their no objection except for the Planning Ministry and the Finance Ministry. I learned that the 10th Finance Commission had recommended against taking over or starting any new institution, which was why those two ministries did not give their no objection to the proposal for taking over ILS. Consequently, the proposal collapsed, and the Secretary of DBT informed us that taking over ILS was not possible. We were shattered. The financial situation at ILS was deteriorating, and it was sometimes even difficult to pay salaries. I went to Delhi to meet the Minister of Science and Technology and the Secretary of DBT. The Minister was very sympathetic. I discussed the situation with the Secretary and ultimately advised her not to pursue the takeover of ILS for another three to four months, after which we could reassess the situation. I returned home, but the staff at ILS, who had been hopeful and trusted me, were saddened by the news. I consoled them, saying that we should forget about this for a couple of months and plan to restart again. It is impossible to live without failing at something; I believe it's more about how we embrace failure. I enjoy being driven toward challenging yet realistic goals and strive to create a healthy and positive environment.

At ILS, we did not have a dedicated library building. I approached the late Dr S. Pattanayak, a member of the Governing Body of ILS, and requested him to donate a library building. He agreed on the condition that the library would be named after his mother. I obtained the necessary approval from the government, and the library building was completed in less than ten months. The Chief Minister inaugurated the ILS library, along with the Minister for Science & Technology (Mr. Ranendra Pratap Swain) and the local MP (Dr Prasanna Patsani). Dr Pattanayak was also invited to this inaugural function.

The previous year, in 2000, a pseudonymous letter was sent to the Chief Minister against me, alleging that I had decorated my office room at a significant expense. The letter was sent in the names of two faculty members: Dr Supakar and Dr Sabat. It was forwarded to me through the Secretary of Science & Technology. I requested the Secretary to personally investigate with Dr Supakar and Dr Sabat to confirm whether they had written that letter. He did so and noted that neither of them was aware of the letter, let alone involved in writing it. They further testified that all the allegations were fabricated. They even provided their original signatures, which did not match those on the letter. Eventually, I discovered the identity of the person who had manipulated the letter. This individual was supposedly close to me and was attempting to secure a promotion that was unlikely at that time. Perhaps out of frustration, they wanted to create some instability. Regardless, I chose not to dwell on these issues. I try to remain happy for no specific reason, and I easily forgive and forget. I hold no grudges and consistently focus on the brighter side of life. It's important to be around people who allow you to be yourself. Children are happy because they do what brings them joy, whereas many of us are often preoccupied with pleasing others. I didn't inform anyone that I knew who had orchestrated this. Being kind and helpful toward others significantly boosts self-esteem. I generally strive to cultivate the qualities I admire in others.

The Orissa Science Academy is an autonomous organization under the Ministry of Science & Technology, Government of Odisha. The Academy has a President and a Secretary who serve as the executive officers. At one point, the Secretary of the Academy created some issues, leading the Government to transfer him to a government college in Koraput. I was then given the charge of Secretary. This was my first visit to the Orissa Bigyan Academy office, where I took on the role of Secretary in addition to my position as Director of ILS. Later, I was appointed both President and Secretary of the Academy, alongside my responsibilities as Director of ILS. The Academy was conceptualized as early as 1981 by a group of senior scientists from Odisha and was formally adopted by the Government of Odisha in 1984. It commemorates and honours scientists who have made significant contributions in various fields of science and technology by conferring them with various awards.

Every year, an award investiture ceremony is organized to present these awards. I was in charge of the Academy until around 2002.

With Chief Minister of Odisha in an award investiture ceremony of Odisha Science Academy

In 2001, Dr V.P. Sharma wanted to visit ILS, and we invited him. By that time, Dr Sharma had retired. The library of ILS was completed, and he took photographs of it to show DBT Secretary (who was his wife) that we had established the library through a donation from Dr Pattanayak. During his visit, he met everyone at ILS and repeatedly stated that taking over ILS was not possible. Although he was an invited guest, he presented himself as a representative of DBT and the Government of India. I sensed that this behaviour stemmed from an identity crisis on his part, so I chose not to engage with his comments. As I mentioned earlier, Dr Renu Swarup was a senior scientist at DBT and served as the nodal point for matters concerning ILS, including the proposal for its takeover. During my frequent visits to DBT, I would see her in her office each time. She often shared her fondness for Odisha, as she had spent her childhood there; her father was in the defence services and worked in Charbatia. This connection to Odisha was significant for her, and she genuinely wanted to assist us. As I mentioned earlier, the proposal to take over ILS did not materialize in the first attempt, as the Finance and Planning Ministries did not recommend it. At that time, Mr. Yashwant Sinha was the finance minister.

I resumed my efforts in early 2002 after a brief pause. By that time, all formalities for the handover of ILS by the Government of Orissa had been completed during the first attempt. The next step was to reinitiate the proposal for Cabinet approval at the right moment. I had a close rapport with the Minister of Science and Technology, thanks to a previous introduction by the former Chief Justice of India, the late Justice Ranganath Mishra.

In early 2002, I discussed the matter with the Minister Science & Technology, who extended his full support and took up the issue with the Secretary of DBT to make a fresh attempt at taking over ILS. During my subsequent discussions with the Secretary of DBT, she indicated that a new letter from the Chief Minister of Orissa to the Prime Minister was necessary to restart the process. With the change in Finance Minister to Mr. Jaswant Singh and the addition of Mr. Mishra, IAS (son of late Justice G.K. Mishra, who was a classmate of my father), in the Finance Department, I saw an opportunity to make progress.

By then, Mr. S.P. Nanda was the Secretary of Industries. I met him, and he was very supportive and discussed with the Principal Secretary to the Chief Minister. The Chief Minister, being a coalition partner in the then-NDA Government, sent a polite but firmly worded letter, pointing out that the previous attempt had been stalled because the Finance and Planning Ministries did not grant the NOC. It requested the Prime Minister's personal intervention this time. I obtained a copy of the letter and delivered it to the Minister of Science and Technology and the Secretary of DBT.

The Prime Minister's Office took the matter seriously. Prior to this, I had met the Chief Secretary, Mr. Bagchi, who was serving as the Secretary in the Textile department and the Minister of Textiles was also the minister for Planning, Personnel, Minister of State in PMO and probably looking after external affairs (Smt. Vasundhara Raje). He arranged a meeting with the Honorable Minister, during which I provided details about the ILS takeover. She quickly took action to have the Planning Ministry recommend the proposal. The Prime Minister's Office then convened a meeting with the Minister of Science and Technology, the Secretary of the Department of Biotechnology, representatives from the Finance and Planning Departments, and the Chief Minister of Odisha. Fortunately, Mr. Mishra from the Finance Department was in attendance. The meeting was productive, and the recommendation for the Government of India to take over ILS was put forward.

The proposal was then submitted as a Cabinet note for approval, and it was scheduled for discussion during a Cabinet meeting on the evening of August 1, 2002. The Prime Minister chaired the meeting, with our proposal as agenda item No. 4. There was a moment of silence when the item came up, and even the three Cabinet Ministers from Orissa who were present did not speak up. Finally, the Prime Minister declared, "Agenda item No. 4 is approved." The decision was unanimous, and the minutes were issued.

I learned about the Cabinet's approval at 9:30 PM that night when the Minister of Science and Technology called to congratulate me. Interestingly, no one from the Department of Biotechnology (DBT) had informed me yet. Mr. Ranendra Pratap Swain, the Minister of Science and Technology in Odisha, heard the news from another Cabinet Minister from Odisha and immediately conveyed his happiness to me. I had expected the DBT Secretary to inform me first, but she did not. When I called the DBT Secretary at 10 PM, she gave a brief reply of "yes." To this day, I am unclear whether she was pleased about this monumental achievement for ILS.

On August 2, 2002, the Government of India officially took over ILS under the Department of Biotechnology. There was a sense of joy and relief all around. I travelled to Delhi to personally thank the Minister of Science and Technology, the Secretary of DBT, and Dr Renu Swarup for their support.

During the process of ILS's takeover by the Government of India, there was some internal complexity. A 1971-batch IAS officer from Assam was serving as the Joint Secretary (JS) to the Prime Minister, the late Mr. A.B. Vajpayee, while Mr. Brajesh Mishra was the Principal Secretary. Given his background, the JS was more interested in securing the takeover of the Centre of Plasma Physics, located in Assam, by the Government of India. This interest was indirectly at odds with the proposal for the takeover of ILS, as it created a competing priority. Nonetheless, the persistent efforts and support from various allies helped in successfully advancing the proposal for ILS.

The Centre of Plasma Physics, now known as the Centre of Plasma Physics – Institute for Plasma Research (CPP-IPR), is a prominent research organization in Northeast India. Established in 1991 under the Department of Science and Technology, Government of Assam, it operates as an autonomous institute dedicated to basic research in both theoretical and experimental plasma physics and related areas. The Centre began its activities in April 1991, based in Guwahati. At the same time as our efforts for the takeover of ILS by the Government of India, there were initiatives to bring the Centre of Plasma Physics under the central government's fold. While ILS successfully achieved this milestone in August 2002, the Centre of Plasma Physics followed a different trajectory. After continued efforts, the Government of India decided to integrate it under the Department of Atomic Energy, making it a sister organization of the Institute for Plasma Research (IPR), based in Ahmedabad. This formal merger took place on May 29, 2009, with the Centre adopting its new name, CPP-IPR. Unfortunately, the Joint Secretary (JS), who had shown interest in the Centre's central takeover, passed away in 2007 at the age of 60 following a heart surgery. His involvement marked a period when parallel proposals for both institutes were in motion, albeit with different timelines and eventual outcomes.

During the efforts to secure the takeover of the Institute of Life Sciences (ILS) by the Government of India, we encountered significant competition from other institutions aiming for the same central support. The Rajiv Gandhi Centre for Biotechnology (RGCB) in Thiruvananthapuram was one such challenge. Originally established in 1990 as the Centre for Development of Education, Science and Technology (C-DEST), it was restructured into RGCB by the Government of Kerala in 1994. The transformation aimed to create a comprehensive biotechnology research centre, and the foundation stone for its new building was laid by Prime Minister Narasimha Rao in 1995.

Prof. M.G.K. Menon was actively working towards having RGCB taken over by the central government. This posed a direct challenge to our proposal for ILS, as RGCB was already gaining momentum and support at the national level. Along with the Centre for Plasma Physics in Guwahati, these two institutions represented significant threats to the priority of the ILS takeover. Nevertheless, our strategy to secure the takeover of ILS was effective, culminating in the successful transfer of the institute to the Government of India under the Department of Biotechnology on August 2, 2002. The outcome marked a crucial achievement amidst strong competition and multiple contenders for central support in the realm of scientific research and development.

Indeed, the Rajiv Gandhi Centre for Biotechnology (RGCB) was eventually taken over by the Government of India on August 2, 2007, under the Department of Biotechnology (DBT). This happened five years after the successful takeover of the Institute of Life Sciences (ILS) by the central government in 2002. The Plasma Research Centre in Guwahati, which had also been vying for a similar central takeover, was taken over later. It formally became part of the Department of Atomic Energy as the Centre of Plasma Physics – Institute for Plasma Research (CPP-IPR) in 2009.

Before the takeover of the Institute of Life Sciences (ILS), there was a small team of scientists holding academic designations such as Professor, Reader, and Lecturer. During the proposal for the takeover, a recommendation was made to retain these academic titles but update them to Professor, Associate Professor, and Assistant Professor. The plan also included expanding the number of faculty positions to 26 by the year 2020, which was approved by both the Department of Biotechnology (DBT) and the Government of India. After the takeover on August 2, 2002, the DBT provided the necessary funding, enabling the institute to grow and enhance its research capabilities. The Government even approved granting university status to ILS. However, I had to leave ILS when my deputation period ended, and it seems the university status issue may not have been actively pursued afterward. This resulted in a missed opportunity to elevate ILS to a university-level institution, which could have significantly enhanced its academic profile.

After the takeover of the Institute of Life Sciences (ILS) by the Government of India, the reconstitution of the Society and Governing Body marked a significant milestone. The first Governing Body meeting took place in Bhubaneswar and was chaired by the Minister of Science & Technology, who arrived by a special plane provided by Panda and Company. I had secured a special permission from the DG of CISF, to go directly to the aircraft to receive the Minister. In the rush to arrange this permission, however, I forgot to bring a flower bouquet to greet the Minister. Late Justice Ranganath Mishra, who was present at the airport and had a personal connection with both our family and the Minister, stepped in to help. He had brought two small flower bouquets—one for the Minister and one for the Minister's wife. When he noticed me empty-handed, he kindly gave me one of the bouquets to present. From the airport, the Minister and his wife departed directly for Puri, where they had a meeting scheduled.

The next day, key figures including Dr Renu Swarup, Secretary DBT, and other members of the Governing Body arrived in Odisha. The meeting was held at Hotel Swosti on Janpath, with accommodations arranged for all participants, including the Minister. By then, Mr. Surya Narayan Patra had taken over as the Minister for Energy and Science & Technology in Odisha, and he also attended the Governing Body meeting. Since this was the first Governing Body meeting after ILS's takeover, it garnered media attention. The Minister assured the media that there would be ample funding for ILS, provided the scientists continued to work diligently. The meeting was considered a success, setting a positive tone for the institute's future under the Government of India's administration.

With Late Surya Narayan Patra Minister Science& Technology, Odisha

With Minister Science & Technology, Govt. of India & Secretary, Dept. of Biotechnology

Once the ILS was officially taken over by the Government of India, my first task was to fill the existing vacant positions, which I promptly did by advertising and recruiting for those roles. I then requested additional positions, which were subsequently sanctioned. Following this, the Scientific Advisory Committee (SAC) for ILS was constituted, with Prof. G. Padmanaban as the Chairman. The committee members included distinguished personalities such as Prof. Asis Dutta (Vice-Chancellor of JNU), Dr. Sandeep Basu (Director of NII, New Delhi), the Director Generals of ICMR, ICAR, and the Directorate General of Health Services (DGHS), Government of India, as well as the Director of CMAP, Lucknow.

After the Governing Body meeting, I had to organize the first SAC meeting, and the date was set. Known for my inclination to approach things in a novel way, I decided to hold the SAC meeting at Chilika. Chilika Lake is a brackish water lagoon located on the east coast of India, flowing into the Bay of Bengal. It is the largest coastal lagoon in India and the second-largest brackish water lagoon in the world.

At that time, I knew the Minister for Tourism and Culture in Odisha, and I visited his office to discuss the possibility of hosting the SAC meeting at Chilika. During our conversation, I learned about the availability of a boat cruise on the lake. This gave me the idea to not just hold the meeting at Chilika, but to actually conduct it aboard a cruise on Chilika Lake. The Odisha Government extended full support, and we made arrangements to transform the cruise into a conference venue. The boat was equipped with a powerful generator, and we set up a presentation screen and organized the covered space to resemble a conference room. Tea, snacks, and meals were prepared onboard. We brought all SAC members and ILS scientists, along with their presentation materials, to Chilika. The government guest house was booked for accommodation, and since it was the first SAC meeting of ILS, the Secretary of DBT, late Dr Manju Sharma, also attended. We arrived at Chilika by noon and had lunch at the guest house. By 4 PM, the cruise was ready. We boarded and set off into the lake, with the cruise booked from 4 PM to 11 PM. The meeting began with an introduction from me, followed by presentations from the scientists. There was ample time for discussion, and all members actively participated, showing great interest in the work ILS was doing at the time, despite the limited staff. We even enjoyed dinner on the cruise. After the meeting concluded, we returned to the guest house for the night.

Chilika Lake, the largest wintering ground for migratory birds in the Indian subcontinent, offered a great opportunity for sightseeing the next morning. After breakfast, everyone was eager to explore the lake to observe the migratory birds, so we arranged a motorboat excursion.

It was during this outing that I discovered another facet of Prof. Padmanaban; besides being a top scientist, he was also a renowned Carnatic singer. At the request of DBT Secretary, he sang a beautiful song, adding a special touch to the experience. The time spent at Chilika was enjoyable and memorable. We had lunch at the *Barkul* guest house before returning to Bhubaneswar. The following day, the SAC members visited ILS and departed for their respective destinations by evening.

The year 2002 was indeed a turning point for ILS. August marked the beginning of a new chapter, as the institute gained momentum with the Government of India's takeover. Around this time, the Administrative Officer on deputation from the Odisha Administrative Service returned to her cadre, and ILS hired its first dedicated Administrative Officer, like other DBT institutes. With renewed enthusiasm, everyone at ILS worked diligently towards its growth and development.

I was on deputation from ICMR (RMRC, Bhubaneswar) to ILS starting in March 1998, and my initial three-year period was set to end in February 2001. At that time, Prof. N.K. Ganguly served as the Director General of ICMR. The situation regarding the director, RMRC in Bhubaneswar post-cyclone was indeed complex. The super cyclone that devastated Odisha in 1999 had significant impacts on public health and the infrastructure of the region. In response to these challenges a committee was formed to examine the various issues the RMRC was facing, including operational, administration and resource related difficulties. The reluctance of the committee members to accept hospitality from RMRC may have stemmed from several factors, such as concerns about potential conflicts of interest. Ethical considerations, or the desire to remain impartial during their evaluation. It was important for the committee to maintain a level of independence to ensure that their findings and recommendations are credible and unbiassed. This situation highlights the broader themes of crisis management, the importance of integrity in public health initiatives, and the complexities involved in leadership roles during the times of disaster and recovery. Addressing the aftermath of such a significant natural disaster requires not only logistical and material support but also effective governance and ethical considerations among stake holders.

The committee members approached me for assistance, and I arranged accommodations and provided my personal vehicle for their transportation. Based on the committee's recommendations, the director was transferred to another ICMR centre as ' Officer in Charge', retaining the same scale of pay. Additionally, there was another scientist who had worked with us at RMRC in the early 1980s. He had become a director prematurely at another institute, but was also facing problems there and was under inquiry. Although the committee recommended his transfer, he ultimately requested to be transferred to Bhubaneswar, where he wanted to return. Given these circumstances, I did not wish to return to RMRC, Bhubaneswar. I spoke with Dr Manju Sharma and personally requested her to discuss my situation with the DG of ICMR. Thankfully, my deputation was eventually extended until February 2003.

As I mentioned earlier, the Director General of ICMR was a member of our Governing Body at ILS. In early 2002, I invited Prof. N.K. Ganguly, who was the DG of ICMR at the time, to visit ILS. He graciously accepted the invitation and spent a significant amount of time with us. During his visit, he interacted with every scientist and student at ILS, fostering a sense of connection and engagement within the institution.

CHAPTER – 20

Back to ICMR

At the end of Prof. Ganguly's visit, he urged me to return to ICMR, as the institutes were struggling due to a lack of strong leadership. I also had a personal interest in going back to ICMR since positions in DBT institutes were not pensionable, while those in ICMR were. By that time, I had completed the crucial tasks needed at ILS. I told Prof. Ganguly that I would only return to ICMR as a Director, and he agreed. He informed me that the post of Director at RMRC, Jabalpur was advertised and encouraged me to apply. I applied for the position and was selected. Until that time, only medical scientists had been appointed to RMRCs in ICMR, so I was the first biologist to be selected as Director of one of the RMRCs. My selection raised many eyebrows, and there were several anonymous complaints, including one from a professor at AIIMS, New Delhi. The appointment of Institute Directors in ICMR required approval from the Appointment Committee of the Cabinet (ACC), which included the Prime Minister as Chairman, along with the Home Minister, the Personnel Minister, and the departmental Minister. My selection was sent to the ACC, but by the time it reached them, the Health Minister had changed, and Mr. Shatrughna Sinha had taken over. The

PMO referred the file to the new Minister, but ultimately, my appointment was approved by the end of 2002.

Once I received the appointment letter, I prepared to move. I went to Delhi to meet the Secretary of DBT, who was upset about my decision to leave ILS, stating that the institute was taken over because of my efforts. She urged me to stay in DBT and assured me I could build a successful career there. I explained my concerns about pension and the financial security I would need after retirement, which I wouldn't have if I remained at ILS. Additionally, I hadn't completed 20 years of service in ICMR, which would have allowed me to resign and receive a reduced pension upon joining ILS. The Secretary of DBT then proposed that the Minister of Science & Technology write to the Minister of Health to request an extension of my deputation, enabling me to complete 20 years in ICMR and qualify for some pension. I agreed, and a letter was sent from the Minister of Science & Technology to the Minister of Health. However, since rules did not permit extensions of deputation beyond five years at that time, the request could not be granted.

I discussed my situation with the Financial Adviser of DBT, who was the brother-in-law of an Orissa cadre IAS officer. He strongly advised me that for my own financial protection, I should return to ICMR. I took his advice to heart. I met again with the Secretary of DBT and the Minister of Science & Technology to explain my position. The Minister understood my concerns and agreed to relieve me, but he wrote a letter to the Minister of Health, copying the DG of ICMR, to allow me to serve as the Director in charge until a new Director for ILS was selected and joined. ICMR accepted this proposal, and I was finally relieved to join ICMR on 26th February 2003 as the Director of RMRC, Jabalpur. I took charge of the Director position at RMRC,

Jabalpur, in Delhi on the afternoon of 26th February 2003, while also continuing as the Director in charge of ILS, Bhubaneswar.

I am not a light-hearted person; I am serious and have deep concerns. I firmly believe that everyone in this universe possesses both positive and negative vibrations. If we could channel the positive aspects, they could transform into a powerful force capable of changing lives. My five years of hard work at ILS, directed positively, brought happiness into my life for many years to come.

Before joining in Jabalpur, I wanted to leave the RMRC campus where I had been staying. My wife decided to move with our children to her mother's place in Saheed Nagar. ILS assisted with the relocation, and my family settled in Saheed Nagar with my mother-in-law while I left for Jabalpur. After taking over charge in Delhi, I stayed for a day, as my train to Jabalpur was scheduled for the following day. At that time, there were no flights to Jabalpur, so I opted for the Gondwana Express train from Delhi. The first director of Jabalpur, Colonel Tewari, had retired in February and was now settled in Noida. Upon learning that I was in Delhi, he invited me to his home, where he briefed me about the Jabalpur institute and Dr Neeru Singh, who was to hand over charge to me. He expressed many grievances about various individuals, and I listened attentively before returning to Dr Pattnayak's house in Swasthya Vihar for dinner. Afterward, I returned to Orissa Bhawan to prepare for my train journey the next day.

I needed to catch the train to Jabalpur, which was scheduled to depart at 3:30 PM. Unfamiliar with the food options on the train, I simply went to the station and boarded the train. Fortunately, Mr. P. Pattanayak, the son of Dr S. Pattanayak, was at the station with a packet of food.

He kindly informed me that good food would be hard to come by, so he brought some from his home. I accepted his offer and boarded the train. The first-class compartment was small and sparsely populated. The train was set to arrive the next morning at 5 AM, and I reached Jabalpur on time. Upon arrival, I was warmly welcomed by several staff members from RMRC, who escorted me to the RMRC guest house. The campus was expansive, featuring a large building for laboratories and offices. That same day at 9:30 AM, I went to the office and met the staff members who were eagerly waiting to see me. The Centre had a solid number of scientists, and the field station of the Malaria Research Centre was also operational there, with Dr Neeru Singh serving as Officer in Charge. She took me to the Director's office and made me comfortable.

I resumed the Directorship of the Regional Medical Research Centre (now the National Institute for Research on Tribal Health) at Jabalpur after the centre's building had been destroyed by a significant earthquake. My role was to restore functionality to the institute, which I successfully accomplished. At that time, as per the directions of the DG of ICMR, every institute was required to maintain its scientific profile. Surprisingly, RMRC, Jabalpur ranked at the bottom, with hardly any extramural projects and no practice of weekly seminars. There was a considerable amount of work needed at the institute.

Tribal populations are known for their homogeneity and inbreeding, resulting in unusual genetic parity. Therefore, studying genetic diversity among these tribes is essential. We do not yet know whether some tribes possess intrinsic resistance to specific diseases. I had to establish a research culture at the Regional Medical Research Centre, now National Institute for Research on Tribal Health

(NIRTH). I made significant efforts in underserved tribal areas of Madhya Pradesh and Chhattisgarh, arranging work elements deep within Naxal-affected regions. I discussed with each scientist and assigned different areas for them to focus on. Soon, a work culture began to take shape, leading to the generation of extramural projects and the publication of research papers. The Scientific Advisory Committee (SAC) of RMRC, Jabalpur was chaired by General Raghunath from Bangalore, and I convened the SAC meeting, which went well. However, I was not satisfied with the constitution of the SAC; I wanted it to be more meaningful. After discussing this with the DG, he agreed to my proposal.

At ILS, the SAC met only once a year, with members doing their jobs and then leaving without interfering in the management of the institute. However, I found a different dynamic at NIRTH, Jabalpur. The then Chairman of the SAC wrote a letter to the DG of ICMR, complaining that I was not in regular contact with him and that I had not consulted him sufficiently.

In response, I travelled to Delhi, met with the DG, and reconstituted the SAC with scientists who had proven records. Dr Sandeep Basu was appointed as the new Chairman, and several other distinguished scientists, including Dr G.C. Mishra, then Director of NCCS, Pune, were added as members. This change might have irritated some, but the new SAC performed exceptionally well in uplifting the centre. Within one year, RMRC ranked 8th among ICMR institutes. Almost every scientist secured an extramural project and began publishing research papers.

During my tenure as Director of NIRTH, Jabalpur, I also held the additional position of Director in charge of ILS, Bhubaneswar, which required me to visit ILS every month while overseeing the functioning of both institutes. In May 2003, the Director of the Centre for Research in Medical Entomology (CRME), Madurai, was set to retire. The DG of ICMR called me and requested that I take on the additional role of Director at CRME. Following this directive, I hurried to Madurai to assume charge from Dr K. Satyanarayana, who was heading the CRME. After taking over at CRME, I convened a meeting with the scientists to establish an excellent work culture. Subsequently, I returned to Jabalpur via ILS, Bhubaneswar. My official headquarters remained in Jabalpur, but I had to travel to ILS, Bhubaneswar, and CRME, Madurai, each month. On one occasion, while traveling from Bhubaneswar to Madurai, my wife accompanied me. We took an Air India flight connecting Bhubaneswar to Chennai, where we were picked up by a vehicle from VCRC, Pondicherry, and transported to Pondicherry. We spent some time visiting VCRC, and the following day, a CRME vehicle collected us for the journey to Madurai. At that time, I had three mobile phones provided by the three institutes: NIRTH, Jabalpur; ILS, Bhubaneswar; and CRME, Madurai. Throughout our travel from Pondicherry to Madurai, each phone rang continuously, and I found myself giving instructions to various institutes. I barely spoke to my wife during the entire journey, which, I believe, led her to avoid accompanying me on official trips in the future.

Finally, I returned to Jabalpur, my official headquarters. Jabalpur is an important administrative, industrial, and business centre in Madhya Pradesh. It houses the High Court of Madhya Pradesh and several departmental headquarters of the State Government. Notable sites in Jabalpur include the famous Jain temple, *Dhuandhar* falls, *Chausta Yogini*, Marble Rocks in *Bhedaghat*, and the Balancing Rock near Madan Mahal Fort. Additionally, the world-renowned tiger reserves, such as Kanha National Park, Bandhavgarh National Park, and Pench National Park, can be easily accessed from Jabalpur.

The NIRTH in Jabalpur was situated in a beautiful location with ample space and excellent gardens filled with various flowers. The guest house was also surrounded by a lovely garden and equipped with all necessary amenities. Important visitors to Jabalpur often made a point to visit the RMRC campus. One notable occasion was during a national judiciary conference when Justice S. Rajendra Babu, the senior-most judge of the Supreme Court of India who would later become Chief Justice of India, visited us. He was accompanied by his wife, who was studying in Berhampur, Odisha. They spent considerable time exploring the laboratory and facilities. Another Judge of the High Court, who later became Chief Justice of India, was serving in the Madhya Pradesh High Court at the time, also visited the institute located in Jabalpur.

As I mentioned earlier, there were no flights to Jabalpur, so one had to travel by train. Once, while traveling from Delhi to Jabalpur, I found myself in the same compartment as Mrs. Jaishree Banerjee, the MP for Jabalpur Lok Sabha. She had issues with the RMRC, where the late Dr Neeru Singh was the Officer in Charge. As soon as she learned that I was the Director of RMRC, Jabalpur, she began expressing her grievances about the institute and its leadership. I listened patiently as she voiced her concerns, particularly her disappointment at not being invited to RMRC. She insisted that I invite her to the institute, but I told her I would consider it for an appropriate occasion. However, she pressed for a specific date. I managed to deflect her insistence by saying I would check my schedule and let her know. A few days later, she invited me to her home for tea, where she again brought up the invitation to RMRC. At that time, one of her grandchildren was running a fever, and she wanted to have them checked for malaria. I suggested she send the child to RMRC for a blood sample, which she did, but I never extended the invitation to her. After a couple of months, I began receiving threatening messages from her side. I chose to ignore them. Eventually, the 2004 elections arrived, and she did not receive a ticket to contest.

I continued my usual work and initiated weekly seminars at NIRTH, Jabalpur, successfully establishing a positive work culture within a year. During a previous visit to ILS, Bhubaneswar, in May 2003, I had the opportunity to meet the Chief Minister. I briefed him on the progress of ILS since its takeover by the Government of India and requested his assistance in inviting the PM to dedicate ILS to the nation the institute and dedicate it to the nation. The Chief Minister kindly agreed, and a letter to the Prime Minister was promptly drafted . I took a copy of this letter to share with the Minister of Science & Technology and the Secretary of the Department of Biotechnology (DBT). After returning to Madurai and then to Jabalpur, I resumed my responsibilities. In early July, I received a call from the Prime Minister's Office, informing me that the Prime Minister would be visiting Bhubaneswar on July 15, 2003, to inaugurate AIIMS and would also visit ILS to dedicate it to the Nation. I was instructed to prepare accordingly. Since the preparations required a few days, I discussed the situation with the DG of ICMR, who understood the urgency and asked me to head to ILS, Bhubaneswar, immediately to oversee the arrangements and return to Jabalpur after the Prime Minister's visit.

At that time, the DBT was unaware of the Prime Minister's program, but the Chief Minister's Office had been informed. I promptly contacted the Secretary of DBT to update her on the Prime Minister's visit so she could also attend. I arrived in Bhubaneswar in early July 2003, where CPWD officials and state police frequently consulted with me regarding the preparations. The CPWD refined the roads and constructed a temporary bathroom near the meeting space. I spent my days at ILS from 8 AM to 9 PM, meeting with various officers who provided a range of suggestions.

We prepared a meeting space on the ILS campus, outside the main building, accommodating up to 400 people. We arranged chairs, colourful canopies, and a dais for around ten dignitaries, as advised by the Prime Minister's Office. One day, the Chief Minister visited ILS to review the arrangements for the Prime Minister's visit, accompanied by the Minister of Science & Technology. They inspected the entire campus and all the arrangements. We then proceeded to the ILS guest house, which at the time had only two rooms. The Minister of Science & Technology expressed disappointment at the limited capacity for such an important event, stating it was too small for the Prime Minister's meeting. I reassured him that this was not a public meeting but rather an academic gathering attended solely by academicians, which we had accordingly arranged. The Chief Minister agreed but made a polite comment: "Don't you think that this colourful canopy gives the impression of a different type of function?" He suggested that we change the colours of the canopy. We made the adjustments to blue and white, which ultimately created a more fitting atmosphere for an academic event.

Both the Collector and Superintendent of Police (SP) were visiting us every day as we remained extremely busy making various arrangements. We also aimed to find a good anchor for the event. I remembered that during the visit of the late Mr. Rajiv Gandhi to Cuttack in the 1980s, a schoolgirl had done an excellent job of anchoring. I discussed this with Dr B.K. Das from SCB Medical College, and he mentioned that he knew the person. With his help, we finalized the anchor. Dr Das brought her to ILS, where we explained everything to her. She took notes, and after two days, she returned with the script, which was excellent. By that time, security personnel from the Prime Minister's Office (PMO), led by a DIG, had arrived at ILS. They visited various locations on the campus and held several discussions with me. From ILS, Mr. Samal was entrusted with coordination, and he did a wonderful job. The security staff wanted to see a rehearsal of the anchoring and requested the anchor to come back. She arrived and performed a rehearsal, which impressed the security staff so much that they requested her to slightly downplay her anchoring style.

On July 14, 2003, all the Governing Body members arrived, including the Director General of Health Services, the late Dr S.P. Agarwal. The Prime Minister was scheduled to first visit ILS to dedicate the institute to the nation before heading to the AIIMS site in *Patrapada* to lay the foundation stone and address a large public gathering. The program was set for the entire day. A bulletproof car first arrived at Bhubaneswar airport, followed by the Prime Minister. Mr. Rajendra Singh, popularly known as Rajju Bhaiya, was the fourth *Sarsanghchalak* of the *Rashtriya Swayamsevak Sangh* (RSS), serving as the chief of the organization from 1994 to 2000. Unfortunately, he passed away on July 14, 2003. Due to this, the Prime Minister needed to complete his engagements in Bhubaneswar quickly before rushing to Pune for Rajju Bhaiya's funeral rituals. Consequently, all the programs were arranged to take place in Patrapada, where the Prime Minister would lay the foundation stone for AIIMS and address the public gathering.

We were informed on the evening of July 14 that we needed to shift everything, including the inaugural plaque, to Patrapada, as both functions would be combined. This was a monumental task for us. I sat down briefly with the security staff from the Prime Minister's Office (PMO) and my colleagues at ILS. Mr. Samal stepped forward and assured me that he would manage everything, and I authorized him to take the necessary actions. Mr. Samal and his team from ILS spent the entire night working in Patrapada, staying in frequent contact with me to provide updates on their progress. On the morning of July 15, I went to the venue along with some Governing Body members, including Dr Pattanayak. Upon our arrival, Mr. Samal greeted us and confirmed that everything was perfectly arranged. He had gone without food and hadn't even brushed his teeth, which made it difficult for Dr Pattanayak to recognize him. He truly accomplished what seemed almost impossible. As we arrived at the venue, the security staff of the PMO escorted me inside to receive the Prime Minister, while the Chief Minister and the others were directed to the audience.

We were all waiting when the Prime Minister arrived, accompanied by the Minister for Science and Technology (Dr M.M. Joshi) and the Minister of Health (late Smt. Sushma Swaraj), led by the Chief Minister of Odisha, Mr. Naveen Patnaik. The Chief Minister introduced me to the Prime Minister and then to the other dignitaries. After our introductions, the Prime Minister and the other delegates proceeded to the dais. The program began with Smt. Sushma Swaraj discussing the proposed AIIMS in Bhubaneswar, followed by Dr Joshi, who spoke about ILS. While addressing the gathering, the Prime Minister inaugurated AIIMS and shared a few words about ILS, explaining how and why it was taken over by the Government of India. He expressed his satisfaction with the institute's progress and dedicated ILS to the nation.

Once the program concluded, the Prime Minister departed for Pune, and everyone began to disperse. We took the ILS plaque and returned to the institute, where I thanked all the ILS staff for their efforts in making the program a success. Everyone was in high spirits, though Mr. Samal appeared extremely tired after the demanding preparations. Among the core ILS staff who supported me throughout the process were B.M. Mishra, Debendra Kar, as well as faculty members like Prof Supakar and Dr Sabat. Dr B.R. Das, an excellent scientist who left ILS in 2001 to join Ranbaxy in Bombay, also contributed significantly during the drafting of the vision document for ILS.

I stayed at ILS for a couple of days after the program, spending time with each staff member. However, I had to return to Jabalpur on July 18, 2003. In the meantime, the selection committee convened to choose the new Director of ILS, and Dr Satish Gupta from the National Institute of Immunology (NII) in New Delhi was selected. I was informed that I needed to return to ILS, Bhubaneswar, to officially hand over the charge to Dr Gupta. I arrived in Bhubaneswar on August 1, 2003, and handed over the responsibilities of ILS to Dr Gupta on August 2. I returned to Jabalpur on August 4 and continued my work at RMRC, Jabalpur, and CRME, Madurai.

As time passed, the ICMR advertised the position of Director of the Malaria Research Centre (MRC), now known as the National Institute of Malaria Research (NIMR), in Delhi, and I decided to apply. Dr Sarla Subbarao had been the Director of MRC since September 1998, following the retirement of Dr V.P. Sharma in April 1998. During the interim, Dr Ansari, who was senior to Dr Subbarao as Deputy Director, served as the Officer in Charge. However, when Dr Subbarao was selected as Director, Dr Ansari filed a lawsuit but ultimately lost. He continued in his role as Deputy Director.

The Director of MRC (Dr Subbarao) retired in April 2003, and once again, Dr Ansari assumed the position of Officer in Charge, being the senior-most staff member. He had also applied for the Director position, along with several others, including Dr Y.D. Sharma, who was then a senior professor of biotechnology at AIIMS, New Delhi. However, Dr Ansari was actively campaigning for the role. As the Officer in Charge, he frequently invited influential individuals to lunch at MRC, effectively creating a lobby of support around him, making it seem almost certain that he would be selected.

During this time, the selection committee for the Director position was chaired by the DG of ICMR and included the Director General of Health Services (DGHS) along with five top experts in the field. The recommendations of the selection committee were then presented to the Executive Committee of ICMR, and after their approval, the selected candidate's name was sent to the Appointment Committee of the Cabinet (ACC) for final approval (this was the practice at that time). It was quite a lengthy process. The selection committee meeting took place in October 2003, and I attended. There were seven experts present, including the DG of ICMR and the DGHS. The atmosphere of the selection committee was rigorous. One of the experts, a regular visitor to MRC, supported Dr Ansari, arguing against my selection by saying that I was already a director and that it would be disruptive to change that. However, I later learned from a very reliable source that all the other experts unanimously supported my candidacy. I also found out that during the final discussions, the DG of ICMR asked the DGHS (the late Dr. Agarwal) for his opinion on whom to select. Dr. Agarwal responded, "If you want the MRC to continue as it is, you can select Dr. Ansari. But if you want to further develop the MRC and take it to new heights, please select Dr. Dash." Ultimately, I was selected for the position. After the interview, I returned to Jabalpur.

The papers were submitted to the Appointment Committee of the Cabinet (ACC) by December 2003. However, there was another representation against my selection. It was clear who the petitioner was, and this representation also had some political backing, which further delayed the process in the Ministry of Health. After a thorough scrutiny, the Health Ministry finally recommended the case to the ACC for the necessary approval. Dr Ansari was approaching the end of his term as Officer in Charge, completing one year in that role on April 30, 2004.

I continued to serve as the Director of NIRTH, Jabalpur, while also being in charge of the Centre for Research in Medical Entomology (CRME), Madurai. I remember being in Jabalpur when I was informed by ICMR on April 28, 2004, to proceed to Delhi and take over the charge of MRC by April 30. I arrived in Delhi on the night of April 29 and officially assumed my role as the Director of MRC at the ICMR headquarters. The Administrative Officer (AO) of MRC was called to assist me, and he took me directly to the Madhuban office. On the way, I asked the AO to inform all scientists to gather at Madhuban for a meeting, as I wanted to address them. Arrangements were promptly made. MRC was operating from four different locations: Shamnath Marg, Madhuban, Mukherjee Nagar, and Azadpur. Dr Ansari was situated at the Madhuban office.

Upon arriving at the office, I found that all the scientists were present except for Dr Ansari and Dr Adak, who were on a field tour. I addressed the scientists, encouraging them to pursue innovative work. Dr Ansari and Dr Adak returned the next day to meet with me. Initially, I stayed at Orissa Bhawan for a few days before moving to the NICD guest house on Shamnath Marg. After working for a few days at MRC, Delhi, I returned to Madurai and then back to Jabalpur.

The NIRTH, Jabalpur, had been publishing a Tribal Health Bulletin, which was discontinued for some reason. I took the initiative to revive it. Alongside the scientists from NIRTH, I visited numerous tribal villages, where we collected various types of samples. Since it was not feasible to collect these samples frequently, I decided to establish a tribal cell line at NIRTH, Jabalpur. Dr G.C. Mishra, the Director of NCCS in Pune, was a member of our Scientific Advisory Committee (SAC). During the next SAC meeting, I presented the proposal to establish a tribal cell line and requested assistance and support from Dr Mishra. He readily agreed, and the SAC approved the proposal.

Jabalpur is a beautiful place, known for its natural attractions such as *Bhedaghat, Dhuandhar* Falls, Chaunsath Yogini Temple, and Kanha Forest. *Bhedaghat* is located alongside the River Narmada. The *Chaunsath Yogini* Temple is one of the four major extant temples featuring carvings of sixty-four *Yoginis,* female yoga mystics. Built in the 10th century, it commands a panoramic view of the surrounding area and the river flowing through the marble rocks.

Dhuandhar Falls creates a stunning visual effect, resembling smoke rising from the river. Another significant attraction is "Bandar Kodini." When traveling by boat between the marble rocks, the mountains on either side narrow to the extent that monkeys can jump across them, hence the name "Bandar Kodini." A moonlit boat ride through the marble rock mountains on the Narmada River is a popular tourist activity in the area. Kanha Forest, known as a tiger reserve, is one of the largest national parks in Madhya Pradesh. Established on June 1, 1955, it was designated as a tiger reserve in 1973. The regions surrounding Kanha Forest were highly endemic for malaria, requiring our teams to collect samples for malaria research. I fondly remember staying in the forest department guesthouse in Kanha; it was truly enjoyable.

As I mentioned earlier, I took over as Director of the Malaria Research Centre (MRC) in Delhi, now National Institute of Malaria Research (NIMR) on April 30. My papers were submitted to the Appointment Committee of the Cabinet (ACC) for approval, but the process was delayed due to representations from a candidate who was not selected for the post. By May 2004, the government changed, and the UPA government led by Congress came to power. Consequently, the ACC returned the papers to the Health Ministry to restart the approval process. Finally, in August 2004, I received full approval and became the full-time Director of MRC (now NIMR) while remaining in charge of NIRTH, Jabalpur, and CRME, Madurai. By the time I joined NIRTH, Jabalpur in 2003, the institute had already made significant contributions to the Yaws eradication program, particularly in Chhattisgarh. The Yaws eradication program in India began long ago, as Yaws is a chronic bacterial infection caused by treponemes.

It was first reported in Assam in 1887, and since then, cases have been documented in Odisha, Chhattisgarh, Madhya Pradesh, Andhra Pradesh, Uttar Pradesh, Jharkhand, and a few other states. The number of Yaws cases in India dropped from 3,600 in 1996 to zero in 2004, leading to India's declaration of Yaws elimination in 2006. Later, when I joined the World Health Organization (WHO) in 2009, I continued to oversee Yaws alongside other health issues. Eventually, WHO certified India as free from Yaws in 2016.

While at NIMR, Jabalpur, I initiated a Ph.D. program within the institute. The MRC Field Station was relocated to the RMRC building, with the late Dr Neeru Singh serving as the Officer in Charge. Although my official headquarters became Delhi, I travelled to CRME, Madurai, and NIRTH, Jabalpur, every month since I was also the Director in charge of these two institutes.

CRME, Madurai was undertaking several important research projects on lymphatic filariasis elimination and Japanese encephalitis (JE). Established in 1985 as a permanent institute of ICMR to address the endemic nature of JE at the time, CRME's first Director was the late Dr Rachel Reuben. In the 1990s, the WHO targeted lymphatic filariasis for elimination using a strategy of annual single-dose mass treatment with diethylcarbamazine (DEC), later combined with Albendazole. However, India opted for the single annual treatment of DEC alone. The substantial work conducted by scientists at CRME, Madurai, demonstrating that DEC combined with Albendazole was more effective than DEC alone, ultimately led to a change in the Government of India's program from administering DEC alone to the combined treatment of DEC and Albendazole.

During my time in Jabalpur, issues arose at the Institute of Life Sciences (ILS) in Bhubaneswar, creating a significant conflict between the Director and the staff. In early 2004, during a personal visit to Bhubaneswar, I met with the staff of ILS, who expressed their serious concerns about the situation with the then Director. I felt caught in a difficult position, as I represented the Governing Body of ILS on behalf of the Director General of ICMR, and the staff expected me to take action to resolve the conflict.

The Governing Body meeting took place in Delhi in late 2004, with the Minister of Science and Technology in Chair. During this meeting, the staff agitation against the Director was brought up, and the Director was present as well. The Minister directed the Secretary of the Department of Biotechnology (DBT) to consult with me, as the former Director, to help diffuse the situation. The Secretary took me to her residence for a detailed discussion. After carefully considering the issues, I concluded that the only viable solution was to remove the Director. This recommendation was acted upon, and within a month, the Director was asked to resign. Subsequently, the late Professor Supakar was made Director in charge of ILS, and the position was advertised again. I remained involved in the selection process for scientists at ILS until early 2006.

I was diligently managing the NIMR, Delhi; NIRTH Jabalpur, and CRME Madurai during this period. Between 2003 and 2005, the publication profile of CRME Madurai significantly improved. In December 2004, I convened the Scientific Advisory Committee (SAC) meeting for CRME in Madurai, which was attended by the Director General of ICMR. At that time, the NIMR, Delhi, operated a field station in the Nicobar Islands, one of 13 field stations located across the country. Each field station had an officer (scientist) in charge. I had called for a meeting of all officers in charge of the 13 field stations in Delhi. The officer in charge of the Nicobar field station was scheduled to travel from Port Blair to attend the meeting on December 26, 2004. On that day, the officer in charge of Nicobar Islands contacted me, reporting a devastating tsunami that had affected the Andaman and Nicobar Islands. He expressed concern about his family, as he was unable to reach them. Recognizing the gravity of the situation, I instructed him to stay back and cancelled the proposed meeting. Until that moment, there had been no news of the tsunami in Delhi. I immediately informed the DG of ICMR, who directed me to notify the Director of RMRC, Port Blair, who was also in Delhi at the time and unaware of the tsunami. Gradually, by the afternoon, we began to learn more about the disaster's impact. According to official estimates, over 10,000 people were killed in India, and hundreds of thousands were left homeless due to the tsunami.

After joining the NIMR in Delhi, I stayed at the NICD guest house and occasionally at Orissa Bhawan. One day, the Director General (DG) called me and said, "I brought you from ILS to ICMR, and it is my duty to take care of you." He instructed the ICMR administration to allocate me a house in Connaught Place.

There was a lady doctor in Bombay named Dr Engineer, who was living alone. Many years earlier, she had visited Delhi and requested a room in the ICMR guest house, but it was unavailable. She owned a four-bedroom flat in Ashadeep Building on Haily Road, Connaught Place, which she rented to Coal India Limited for their guest house. In her will, she donated the flat to ICMR. After her death, Coal India continued to occupy the house and did not vacate it. ICMR had to issue a notice for the flat to be returned, and after much difficulty, it was finally handed over.

Due to its size and prime location, many people were interested in occupying the flat, and rumours suggested that even the ministry wanted it. However, the DG of ICMR allocated the flat to me, instructing me to occupy it as soon as possible. The ICMR engineer handed me the keys, and I immediately took possession of the flat. It needed some work to make it habitable, so I constituted a committee to oversee the renovations, appointing Dr Ansari—who was initially opposed to my appointment at MRC—as the chairman. To my surprise, he did an excellent job, and by September 2004, I moved into 104 Ashadeep Building, 9 Haily Road, Connaught Place.

During this time, my family remained in Bhubaneswar, as my children were studying engineering and my wife was working there. They visited me in Delhi in December. By then, the flat was properly arranged. My children completed their examinations in April 2006, and in the same year, my wife received a UGC Research Scientist Award for three years in the Zoology Department at Delhi University. Consequently, my entire family relocated to Delhi in 2006. My daughter was selected during campus recruitment by Accenture in Bangalore and joined the company there, while my son gained admission to a management institute in Delhi.

As I mentioned earlier, the MRC was operating from four different buildings across Delhi: Shamnath Marg, Mukherjee Nagar, Madhuban, and Azadpur. The Government of India had allocated land for MRC in Sector 8 of Dwarka, New Delhi, long before my joining. However, no construction had commenced, and due to the non-utilization of the land, the Municipal Corporation of Delhi (MCD) imposed a heavy fine on MRC, which was gradually increasing. I realized that my first task was to resolve the land issue and initiate construction. Therefore, in 2004, shortly after joining, I organized a *"Bhumi Pujan"* on the day of the return car festival of Lord Jagannath. Almost all staff members of MRC, including Dr Ansari, attended the ceremony. It was heartening to see Dr Ansari participate and offer *"Aahuti"* during the *"Bhumi Pujan."* After the ceremony, my next step was to meet with MCD officials and present them with photographs of the "Bhumi Pujan" to demonstrate our commitment to starting construction soon. I met with a senior MCD official, Mr. Padhy, who was in charge of land and happened to be from Orissa. Along with Dr. Ansari, I discussed the significance of the "Bhumi Pujan" and assured him that construction activities would begin shortly. We requested him to consider waiving the fine as a special case. Mr. Padhy appeared convinced by our discussion, and the following month, we received a letter confirming the waiver of the fine that had been pending for some time.

When the land was allocated to the MRC, a World Bank project was underway with the National Vector Borne Disease Control Programme. The Government had decided that the construction of the NIMR building would be funded through this World Bank project. An architect, Gherzi Eastern Ltd., was engaged to create the architectural drawings for the NIMR building, and an advance payment was made to them. Although the World Bank project was completed, the building construction had not yet begun. It was alleged that out of the four campuses of NIMR, three were private buildings owned by influential individuals, taken on substantial rent, and few retired officers of MRC were reluctant to vacate those premises.

However, I was determined to initiate the construction of the new building, ensuring that once completed, all four campuses of MRC would be consolidated under one roof in Dwarka, New Delhi. Since World Bank funds were not available at that time, the construction had to be financed by ICMR. My first task was to obtain government approval for the architect, who had already commenced some preliminary work. Gherzi Eastern Ltd. approached the ministry, and the matter was presented to the Executive Committee of ICMR, where the architect was ultimately approved. Next, I met with Prof. N.K. Ganguly, the Director General of ICMR, who was an esteemed scientist and progressive thinker, having received numerous national and international awards, including the prestigious Padma Bhushan Award in Medicine. Upon my return to ICMR, a tremendous trust was established between us. He agreed to my proposal, and subsequently, the funds for the construction were approved.

NIMR issued a tender for the building, adhering to all relevant norms, including those set by the Central Vigilance Commission (CVC). Several companies submitted bids, including the Hospital Services Construction Corporation (HSCC), which was a government entity under the Ministry of Health, with the Health Minister as its Chairman at that time. The National Building Construction Corporation (NBCC) also participated in the bidding process. I faced significant pressure to award the contract to HSCC, which was not the lowest bidder; the lowest bid came from the Rajasthan State Road Development Corporation (RSRDCC), owned by the Rajasthan Government. Therefore, the contract was awarded to RSRDCC.

Before issuing the work order, an agreement was signed that included several clauses: a penalty clause for failing to complete the building within the stipulated time, a provision for a monitoring committee to oversee construction quality and progress, and a requirement to send construction samples to IIT for certification. Funds would only be released after receiving satisfactory reports from the monitoring committee. I opted out of serving on the monitoring committee and established a building committee chaired by Dr Sandeep Basu, Director of NII, Delhi, to supervise the construction.

The agreement was thoroughly discussed with the Financial Adviser, Senior Deputy Director General (Administration), the DG of ICMR, myself, and officials from RSRDCC. I took all necessary precautions, knowing that there would be opposition and that some individuals might attempt to undermine my efforts through unfounded rumours. Construction finally began in 2006, with plans for a four-story building that included an underground basement and was fully air-conditioned. The monitoring committee commenced its work, and everything progressed as planned.

In 2004, I engaged in an extensive discussion with the DG of ICMR regarding the operations of NIMR. I explained that NIMR was the largest institute under ICMR, boasting 13 field stations across India. Prior to my role as Director of NIMR (then MRC), I had served as the Director of the Institute of Life Sciences in Bhubaneswar. Given the scale of staff and operations at NIMR, I proposed that its name be changed to the National Institute of Malaria Research. The DG informed me that the name change would require a lengthy process. It first needed to be recommended by the institute's Scientific Advisory Committee (SAC), followed by approvals from the Scientific Advisory Group (SAG) of ICMR, the Scientific Advisory Board (SAB) of ICMR, the Executive Committee of ICMR, and finally, the Governing Body of ICMR. However, he encouraged me to initiate the process. I promptly convened the SAC of ICMR, which approved the proposal to rename the Centre to the National Institute of Malaria Research. The proposal was then forwarded to ICMR's SAG, SAB, and Executive Committee, all of which approved it. The finalized proposal was presented to the next Governing Body (GB) in 2005, where it received approval as well.

In the meantime, I was planning an international conference on malaria to commemorate the 125th anniversary of the discovery of the malaria parasite. Charles Louis Alphonse Laveran, a calm and reserved French military physician, won the Nobel Prize for Medicine and Physiology in 1907 for his discovery of the malaria parasite and significant contributions to parasitology. On November 5, 1880, while working at a military hospital in Constantine, Algeria, he discovered that the cause of malaria was a protozoan, after observing the parasites in a blood smear taken from a patient who had just died of the disease. He initially named the causative organism *Oscillaria malariae*, which was later renamed *Plasmodium*.

Shortly after Laveran's discovery, another landmark finding occurred in India in 1897, when Ronald Ross, born in Almora, became a pivotal figure in understanding malaria transmission. The eldest of ten children of Sir C.C.G. Ross, a general in the British Indian Army, Ross received the Nobel Prize for Physiology and Medicine in 1902 for his groundbreaking work. On August 20, 1897, in Secunderabad, he made his landmark discovery by dissecting the stomach tissue of an *Anopheles* mosquito that had fed on a malarious patient four days earlier. He found the malaria parasite and proved the role of *Anopheles* mosquitoes in transmitting malaria to humans, establishing that the malarial parasite was transmitted by the bite of infected mosquitoes. Both Laveran and Ross were military personnel, and their shared backgrounds have led to malaria often being referred to as "military disease."

My intention was to convene an international conference in November 2005 to mark the 125th anniversary of the discovery of the malaria parasite. I discussed this proposal with the scientists at MRC, and they all agreed to participate. I aimed to involve everyone in the planning process, so I initiated discussions with the first Director of MRC. Along with two senior scientists, I invited him to the India International Centre (IIC) for a meeting about the proposed conference. However, the first Director was not very enthusiastic. During our discussion, I overheard my predecessor questioning one of the MRC scientists about my motivations for planning such a significant conference. He expressed concern that I might have ulterior motives for organising it, but I had no hidden agenda.

In my view, there was a critical need for organizational affinity, collaboration, and contribution among our teams. We needed to learn to manage egos and mindsets to foster partnerships. True ownership of an organization's mission reflects a passion for the cause, and a power structure should not hinder collaboration. Institutions must remain open to new ideas and change; every organization needs to reinvent itself to thrive. My primary goal was to bring NIMR (then MRC) into the global spotlight, especially since it was established to conduct research on malaria.

Additionally, there was the National Vector Borne Disease Control Programme (NVBDCP), responsible for the management and control of malaria and other vector-borne diseases. Until 2004, the relationship between NIMR and NVBDCP had been poor. After my arrival, I made concerted efforts to establish a cordial relationship with NVBDCP, which proved successful. At that time, Dr Jytsna Sokhe was the Director of NVBDCP, and Dr P.L. Joshi served as the Additional Director. I enjoyed an excellent rapport with both, as well as with all the officers of NVBDCP. By 2005, Dr Joshi had become the Director of NVBDCP, and I involved them in organizing the international conference. Not only did NVBDCP become a partner in the event, but they also offered financial assistance. The conference attracted over 500 delegates from around the world, featuring prominent figures in the field of malaria research. The scientific sessions were robust, and the event took place in the conference hall of ICAR in Pusa. Overall, the conference was a success. The Minister of Health was invited to inaugurate the event on November 5, 2005. During the inaugural ceremony, the Minister announced the renaming of MRC to the National Institute of Malaria Research (NIMR). Consequently, MRC became widely recognized as NIMR with effect from 5th November, 2005.

In the late 1980s, when Prof. M.G.K. Menon was part of the Planning Commission and Mr. Rajiv Gandhi was Prime Minister, the government awarded a significant grant to MRC to launch the Integrated Disease Vector Control (IDVC) project. The project was intended as a long-term initiative, leading to the establishment of 13 field stations across India. Numerous staff, including scientists, were recruited, and a fleet of vehicles was acquired for distribution among the field stations. Funds for the project were released biannually, but delays left staff waiting for salaries for months.

When I joined NIMR (MRC) in 2004, the IDVC project was in poor condition. Funding was erratic, leaving staff unpaid for several months, which even disrupted the education of some of their children. I felt compelled to address the situation and discussed it with the Ministry, where I discovered that the project had initially been approved for five years in the late 1980s and then continued without formal renewal. Consequently, no budget was allocated for it, and the project operated on a six-month cycle, relying on ad hoc funding. The project essentially lacked ownership.

I was advised to draft a comprehensive proposal for the approval of the Standing Finance Committee (SFC) of the Government of India. After consulting with the Director-General (DG) of ICMR, who supported the initiative, I entrusted Dr R.C. Dhiman of NIMR to prepare the detailed SFC report under my guidance. At that time, the purchase of vehicles was prohibited for all government organizations. The existing vehicles at the field stations were outdated and unusable, so I included a request for 30 new vehicles in the proposal.

We submitted the SFC report to the Ministry, and a meeting was convened within a month where I was asked to present the proposal. The meeting was attended by the DG of ICMR, Prof. Ganguly, who was very supportive. The Health Secretary, Mr. P.K. Hota, Additional Secretary Mr. S.Y. Quraishi (later Chief Election Commissioner of India), and Joint Secretary Mrs. Rita Teotia were also present. Mr. Quraishi, a batchmate of Mr. D.N. Padhy from Odisha, had been approached by Mr. Padhy on my behalf to put in a good word.

When I presented the proposal and mentioned the request for 30 vehicles, there was noticeable scepticism. With the ban on vehicle purchases, it seemed unlikely that the SFC would approve them. I explained that for malaria research, extensive fieldwork was crucial, and vehicles were essential equipment rather than luxury items. Reliable transport was more valuable than sophisticated laboratory equipment because it was necessary for collecting biological samples in the field and transporting them to the laboratory. I emphasized the need for a cold chain to maintain sample integrity, which justified the request for 30 air-conditioned "field equipment" i.e., vehicles.

My argument resonated with the committee, and they approved the vehicles. Prof. Ganguly took over from me during the discussion, further stressing the importance of malaria research in India. The proposal not only received approval for the vehicles but also for filling vacant project positions that had been sanctioned from the start. After the government's approval, funding issues were resolved, and the staff was finally relieved.

However, the SFC recommended reorganizing the field stations, as some were located in areas without significant malaria activity. The reorganization was mandatory, but it faced resistance from a few senior and retired faculty members who had benefited from using project staff for personal domestic help. Despite this opposition, the restructuring proceeded as planned.

The SFC approval included a major task for me: reorganizing the field stations. Out of the 13 existing stations, the Car Nicobar field station had been destroyed by the tsunami, and we decided to close it, along with the stations in Delhi and three locations in Uttar Pradesh. To replace these, we planned to open two new field stations, one in Chhattisgarh and another in Jharkhand, both of which were highly endemic for malaria at the time. Senior scientists and a retired director advised against the reorganization, warning that it could provoke serious staff unrest and lead to legal complications. The senior staff members benefiting from the project in Delhi were particularly uncooperative. To navigate the legal aspects of closing the field stations and relocating staff, I sought legal advice. I consulted with ICMR, and the DG suggested contacting Mr. Khuranna, the organization's advocate. Accompanied by the Administrative Officer, I visited his chamber and explained our plans in detail. He requested some time to consider the legal implications.

Meanwhile, we reached out to the governments of Chhattisgarh and Jharkhand about establishing new field stations in each state. Dr Raman Singh, the Chief Minister of Chhattisgarh, and Mr. Arjun Munda, the Chief Minister of Jharkhand, facilitated the process by allocating space for NIMR field stations in Raipur and Ranchi. All staff members in the IDVC project were on temporary appointments, which gave us some flexibility in restructuring. We drafted two letters: one announcing the closure of the five field stations, and the other detailing the relocation of individual staff members to the new and remaining field stations. I kept this process strictly confidential, sharing the details only with the Administrative Officer. I personally typed and sealed all the individual orders.

The next day, we dispatched special messengers to the closing field stations, coordinating a specific date and time for delivering the letters to all affected staff. This included the nearly 100 project staff members at the Delhi field station, and over 200 in total. We also advised our advocate to file a caveat in the Delhi High Court to anticipate any potential legal challenges. This approach ensured that the reorganization was executed smoothly and strategically, despite the initial resistance and potential for unrest.

At that time, my office was located on Shamnath Marg. Two days after the reorganization letters were delivered, I arrived at the office to find hundreds of project staff gathered outside, clearly agitated. My personal staff were prepared to escort me through the crowd to my office, but I chose to step out of the car and engage with the crowd directly. The gathered staff expressed their grievances and pleaded with me to halt the reorganization. I explained to them that the restructuring of the field stations was mandated by the Ministry and was essential for the smooth continuation of the IDVC project. I assured them that no one would be terminated; every project staff member had been reassigned to another field station.

The crowd then mentioned their intention to go to court to challenge the decision. I responded, "You have every right to go to court if you believe it is necessary. However, if a stay order is issued, it will not benefit anyone, as you have already been relieved from your current positions and have not yet reported to your new assignments. In that case, there is a risk of not receiving your salary." I advised them that the best course of action was to join their new posts. Following this interaction, the crowd dispersed, and I continued with my usual work in the office. In the days that followed, all the staff members reported to their assigned locations, and not a single court case was filed.

Although I left the Institute of Life Sciences (ILS), Bhubaneswar in August 2003, people continued to reach out to me regarding various issues at the institute. After my departure, my successor resigned, and late Prof. Supakar took over as Director in charge, during which the institute was running smoothly. When the post of Director was advertised, there was a widespread desire for a competent leader who could guide ILS in the right direction.

I encouraged Prof. Supakar to apply for the position, but he was unwilling, preferring to continue his work in the laboratory. Since he had already been serving as

Director in charge for over a year, I explained the potential consequences if someone else were appointed as Director, which would mean his reversion to his original position. However, he remained firm in his decision not to apply. At that time, Dr M.K. Bhan was the Secretary of the Department of Biotechnology (DBT). Some individuals in Delhi had identified Dr Swapan Datta, who was based in Manila, as a potential candidate for the ILS directorship. Dr Datta even visited ILS with his wife, but his visit made the institute's stakeholders apprehensive. Since Prof. Supakar declined to be considered for the Director post, I approached Dr Ravindran at the Regional Medical Research Centre (RMRC) and encouraged him to apply. Initially, he was hesitant, fearing that the responsibilities of the directorship might negatively impact his research projects. I explained to him that the directorships of DBT institutes were different from those of ICMR institutes, as Directors at DBT institutes often continued to conduct excellent scientific research alongside their administrative duties. He was partially convinced, and I proceeded to nominate him for the Director position at ILS. The interview process took place, with around ten candidates being shortlisted, including Dr Ravindran and Dr Swapan Datta. The selection committee consisted of notable members such as Prof. Padmanaban (Chairman), Dr P.N. Tandon, Dr Bhan, and another committee member. Ultimately, Dr Ravindran was selected and took up the position as Director of ILS in 2006.

In 2005, while managing the National Institute of Malaria Research (NIMR), I was also handling additional responsibilities for the NIRTH, Jabalpur, and the CRME, Madurai. Given the workload, I approached the Director-General of the Indian Council of Medical Research (ICMR) and requested to be relieved from the additional roles to focus solely on NIMR's development. The DG agreed, and I subsequently handed over charge of CRME to Dr Tyagi and NIRTH, Jabalpur, to late Dr Neeru Singh. Both continued as Officers in charge, as there was no Director position at CRME, while the Director's post at NIRTH, Jabalpur, was later advertised.

Dr Ansari, who had been the Officer in Charge at NIMR before my directorship, applied for the Director position at NIRTH, Jabalpur, and was selected. I supported his transition by allowing him to retain his laboratory at NIMR. Meanwhile, the construction of the NIMR building progressed rapidly, and I remained deeply engaged in various activities, striving to elevate the institute's profile. Throughout my tenure at different institutions, I focused on establishing state-of-the-art laboratories, fostering growth, and building a strong institutional identity. I aimed to create a brand name for the institutes I led by nurturing opportunities for academicians, encouraging innovation and research, and producing students recognized nationally and internationally. I also emphasized the involvement of communities in research and disease control programs, as well as enhancing communication and IT skills among the staff. Gender equity, human rights, and ethics were key values that I promoted.

My leadership extended beyond administration, as I also contributed significantly to research at NIMR. I sought to establish a positive "institute culture" that shaped the organization's effectiveness on both national and international levels. This included decentralizing the representation of NIMR in technical meetings, where I nominated scientists to attend instead of assuming the sole responsibility myself. I personally attended conferences only when invited specifically.

Our research efforts covered various areas, including molecular taxonomy of Indian mosquito vectors and the phylogenetic relationships among malaria vectors using DNA sequencing. These findings supported the conclusions of traditional cyto-taxonomy. My collaborative work on malaria parasites involved studying the evolutionary patterns of the chloroquine-resistant gene in *Plasmodium falciparum* and genomic analyses of both *P. falciparum* and *P. vivax*. These genomic studies uncovered significant similarities between the two species, alongside crucial differences in their epidemiology and pathogenicity.

Additionally, we contributed to the development of novel genomic markers for understanding the population structure and demographic history of *P. vivax* in India. The genomic insights into *P. falciparum* and *P. vivax* Indian isolates have become benchmarks in the field. One major contribution in molecular epidemiology was the identification of a high prevalence of mixed-species malaria infections in India. Using various molecular protocols and PCR diagnostic techniques, our research revealed that co-infections with *P. falciparum* and *P. vivax* were much more common than previously thought.

These efforts helped establish new baselines for studying drug resistance, virulence genes, and malaria epidemiology, shaping the understanding of malaria in India and setting the stage for future research advancements. Beyond laboratory research, we actively participated in field trials for various malaria intervention measures. These trials were unique experiences that allowed us to translate scientific research into practical, deliverable products, testing their performance under real-world conditions. It provided valuable insights into how scientific innovations could be implemented effectively to combat malaria in different environments. We made significant contributions to understanding the epidemiology of malaria in India, focusing on the challenges faced by the national malaria control program. Our work addressed issues such as the spread of malaria in different regions, variations in transmission patterns, and factors influencing disease persistence and resurgence. This research helped to inform strategies for more effective malaria control and prevention.

In collaboration with colleagues, we also investigated the histopathology of severe respiratory distress caused by *Plasmodium vivax* malaria in India. This work provided critical insights into the pathological mechanisms behind fatal cases, which were not as well understood for *P. vivax* compared to *P. falciparum*. Our findings highlighted the potential severity of *P. vivax* infections and underscored the need for comprehensive approaches to diagnosis, treatment, and management of malaria.

The Multilateral Initiative on Malaria (MIM) was founded in 1997 with the mission of enhancing research capacity in malaria-endemic African countries through collaborative efforts and training. Its goal was to empower these countries to carry out essential research for developing and improving tools for malaria control and to strengthen the interface between research and control programs. The fourth MIM Pan African Malaria Conference took place in Yaounde, Cameroon, from November 13-18, 2005, drawing around 1,500 delegates from across the globe.

I was personally invited by Dr Joel Breman from the National Institutes of Health, USA, to deliver a lecture on the "Burden of Malaria in India: Retrospective and Prospective View" during a session dedicated to discussing disease burdens. Prior to the journey, I learned that there was no Indian embassy in Cameroon, only an Honorary Consulate located in Douala, which was about 240 kilometers from Yaounde. The two cities were well connected by Highway No. 3, making it a four-hour journey between them.

My travel route involved flying from Delhi to Mumbai, then from Mumbai to Nairobi by Indian Airlines, and onward to Yaounde with Kenya Airlines. With a planned stopover in Nairobi, I took the opportunity to visit the zoo there. Before departing India, I had written to the Honorary Consulate in Cameroon, and he arranged for Mr. Advani to receive me upon my arrival at the Yaounde airport.

After arriving safely in Yaounde, I stayed at the Hilton Hotel, located just 15 minutes away from the Yaounde Conference Centre. On the day of the lecture, I presented a comprehensive overview of malaria in India, covering historical trends as well as future challenges and prospects for controlling the disease. The session provided a platform to highlight the unique aspects of malaria epidemiology in India and discuss strategies that could inform global malaria control efforts.

With key speakers in the malaria burden session at Yaoundé, Cameroun with Dr Joel Breman at the centre behind my back (2005).

During the conference, I attended sessions every day, and working lunches were provided. There was a small Indian community in Yaounde, comprising around 50 families. On the first evening, an official dinner was organized for the delegates. On the second day, all the Indian families came together to arrange a special dinner and invited me as a guest. Subsequently, each evening, different members of the community hosted dinners, providing a warm and hospitable experience throughout my stay.

This visit to Cameroon was my second. The first was in 1994, when I travelled to Maroua and Yaoundé for a WHO project workshop. During my earlier visit, I had heard an interesting local saying: "Anyone who visits Cameroon and eats papaya will inevitably return." I recalled that I had indeed eaten papaya back then, which perhaps was a reason behind my second visit. Determined not to tempt fate, I consciously avoided eating papaya this time. Interestingly, I haven't returned to Cameroon since. After the conference, I spent a day in Nairobi before heading back to India. The trip was a blend of professional engagement at the conference and warm interactions with the Indian community in Yaoundé, making it a memorable experience.

At that time, malaria diagnostic kits were primarily available in the private market, costing over a dollar each. These kits, produced by a company based in Goa, had already undergone field testing by the National Institute of Malaria Research (NIMR), which had developed a strong relationship with the company as a result. In many remote and challenging rural areas across India, microscopic examination for malaria parasites was not practical, making rapid diagnostic kits essential for effective malaria control. Dr Joshi, the Director of the NVBDCP, and I discussed this challenge, recognizing the need to procure these kits to support the program. However, the NVBDCP's budget constraints made it difficult to purchase the large quantities required at the existing high price. To address this issue, we arranged a meeting with representatives from the Goa-based company in Delhi. During the discussions, we emphasized the program's need for the kits and explored the possibility of obtaining them at a lower cost, potentially as part of the company's corporate social responsibility. Given the large volume required for the national program, the company agreed to supply the kits at a significantly reduced rate—less than Rs 20 per kit. This negotiation marked a significant breakthrough, enabling the widespread availability of malaria diagnostic kits for public use in the NVBDCP, facilitating better access to malaria testing in remote and underserved areas.

The National Institute of Malaria Research (NIMR) expanded its focus beyond just malaria, addressing various aspects of vector-borne diseases. One of our key initiatives was the publication of the Journal of Vector Borne Diseases, which holds the distinction of being one of the oldest journals in India. Originally established in 1947 as the Indian Journal of Malariology, the journal transitioned to its current name in 2003. In a relatively short span, it garnered significant recognition within its field, achieving an impact factor of 1.4 in 2019, reflecting its influence and quality. As the Chief Editor of this journal, I played a vital role in guiding its direction and ensuring its relevance in the scientific community. I continued to serve on the editorial board until 2020, contributing to the journal's growth and international reputation.

Recognizing the importance of communication and engagement, we initiated the creation of a biannual newsletter to highlight the activities and achievements of NIMR. We aptly named it *"Plasmodium"*, a nod to the malaria parasite and our institute's commitment to vector-borne disease research. This newsletter served as a platform to showcase our research, disseminate information, and foster collaboration within the scientific community, further establishing NIMR's presence and influence in the field of public health.

In 2007, as the National Institute of Malaria Research (NIMR) celebrated its 30th anniversary, it was an opportune moment to reflect on and showcase the significant progress and achievements of the institute since its inception. To mark this milestone, we dedicated ourselves to compiling a comprehensive volume titled "Profile of NIMR." This extensive publication highlighted all facets of NIMR's activities, achievements, and contributions to malaria research and control over the three decades. It served not only as a record of our past accomplishments but also as a testament to the institute's ongoing commitment to advancing research, improving public health outcomes, and addressing the challenges posed by malaria and other vector-borne diseases.

Upon completion, we officially released and disseminated the profile to stakeholders, partners, and the wider scientific community. This initiative was crucial in reinforcing NIMR's role as a leading research institution and in promoting our future goals and directions in the fight against malaria. The profile not only celebrated our past but also set the stage for continued innovation and collaboration in the years to come.

Releasing of the profile (30 years of progress of NIMR) in 2009 at NIMR

In our pursuit of enhancing global visibility for the National Institute of Malaria Research (NIMR), we identified the ongoing Indo-German collaboration on Science and Technology as a significant opportunity. The Department of Science & Technology served as the nodal department for this initiative, and in 2005, an Indian delegation was scheduled to visit the Gesellschaft für Biotechnologische Forschung (GBF) in Braunschweig, Germany. I was nominated to represent the Indian Council of Medical Research (ICMR) alongside a scientist from the National Institute of Cholera and Enteric Diseases (NICED) in Kolkata. Dr Mukesh Kumar from ICMR Headquarters was also part of our team, which included several eminent scientists from various organizations, including Prof. Hasnain and Dr Katoch, who later became the Director General of ICMR after Prof. Ganguly.

Since Braunschweig did not have an airport, we travelled to Hannover, the nearest airport, via Frankfurt. The journey from Hannover to Braunschweig was pleasant, thanks to the hospitality of the GBF, which arranged for our transportation. Upon our arrival, we settled into our hotel, and the meeting commenced the next morning. During the conference, I delivered a lecture on malaria in India and had the honour of co-chairing a session alongside Dr Rudi Balling, a distinguished German geneticist who served as the Scientific Director of the Helmholtz Centre for Infection Research (HZI), formerly known as GBF. The scientific sessions were highly productive, fostering valuable discussions and collaborations.

One memorable highlight of our visit was a dinner invitation from late Dr Chhatwal, an Indian scientist working at GBF. He had married a German woman, Inge, and had settled in Germany. Dr Chhatwal warmly welcomed us into his home and organized a grand party in his backyard, where we mingled and enjoyed each other's company. As the evening progressed, we were introduced to Dr Chhatwal's wife and two children, as well as their neighbour, the jailor of Braunschweig. The dinner featured a delicious mutton dish, and Dr Chhatwal shared fascinating anecdotes about how he obtained goat meat in Germany. He mentioned that his neighbour, a homeopathic doctor, would slaughter goats for their skins to use in preparing homeopathic medicines, and Dr Chhatwal would source his meat from him. This visit not only reinforced our collaborative ties with international partners but also provided us with rich cultural experiences and lasting memories, further enriching our understanding of global scientific communities.

During our time in Braunschweig, we found that our interactions were not just limited to the scientific community. One of the most memorable experiences was our visit to the local jail, facilitated by Dr Chhatwal. The jailor became quite friendly with us and extended an invitation to explore the facility the next day. The following day, Dr Chhatwal guided us through the jail, allowing us to visit various sections and interact with some of the inmates, who were primarily incarcerated for drug trafficking and similar offenses. To our surprise, the conditions in the jail were quite good, with well-maintained rooms and facilities. It was an eye-opening experience to witness the justice system from such a unique perspective. After our visit, we returned to our hotel, reflecting on the fascinating insights we had gained. On the day of our departure, we made our way back to Hannover to catch our flight to Delhi via Frankfurt.

A year later, we returned to Braunschweig for the same program. This time, we stayed at a different hotel, but we were excited to reunite with Dr Chhatwal for another dinner. On this visit, we managed to take a local tour, which showcased the city's many attractions. We traversed narrow alleyways and charming streets, explored beautiful squares, and admired a blend of historic buildings and modern architecture.

I aimed to expand the network of the National Institute of Malaria Research (NIMR) through several collaborative programs with various countries. At that time, Dr Jane Carlton was gaining recognition for her outstanding work in malaria parasite genomics. After earning her Ph.D. in Genetics from Edinburgh University in 1995, she took on research positions at the University of Florida, the National Institutes of Health (NIH), and the Institute for Genomic Research (TIGR) in Rockville, Maryland. Founded by J. Craig Venter in 1992, TIGR focused on sequencing genomes and analysing prokaryotic and eukaryotic organisms, contributing significantly to human genome research. Now she is the Director, Johns Hopkins Malaria Research Institute.

Recognizing the potential for collaboration, we established contact with Dr Jane, who was also interested in partnering with Indian or Indonesian researchers for her studies on *Plasmodium vivax*, the malaria parasite. In early 2005, she organized a workshop at TIGR and invited us to attend. This meeting provided an excellent opportunity to discuss potential collaborations in detail.

Later that year, we invited Dr Carlton to participate in an international conference on malaria held in November in Delhi, which she graciously attended. This marked the beginning of a strong collaboration between NIMR and Dr Carlton's team, leading to groundbreaking findings in our field. Our joint efforts resulted in the publication of several important research papers, including one in *Nature Genetics*, which garnered attention and contributed to the advancement of malaria research. This collaboration not only enhanced the scientific output of NIMR but also positioned the institute as a key player in global malaria research networks, reinforcing our commitment to combating this persistent public health challenge.

The management of insecticide resistance was increasingly recognised by the World Health Organization (WHO) as a critical challenge in malaria control programs worldwide. In response to this pressing issue, Bayer took the initiative to address insecticide resistance management (IRM) by hosting International IRM Workshops. One such workshop took place in Durban in 2004, where I was invited to deliver a lecture. The workshop was held at a resort on the outskirts of Durban, in collaboration with the Medical Research Council of South Africa. The setting was conducive to productive discussions, and the scientific atmosphere was vibrant. Renowned figures in the field, including Prof. Janet Hemingway, who served as the

Director of the Liverpool School of Tropical Medicine from 2000 to 2019, also attended the meeting.

While in Durban, I made the most of the opportunity to explore the city and its surroundings. As South Africa's third most populous city, after Johannesburg and Cape Town, Durban stands out with its own distinct charm. Johannesburg has a modern, urban edge, and Cape Town exudes a sophisticated glamour, but Durban's relaxed, cool atmosphere truly appealed to me. I enjoyed visiting a variety of local attractions and immersing myself in the vibrant culture, which added depth to my experience during the workshop. The workshop discussions were crucial in developing strategies to combat insecticide resistance, emphasizing the importance of integrated methods for effective malaria control. This experience not only broadened my understanding of the global challenges at hand but also underscored the significance of international collaboration in tackling public health issues like malaria.

I read that Gandhi arrived in Durban in 1893 to serve as legal counsel to a merchant. The merchant asked him to undertake a rail trip to Pretoria, Transvaal, which first took Gandhi to Pietermaritzburg, Natal. There, Gandhi was seated in the first-class compartment, as he had purchased a first-class ticket. A white passenger who entered the compartment quickly summoned the railway officials, who ordered Gandhi to move to the van compartment since "coolies" (a racist term for Indians) and non-whites were not permitted in first-class compartments. Gandhi protested and produced his ticket but was warned that he would be forcibly removed if he did not comply. When Gandhi refused to follow the order, a white police officer pushed him out of the train, and his luggage was tossed onto the platform. The train then steamed away, leaving Gandhi to withdraw to the waiting room. "It was winter," Gandhi wrote in his autobiography, "the cold was extremely bitter. My overcoat was in my luggage, but I did not dare to ask for it lest I should be insulted again, so I sat and shivered." It was truly thrilling to see the place.

When I joined the NIMR, the country was following an outdated drug policy for malaria. We were all aware of the widespread development of resistance in malaria parasites to the most popular drug, chloroquine. My first task was to organize a scientific meeting in collaboration with the NVBDCP and the National Institute of Communicable Diseases (NICD), now National Centre for Disease Control (NCDC) to discuss a change in the drug policy. We organized this meeting in 2005 and invited representatives from the NVBDCP, NICD, and the Director of Communicable Diseases at the WHO South-East Asia Region. I also invited Professor Padmanaban from the Indian Institute of Science to deliver the keynote lecture. The meeting took place, and the proceedings were printed and sent to the Ministry of Health. The ministry was to make a decision based on the recommendations from the Technical Advisory Committee (TAC) of the Ministry, which was headed by the Director General of Health Services, India. As the Director of NIMR, I was also a member of this committee, advocating for a change in the drug policy. One TAC member, who was a director at ICMR and a colleague of mine, made an oblique comment suggesting that I wanted to stop chloroquine for *falciparum* malaria to promote western drugs. His comment was not backed by scientific evidence, and I successfully convinced the committee otherwise.

By 2005, the government agreed to change the drug policy to implement Artemisinin-based Combination Therapy (ACT), which was first initiated on an experimental basis by us. Shortly after, Dr Neena Valecha, my successor at NIMR and later an advisor at the World Health Organization, began the surveillance for the therapeutic efficacy of this combination across the country. Based on the data generated, ACT was introduced for *falciparum* malaria nationwide in 2010, including for use in the second and third trimesters of pregnancy. ACT has proven to be one of the most effective interventions, helping India significantly reduce malaria cases over the past decade.

NIMR soon gained recognition from the global research community for conducting clinical trials of various antimalarial drugs and combinations, along with numerous field trials. I, along with my colleagues; attended a workshop related to clinical trials at the Swiss Tropical and Public Health Institute (STPH) in Basel, Switzerland, which was previously known as the Swiss Tropical Institute. Dr Marcel Tanner, the Director of STPH, was someone I knew from his visit to RMRC, Bhubaneswar, in January 1992, concerning a lymphatic filariasis research project. Before heading to Basel, I wrote an email to Dr Tanner to inform him about my visit. He promptly replied, mentioning that he would be traveling at that time but had arranged for one of his colleagues to take me around the laboratories at STPH during my stay.

During the workshop, I had the opportunity to tour the laboratories at STPH. Under the leadership of Dr Neena Valecha, NIMR initiated many clinical trials in India as part of global trials. Consequently, the NIMR team often had to attend review meetings in various countries, and I would accompany them as the director when required. I visited Bangkok for several meetings and once travelled to Ho Chi Minh City, Vietnam, for a review meeting. Ho Chi Minh City, formerly known as Saigon, is the most populous city in Vietnam and serves as its financial centre. The city is accessible via Tân Sơn Nhất International Airport, the largest airport in Vietnam. After attending the review meeting, we explored the city and were profoundly moved by our visit to the War Remnants Museum. The museum preserved devastating photographs and poignant stories from the war. We also enjoyed a boat tour along the Saigon River, which showcased the diverse lifestyles surrounding this bustling metropolis. Our hotel was conveniently located near the river, and every evening we would stroll along its banks. The city was impressively clean, though at that time, there were very few Indian restaurants. Nonetheless, we had ample opportunities to carry out many multicentric projects and attend numerous review meetings in different countries.

During my tenure as the Director of NIRTH in Jabalpur, we established a close collaboration with the Centres for Disease Control and Prevention (CDC) in Atlanta, USA, with the late Dr Neeru Singh as the primary partner from Jabalpur. The Chief of the Malaria Unit at the CDC, Dr Udhay Kumar, was of Indian origin. Together, CDC and NIRTH launched a combined Ph.D. program, and the ethics committee of NIRTH, Jabalpur, was featured on the CDC website.

Collaborators' meetings were held both in Atlanta and Jabalpur. At one such meeting in Atlanta, I had the opportunity to meet many senior scientists from the CDC. My stay in Atlanta lasted a few days, and after the meeting, I visited the Martin Luther King Jr. Historical Park, which was an exciting experience. During the 1950s and 1960s, Atlanta emerged as a significant organising centre for the civil rights movement, with Dr Martin Luther King Jr. serving as its most visible spokesperson and leader until his assassination in 1968.

On another day, we toured the CNN Centre, the world headquarters of CNN, located in Atlanta, Georgia. The main newsrooms and studios for several of CNN's channels are housed in this building. We received special permission to visit the newsroom and the studio, which was a fascinating experience. I also fondly remember that during this trip, I purchased my first iPhone for my daughter from the USA.

NIMR gained international recognition for its research on malaria, including studies on the impact of climate change. There was no global committee on malaria that did not have NIMR representation. The ICMR constituted a "High Power Committee on Climate Change," chaired by late Dr A. P. Mitra, F.R.S., former Director General of CSIR, with myself as a member. I was responsible for addressing climate change's impact on vector-borne diseases. After a few meetings, Dr Mitra passed away in 2007. At that time, ICMR was working to collaborate with the CDC in Atlanta, USA, on climate change studies.

A meeting was organized at the CDC in Atlanta, and Dr S. K. Bhattacharya was the acting DG of ICMR following Prof. Ganguly's retirement, who became the President of JIPMER in Pondicherry. Dr Bhattacharya and I travelled to Atlanta for the meeting, where I was scheduled to give a lecture on the impact of climate change on vector-borne diseases. By that time, NIMR had concluded a study on climate change's impact on malaria in Uttarakhand, led by Dr R.C. Dhiman. The study, conducted in 2007-08 in the *Bhimtal* area of Uttarakhand, was significant as malaria was not endemic there, even when India faced severe malaria outbreaks. Few malaria vectors had been reported in the area. Through a retrospective study, we observed a rise in minimum temperatures. NIMR initiated further research, discovering several cases of both falciparum and vivax malaria, as well as a notable presence of *Anopheles culicifacies and An. Fluviatilis* a malaria vector. I tailored my lecture based on these findings as we prepared to depart for Atlanta.

We travelled by Air France, with a layover in New York. Unfortunately, our flight was delayed, causing us to arrive late in Atlanta. From the airport, we headed straight to the CDC, as my lecture was approaching. Although I was tired, I delivered my presentation on the impact of climate change on malaria in Uttarakhand. The lecture was well received and appreciated. After the meeting, we returned to our hotel to rest. The conference lasted three days, and we attended various sessions before flying back to Delhi via New York.

After returning to NIMR, I focused on further strengthening climate change studies at the institute and appointed Dr Dhiman to lead this initiative. He excelled in this role, and we soon established a collaboration with Dr Mercedes Pascual and her team. Dr Mercedes Pascual, a Uruguayan theoretical ecologist and a Professor in the Department of Ecology and Evolution at the University of Chicago, visited NIMR, and we reciprocated the visit to foster our partnership. As a result of these efforts, climate change became a flagship program at NIMR.

While working at NIMR, I received an invitation to attend the annual meeting of the American Society of Tropical Medicine and Hygiene (ASTMH) held at the Hilton Hotel in Washington, DC. The event attracted a large number of participants, and I was scheduled to speak on "Malaria Burden in India." After my lecture, I engaged in discussions with various scientists and professors, drawing attention as the Director of NIMR. Washington, DC, is unique among American cities, having been established by the Constitution of the United States to serve as the nation's capital. Founded on July 16, 1790, it was named after George Washington, the first president of the United States. After a couple of days, we took a city tour to visit significant sites and monuments. While we had working lunches at the conference venue, we enjoyed dinner at an Indian restaurant near the Hilton. The annual meeting spanned several days, and many participants from the National Institute of Health (NIH) in Bethesda attended. One day, they took me to NIH, where I encountered many Indian scientists.

During my visit, I met Dr Louis Miller, a prominent malariologist at NIH. Dr Miller was familiar with NIMR and its field stations, specifically the work being conducted at the Rourkela field station. However, he was mistakenly informed by some representatives from the International Centre for Genetic Engineering and Biotechnology (ICGEB) in New Delhi that the Rourkela field station belonged to ICGEB. Long back, NIMR had initiated collaborative work with ICGEB for a vaccine trial that ultimately did not come to fruition. Despite the effort, substantial data on vector biology and transmission was generated by the NIMR staff at the Rourkela field station. However, a couple of ICGEB scientists insisted on sharing authorship of papers outside their area of expertise. While I didn't object to this during my tenure as director, it was unethical for those individuals to claim the Rourkela field station as their own at NIH. I clarified the situation to Dr Louis Miller before returning to Delhi to continue my work at NIMR.

While serving as the Director of NIMR, I received several invitations from the WHO in Geneva. One visit, in particular, stands out in my memory. It included two meetings: the first from Monday to Friday, followed by a weekend break, and then another meeting from Tuesday to Thursday. I decided to stay in Geneva to attend both meetings, giving me three days off in between. On Saturday, I explored Old Geneva, known in French as Vieille Ville. This area is a charming maze of narrow streets and picturesque squares, filled with cozy cafés, restaurants, galleries, museums, and historical landmarks. Walking through Old Geneva felt like stepping back a thousand years into the city's ancient past.

On Sunday, I visited Lake Geneva, a deep lake shared between Switzerland and France and one of the largest lakes in Western Europe. Both days were truly enjoyable. On Monday, I returned to the WHO office to catch up with some friends. Typically, when traveling abroad for official duties, my routine consisted of going from the airport to my place of stay, attending meetings, and then returning to the airport. I rarely had the opportunity to visit important places in any country. This was one reason I had never taken my wife with me on official trips; I simply didn't have the funds for family holidays. However, my extended stays in Geneva, Washington, and Atlanta were rare and memorable occasions.

One of the major objectives of NIMR was to provide scientific support to the National Vector Borne Disease Control Programme (NVBDCP), which served as an umbrella initiative for the control and elimination of vector-borne diseases. At the dawn of the 21st century, India lacked a structured public health system. It was noteworthy that Bill Gates had to come to India to establish the Public Health Foundation because we were unable to do it ourselves. Public health cannot thrive without academic research. For instance, in the child health program, 80% of the innovative ideas originated from AIIMS, Delhi, where they conducted applied research programs in a clinical context.

As mentioned earlier, the Scientific Advisory Committee (SAC) convened annually to review all projects at NIMR. When late Dr V.P. Sharma served as director, he initiated the annual SAC meetings, which spanned three days. The first day focused on reviewing projects categorized into three groups: Vector Biology and Control, Clinical Studies and Epidemiology, and Parasite Biology. The second day was dedicated to assessing the work of IDVC field stations, culminating in the final SAC meeting on the last day. I continued this tradition upon my joining.

NIMR typically hosted an official dinner the evening before the final SAC meeting, inviting senior ICMR officials and eminent scientists, such as the Secretary of the Department of Biotechnology (DBT), to join SAC members and NIMR scientists. At the SAC dinner in 2005 or 2006, Dr Bhan, the DBT Secretary, was invited. During the event, Prof. Ganguly, the then DG of ICMR, introduced me to Dr Bhan as the former Director of ILS. Dr Bhan briefly discussed the role of the Director at ILS with me, and I shared my views. Dr Bhan initially did not hold a high opinion of ICMR scientists. However, his view changed after a new director joined the organization around that time. This director impressed Dr Bhan significantly and eventually became his most favoured director.

Dr Ansari had been appointed as the Director of RMRC, Jabalpur, but he retained his official residence in Delhi, leaving his family there and traveling back on weekends. I was familiar with his family, as I was often invited to dinner by Dr Ansari. Another senior scientist at NIMR, Dr Adak, was his neighbour. Both Dr Ansari and Dr Adak began their careers in the WHO/ICMR genetic control project in Delhi alongside Dr P.K. Das, who later became the Director of VCRC. They were all under the mentorship of late Dr V.P. Sharma and late Dr P.K. Rajagopalan, both of whom were awarded the Padma Shri by the Government of India on the recommendation of the late Professor M.G.K. Menon.

In 2006, I had an important field visit to Guwahati, accompanied by Dr Adak and Mr. Verma. We were planning to shift the field station in Assam from Sonapur to Guwahati, and our journey took us through Kolkata. After completing our work in Guwahati, we were on our way back to Delhi. Since there was no direct flight, we travelled to Kolkata and stayed at the ICMR-NICED guest house. On our way there, we received the devastating news that Dr Ansari had fallen seriously ill and was taken to AIIMS. We immediately began contacting the driver for updates, and just a few minutes later, we heard the heartbreaking news that Dr Ansari had passed away. The next morning, we rushed back to Delhi. Dr Ansari was originally from Uttar Pradesh, and his body was taken to his village along with his family. Unfortunately, we did not get the chance to see him one last time. It was indeed a tragic loss.

By early 2008, the construction of the NIMR building was nearly complete, but the furnishing of the laboratories still needed to be arranged. We advertised for the furnishing work, keeping in mind the previous experience of the ICMR, which had furnished the National Institute of Epidemiology (NIE) in Chennai using a Chennai-based contractor. I received a call from the Minister's office, suggesting that the work order for furnishing NIMR should be awarded to the same contractor who had furnished NIE, and I was informed that the contractor would be visiting NIMR for discussions. Anticipating the visit, I called a meeting with the Administrative Officer, Accounts Officer, and a few others. The contractor arrived and gave a presentation. He seemed confident of securing the work, given his referral from someone in the Minister's personal staff. However, the quote he provided was nearly equivalent to the cost of constructing the entire building. I chose not to comment during the presentation, but after careful consideration, we ultimately awarded the work to another bidder who had quoted the lowest price. The decision to choose a different contractor for the laboratory furnishing did not sit well with some people, leading to discontent over the matter.

Professor Ganguly joined as the Director General (DG) of the Indian Council of Medical Research (ICMR) in early 1998. By then, I had left the Regional Medical Research Centre (RMRC) in Bhubaneswar and joined the Institute of Life Sciences (ILS). My initial deputation to ILS was approved before Professor Ganguly's tenure began, but he extended my deputation year by year until it reached the maximum permissible period. Professor Ganguly also received an extension past his retirement date, continuing as DG until November 2006.

When the Ministry initiated the process to select the next DG, nominations were invited from state governments, directors, and vice-chancellors, and a search-cum-selection committee was formed. By then, I was well-known in scientific circles and among state governments. Many encouraged me to apply for the position, and I received more than 70 nominations. However, Professor Ganguly was rightly granted another year of extension, remaining in his role until 2007. During his tenure, Professor Ganguly made efforts to elevate the DG, ICMR position to include the title of Secretary, Health Research, similar to the structure in organizations like the Indian Council of Agricultural Research (ICAR) and the Council of Scientific and Industrial

Research (CSIR), where the DGs also serve as secretaries. Though earlier attempts by Professor Ramalingaswamy had been unsuccessful, Professor Ganguly eventually succeeded in having the DG, ICMR role re-designated as DG, ICMR cum Secretary, Health Research, but he himself did not assume the Secretary title, leaving it to his successor.

Professor Ganguly retired in November 2007, and Dr S.K. Bhattacharya, Additional DG, took over as the officiating DG, ICMR. The Ministry then restarted the selection process for a new DG. Once again, nominations for me came in, with late Dr Neeru Singh from RMRC, Jabalpur, personally visiting states to secure nominations on my behalf. The selection committee for the post, now titled Secretary, Health Research cum DG, ICMR, included the Cabinet Secretary as Chairman, the Principal Secretary to the Prime Minister, and experts such as Professor C.N.R. Rao, Professor P.N. Tandon, and the late Dr M.K. Bhan. A former union secretary and Chief Secretary of Orissa, who knew the Chairman, submitted my CV to the committee.

During the initial committee meeting, while my name was considered for the panel, one member objected to my candidacy (being a non-medical person), though others supported it. As reported in the early 2008 issue of a fortnightly magazine, under the title "The Unhealthy Vacuum," I was empanelled along with three others. However, the then-Minister insisted on cancelling the panel and advertised the position, citing the new Secretary status attached to the post. The re-advertised position required a medical qualification, making me ineligible to apply, effectively removing me from contention.

During Dr Bhattacharya's tenure as the officiating Director General (DG) of ICMR, there were some issues at the Desert Medicine Research Centre (DMRC) in Jodhpur (now known as National Institute for implementation research on non-communicable diseases), and I was asked to take on the additional responsibility of Director there. I was previously selected as Director-in-charge at DMRC in May 1994, so I was familiar with the centre. Upon arriving in Jodhpur, I officially took over the role. At that time, the laboratory and administrative buildings were still under construction by a Government of India agency, despite funds being allocated for the project. The construction was incomplete, and there were only a few scientists and staff. I held a meeting with the scientists to understand the nature of their work and identify any challenges. There were significant issues among the senior scientists, with some of them behaving as if they were untouchable, like the "cacti of the desert." I had to gradually address and streamline the situation, resolving conflicts and improving the functioning of the centre. The construction of the building was eventually completed, and I continued to travel from Delhi to Jodhpur three times a month to oversee the centre's progress. Before the completion of the new building, the DMRC had been operating out of staff quarters.

In 2007, while I was serving as the Director of the National Institute of Malaria Research (NIMR), I received an invitation from the World Health Organisation's South-East Asia Regional Office (SEARO) to join as a consultant, then known as a Temporary International Professional, for a three-month assignment. WHO has its headquarters in Geneva, Switzerland, along with six regional offices around the world and smaller country offices in each member nation. The regions include the Americas, Africa, Eastern Mediterranean, Europe, South-East Asia (SEAR) , and the Western Pacific. SEAR's headquarters is in New Delhi, India.

In 2007, SEARO aimed to develop clear guidelines for Integrated Vector Management (IVM), which was a new approach within malaria control programs. I was approached in June for this role. After discussing the opportunity with the Director General of ICMR, I received permission to accept the invitation, on the condition that I would continue my work at NIMR from 4:30 PM onwards after my WHO hours, which ran from 8 AM to 4:30 PM. After undergoing a medical examination at RML Hospital in New Delhi, I reported to the WHO/SEAR office on November 20, 2007. In my role at SEARO, I held a P-5 position, reporting to Dr Sangay Thinley, the Coordinator, while Dr Krongthong from Thailand served as the Malaria Adviser. Dr Samlee Plianbangchang from Thailand was the Regional Director. My workstation was shared with another person from Nepal, who held a P-4 position and had been there as a temporary international professional for about three months. Initially, he underestimated my presence, avoided conversation, and seemed aloof. He had studied in Bangkok, earned his Ph.D. there, and was fluent in Thai language.

At the same time, Dr Chusak, a senior scientist from Thailand who was familiar with my work from previous WHO projects, was away on official duty when I joined. I began my work at SEARO, and Dr Thinley expressed satisfaction with my contributions. A couple of weeks later, Dr Chusak returned. The next day, just before lunch, he approached my desk, greeted me respectfully, and invited me to join him for lunch. This surprised my office roommate, who had been dismissive of me until that point. After lunch, the dynamics shifted significantly; my roommate's attitude towards me changed completely. He began to engage with me, and other scientists also started reaching out.

Our relationship grew stronger, with my office roommate becoming a close colleague. During technical discussions, he would take notes on my statements, demonstrating newfound respect. I also came to appreciate him, and we developed a productive working relationship that enriched my experience at SEARO.

Before embarking on my temporary assignment with SEARO, I had already committed to attending the Vivax vaccine meeting in London, organized by GlaxoSmithKline (GSK). I informed Dr J.P. Narain, who was the Director of Communicable Diseases, about my upcoming engagement. He was supportive and submitted the necessary paperwork for approval to the Regional Director, which was granted. Once I received the green light, I travelled to London for the meeting, where I had the opportunity to connect with several prominent figures in the field. Among them was Dr Kamini Mendis from Sri Lanka, who was also working with WHO in Geneva, and we had insightful discussions throughout the event. Additionally, I met Dr Kevin Baird, the Head of the Eijkman-Oxford Clinical Research Unit in Jakarta, Indonesia. Despite being British, he was staying in the same hotel as I was, and he kindly looked after me during my time there. Our interaction proved fruitful, leading to a collaboration that resulted in a published paper featuring contributions from both NIMR and Dr Baird. This experience not only enhanced my knowledge about *Vivax* vaccine research but also strengthened professional ties that would benefit future projects.

In India, malaria is primarily attributed to *Plasmodium falciparum* and *Plasmodium vivax*, with occasional cases of *P. malariae* and one reported instance of *P. ovale*. While *P. falciparum* is notorious for its potential to cause severe illness and even death if not treated promptly; *P. vivax* is typically regarded as a relapsing species that does not usually lead to complications or fatalities. However, in June 2008, we received alarming reports of two deaths in Goa attributed to *P. vivax* malaria. Given that NIMR had a field station in Goa, Dr Neena Valecha and I promptly travelled there to investigate the cases. One of the deceased was a 20-year-old woman who had succumbed to the infection while hospitalized. Family members revealed that in the week leading up to her death, private practitioners had treated her with ampicloxacillin, diclofenac, and antipyretics for what was initially diagnosed as an upper respiratory tract infection. Unfortunately, she was actually suffering from a *vivax* infection.

Following our investigation and the collection of samples, we returned to Delhi. While deaths due to *P. vivax* malaria are exceedingly rare, previous reports by Dr Dhapat Kochar had documented a few fatalities in Bikaner, Rajasthan. Nevertheless, this case represented the first histopathological study of a deceased *P. vivax* malaria patient in India. Our findings were published in the *American Journal of Tropical Medicine and Hygiene* under the title "Histopathology of fatal respiratory distress caused by *Plasmodium vivax* malaria," in collaboration with Dr Kevin Baird. This study was pivotal in shedding light on the serious consequences of *P. vivax* malaria, challenging the previously held belief that it rarely led to fatal outcomes.

My assignment at the WHO's South East Asia Regional Office (SEARO) continued until February 19, 2008. During this time, we organized the 8th Conference on Vectors and Vector-Borne Diseases, which took place in the first week of February 2008 at Hotel Mayfair in Puri. The conference attracted over 600 participants, necessitating the booking of all available hotels and guest houses in

Puri. Many international attendees joined the event, highlighting its significance. Dr Narain from WHO/SEARO also participated in this meeting, and three ministers from Odisha graced the inaugural session with their presence. One of the notable traditions of the National Academy of Vector Borne Diseases (NAVBD) is to recognize significant contributors in the field of vector-borne diseases with awards. In 2008, there was a decision to honour the late Dr Ansari with an award, but the then-President of the Academy, the late Dr V.P. Sharma, was initially opposed to the idea. Fortunately, Dr Altaf Lal, who was present at the meeting, persuaded Dr Sharma to agree to the award for Dr Ansari. This conference was particularly memorable for all attendees, as it fostered collaboration and celebrated the contributions of individuals dedicated to advancing the fight against vector-borne diseases. The positive atmosphere and collective commitment to the cause made it a standout event in the community.

The 8th Conference on Vectors and Vector-Borne Diseases in Puri featured vibrant cultural programs that added to the joy and enthusiasm of the participants. Everyone left the event with a sense of fulfilment and camaraderie. After returning to Delhi to complete my assignment at WHO/SEARO, I learned about an opening for the position of Regional Adviser for Vector-Borne Diseases. By then, I had established a good rapport within the SEAR Office, and many colleagues encouraged me to apply for the position. However, some expressed concerns, suggesting that being Indian might hinder my chances since the Indian quota for the role was already filled. Despite these reservations, I had received approval from the Director General of ICMR to pursue any international position, so I decided to go ahead and filled out the online application for the post in WHO while still at SEARO, before my assignment ended on February 19, 2008. I submitted my report on my work, which was deemed highly satisfactory by SEARO. Afterward, I returned to NIMR, where exciting developments were taking place. The new building had been inaugurated, and we were in the process of moving different laboratories to the new facility. This transition marked an important chapter for NIMR, promising enhanced capabilities for our research and work in vector-borne diseases.

After the MRC was converted into NIMR on November 5th, 2005, we began celebrating NIMR's annual day during the first week of November. In 2007, we invited Prof Hasnain, Vice Chancellor of Hyderabad Central University, as the chief guest. Starting that year, we established the tradition of honouring NIMR staff who had completed 25 years of service—a tradition I initiated. In November 2008, Prof. Ganguly, former Director-General of ICMR, and Dr G.C. Mishra, Director of NCCS, Pune, were invited as Guests of Honour, while Dr Katoch, Director-General of ICMR, presided over the event. During this period, in addition to my duties at NIMR, I was frequently traveling to Jodhpur to oversee the DMRC. It is worth mentioning that I never invited any Minister or politician to NIMR, NIRTH, CRME and DMRC, which may be why I was not favoured by politicians at that time.

As I mentioned earlier, I applied for the position of Regional Adviser in Vector-Borne Diseases at WHO while working at SEARO. Despite the Indian quota being full, I was shortlisted. The process involved a written test, followed by an interview with an oral presentation lasting 15 minutes, along with subsequent questions. All shortlisted candidates were invited to take the written test in the first week of September 2008. I performed well in the test and was subsequently called for the interview. The selection committee was chaired by Dr Mint Htwe, Director of Program Management at WHO, who later became Myanmar's Health Minister. Interestingly, sometime earlier, the National Institute of Communicable Diseases (NICD), now the National Centre for Disease Control (NCDC), had invited me to be a guest at their annual function. Dr Mint Htwe was also present, and I delivered a lecture on the impact of climate change on vector-borne diseases.

During the interview, I was asked to make an oral presentation on the topic "Climate Change impact on Malaria," which was given to me on the spot. I paused briefly, and the Chairman reminded me that I had already delivered a comprehensive lecture on this subject at NCDC. I explained that while my previous talk had been an hour long, I was now preparing for a 15-minute presentation. I completed the presentation on time, after which the interview commenced. After the interview, I returned to NIMR. Some of my well-wishers informed me that it would be difficult for an Indian to secure the position. With no news for a couple of months, I began to put the interview out of my mind and resumed my work at NIMR, where our research efforts were in full swing. I inquired about the interview results, but no one seemed to have any information.

CHAPTER 21

An Unexpected Call from the United Nations

In November 2008, while visiting DMRC, Jodhpur, I returned to the place of my stay after finishing my work at the office. After evening tea, I was resting when I received a phone call from someone in the Personnel Department of WHO. He informed me that I had been selected for the position, and the offer letter was being sent. At first, I couldn't believe it and asked him to repeat what he had said. To be sure, I cross-checked this information with another person, who confirmed it. After completing my tasks in Jodhpur, I returned to NIMR in Delhi. At that time, Dr Bhattacharya was still serving as the Acting Director-General (DG) of ICMR. Dr V.M. Katoch, then Director of the JALMA Institute of Leprosy, had already been selected as the new DG of ICMR, but his official appointment orders had not yet been issued. As soon as I received the offer letter from WHO, I rushed to ICMR and submitted my application for voluntary retirement (VRS). I met with Dr Bhattacharya and showed him the letter. He was delighted and wrote on my VRS application, "Since Dr Dash has been selected for a prestigious position at the UN, his VRS may be accepted, and he may be relieved soon," and sent it to his office for processing. My application was then forwarded to the Ministry, where it was approved. From that point, it was up to me to decide when to be relieved and join WHO.

The first step before moving forward was a medical examination. I completed my medical examination at Ram Manohar Lohia (RML) Hospital in New Delhi and submitted the reports to SEARO, which forwarded them to WHO in Geneva. Once my medical reports were approved by WHO Headquarters, I received my final appointment order. By that time, Dr Katoch had joined ICMR as DG. The day he took office; I went to meet him and informed him about my selection at WHO. Since my VRS had already been approved before he took over, there wasn't much he could do, but he requested me to stay and promised me his full support. Before becoming DG, Dr Katoch had been a good friend of mine. I asked him, "Are you asking me to stay as a friend or as the DG?" He replied that he was speaking both as a friend and as the DG of ICMR. In that moment, I saw the power in his eyes.

By that time, I had already held the position of Director at five of the nation's top research institutes and enjoyed a distinguished career as a highly successful Director. My life had taken many turns, leading me through various paths. So, when the opportunity arose, I had no hesitation in accepting the position at WHO.

The buildings of DMRC, Jodhpur, were constructed by NPCC, and I accompanied Dr Katoch, DG of ICMR, to Jodhpur for the inauguration. Over the years, I had interacted with several Science Secretaries such as late Dr Manju Sharma, late Dr Bhan, Dr Vijayraghavan and Dr Soumya Swaminathan; who were quite informal during their travels. However, I noticed that Dr Katoch was more formal and seemed keen to enjoy the hospitality of the state governments. By January 2009, I was ready to be relieved and join WHO. However, Dr Katoch requested that I complete several important tasks before my departure, including the SAC meeting of DMRC, Jodhpur, the SAC meeting of NIMR, New Delhi, and the SAG meeting at ICMR headquarters in February 2009. I completed these responsibilities one by one. The scientists and staff at NIMR were saddened by my decision to take voluntary retirement (VRS).

The next challenge was deciding to whom I should hand over my responsibilities. After discussions with ICMR officials, it was decided that I would hand over the charge to Dr V.K. Dua, the next senior-most officer and in charge of the Haridwar field station. As NIMR was in the process of moving into a new building, I wanted to ensure there would be no disputes over space allocation. To prevent any issues, I formed a committee consisting of a few SAC members to assess the building and recommend how space should be allocated among the scientific and technical groups. The allocation was done fairly and later approved in the SAC meeting. I handed over charge to Dr Dua and left NIMR amidst a rather sad atmosphere. I promised the staff that for the next few days, I would visit NIMR after 4:30 PM before going home. In fact, I did this for about two weeks before finally leaving NIMR in the capable hands of Dr Dua and the senior scientists.

I visited Bhubaneswar on February 22nd, 2009, where my wife was staying. We returned to New Delhi together on the 24th, and I officially retired from NIMR on the 25th. The next day, on February 26th, I joined the SEAR Office of WHO. Around that same time, I received a call from the Global Malaria Programme at WHO Geneva regarding a

P-6 position I had applied for a few weeks earlier. Soon after I joined, my well-wishers at WHO advised me to submit a representation to the Chief of WHO/SEARO, highlighting my qualifications and extensive experience for consideration for the P-6 position. I followed their advice and submitted the representation. On the same day, my letter was forwarded by the Personnel section and recommended by the appropriate authorities, resulting in a significant increase in my salary. Although I was appointed at the P-5 level, I was placed at step 5 instead of step 1, which meant my salary was nearly equivalent to that of a P-6 position. As a result, I chose not to attend the interview for the P-6 role in Geneva.

My first day at WHO was spent on paperwork and verification. The next day, I was assigned a comfortable office (Room No. 115) on the first floor of the main WHO/SEARO building. I began organizing myself in the new environment, with the first week dedicated to briefings. After that, I started working within the international system. The WHO cafeteria was excellent, and I often had lunch there with colleagues. However, unlike in my previous roles at research institutes, we were responsible for collecting our own plates, getting water, and returning the plates to the designated area after lunch. This was something new for me, but everyone followed the same system. The office had a very different atmosphere compared to what I was used to. Everyone was focused on their own tasks, and people addressed each other by their first names, which felt quite different from the more formal Indian workplace culture. Our work hours were from 8 AM to 4:30 PM, and at first, I felt uneasy and somewhat suffocated by the new environment. However, after a couple of months, I adjusted and began to enjoy my work.

At the time I joined WHO, I was staying in the official accommodation provided by ICMR on Haily Road, Connaught Place, New Delhi. It was an excellent residence in a prime area of the city. Although I could have continued staying there for a while by paying higher rent, I did not want to ask for any favours. The standard allowance permitted me to stay for two months without needing special permission, and this could have been extended upon request. However, I made up my mind to vacate the house after the initial two months. I began searching for a flat to purchase, as I had some retirement benefits and planned to take out a loan to cover the rest. Fortunately, I found a decent flat in Indirapuram, opposite Sector 62 in Noida. I applied for a loan from the State Bank of India, and my Private Secretary from NIMR was helping me through the process. However, the bank required some form of mortgage, and I didn't have anything to offer as collateral. Despite having served as Director of five research institutes, my financial situation, with two children in college, didn't allow me to own a house. In fact, while I was still working as Director, I wasn't even sure where I would live after retirement. My Private Secretary, who had always been incredibly loyal and knew my situation well, was from Delhi and owned a house. To my astonishment, he offered to mortgage his own home to secure my loan. I couldn't believe it—no one would ever do such a thing. But thanks to his extraordinary generosity, I was able to secure the loan and purchase the flat. Exactly two months later, I vacated my official accommodation and moved into my new flat in Indirapuram, shortly after retiring from ICMR.

I joined SEARO/WHO as the Scientist and Regional

Adviser for Vector Borne Diseases. Before my appointment, someone else had been handling lymphatic filariasis (LF), and the 6th Regional Programme Review Group (RPRG) meeting on LF was scheduled to take place in Dhaka, Bangladesh, in April 2009. The meeting had been planned by my predecessor, and since I was new to the role, I was neither included in the planning nor aware of the meeting. Just two days before the meeting, I was asked to participate and conduct it. This required me to quickly familiarize myself with all the details of the upcoming meeting, as well as the outcomes of previous ones. The WHO travel agent, located on the first floor of our building, arranged my tickets and visa. Since I had not yet received my UN passport, I had to travel with my personal passport. There were limited flight options from Delhi to Dhaka. Jet Airways had one flight, but due to a lack of available seats, the travel agent booked me on *Biman*, the national carrier of Bangladesh. It was my first experience flying with *Biman* in April 2009, and while the experience wasn't the best, I arrived safely at Dhaka airport and proceeded to the "Hotel Sonar Bangla". The hotel, a Japanese establishment in Dhaka, provided a comfortable stay.

The meeting began the next day, with the WHO Country Office in Dhaka handling the logistics. It went well, and the staff from the WHO office were very helpful, even assisting me with some shopping. Interestingly, when I tried speaking in Hindi in Dhaka, many people acted as though they didn't understand the language at all. However, my experience at the hotel was quite different. In the evenings, the hotel club featured Hindi film songs and dances. Families gathered there, singing along and enjoying the Hindi music.

My first lecture as Adviser, WHO; at Dhaka, Bangladesh. Addressing the Expert members in the RPRG meeting for Lymphatic Filariasis

The meeting in Dhaka was the first WHO meeting I conducted, shortly after joining. On my return, I was able to secure a seat on Jet Airways from Dhaka to Delhi. As mentioned earlier, I joined the South-East Asia Regional Office of the World Health Organization (WHO) in February 2009 as the Regional Adviser for Vector Borne Diseases (VBD). My initial responsibilities were focused on managing vector-borne diseases such as malaria, lymphatic filariasis, kala-azar, and dengue. I approached the work with great dedication. However, after four months, my role was expanded, and I was re-designated as Regional Adviser for Vector Borne and Neglected Tropical Diseases (VBN). This added significant responsibilities, including managing additional diseases like yaws, trachoma, soil-transmitted helminthiasis, schistosomiasis, lymphatic filariasis, Kala-azar and other neglected tropical diseases, except for leprosy. It was a substantial task, and I had to read extensively to update my knowledge. In addition to these responsibilities, I was also given the charge of managing the impact of climate change on communicable diseases and overseeing Tropical Disease Research (TDR).

An international conference on *Plasmodium vivax* was held in Panama from May 24th to 28th, 2009. Before joining WHO, I had been invited by the organizers to deliver a lecture on vivax malaria in India, which I had agreed to. After joining WHO, I submitted a note to the Chief of WHO outlining my commitment, and he granted me permission to attend the conference.

I first learned about the Panama Canal during my Master's studies and later when I entered the workforce in 1978. The control of malaria and yellow fever played a crucial role in the construction of the Panama Canal. The groundbreaking discovery by Major Ronald Ross, which revealed that malaria was transmitted by mosquitoes, had a profound impact on development programs in tropical regions. One of the first major initiatives following Dr. Ross's discovery was the construction of the Panama Canal, which began just a few years later. During the American occupation of Havana, Cuba, the United States Army implemented measures to control yellow fever, including house screening and extensive drainage systems to reduce mosquito breeding. These efforts not only eliminated yellow fever but also significantly reduced malaria transmission

Panama, officially known as the Republic of Panama, is a transcontinental country situated between Central and South America. It is bordered by Costa Rica to the west, Colombia to the southeast, the Caribbean Sea to the north, and the Pacific Ocean to the south. Panama City, the capital, is also the largest city in the country. I was truly excited to visit Panama, and during my trip, I made sure to see the famous Panama Canal. However, there were no direct flights available to Panama, so I had to first fly to the USA and then continue on to Panama, with my return trip routing through Amsterdam.

The work on climate change research at WHO/SEARO began in 2009, with a primary focus on developing generic protocols to study the impact of climate change on communicable diseases. To kickstart this initiative, we organized an expert consultation in Kolkota in September 2009. The National Institute of Cholera and Enteric Diseases (NICED), a WHO collaborative centre, was selected as the venue for the meeting. During the expert consultation, we identified the need to create three specific generic protocols: one for retrospective studies, another for prospective studies, and a third for mitigation strategies. To facilitate this process, we formed three sub-groups, and I took on the role of coordinator. Through collaborative efforts, we successfully developed and finalized these three generic protocols. This initiative marked the beginning of climate change research in the South-East Asia Region, laying the groundwork for future studies and interventions aimed at understanding and addressing the effects of climate change on public health.

Until I joined WHO, the Environmental Health Department of SEARO was overseeing Integrated Vector Management (IVM), with Dr Alex in charge. Given that IVM was a new concept, there was a pressing need to train country representatives on its principles and practices. To address this, the department awarded an APW (Agreement for Performance of Work) in 2006-2007 to the Vector Control Research Centre (VCRC) in Pondicherry, a WHO Collaborative Centre, with the goal of developing a comprehensive course curriculum for training national experts and technical staff, as well as trainers from various countries.

However, this assignment remained incomplete by the time I joined. The Director of VCRC had also changed, and a new director had taken over. Shortly after my arrival, I was instructed to travel to VCRC to expedite the completion of this project. Upon my arrival, I engaged in discussions with the team there. Together, we constituted a group and dedicated several days to developing a six-week course focused on IVM, along with a 15-day crash course. I returned to WHO with the finalized documents and submitted them for approval, ensuring that the training initiatives for IVM were set in motion across the region.

As I mentioned earlier, I was assigned multiple responsibilities after joining WHO, each with specific activities and objectives. One of the major tasks involved conducting inter-country meetings, and the process was strictly structured. Larger meetings required approval from the Planning Committee, and it was mandatory to constitute the relevant planning committees for each event. When I first joined WHO in 2009, I was unaware of the internal dynamics and politics among the professional staff. There were clear divisions and personalized groups within the organization. I learned about this the hard way when I organized a meeting and formed a planning committee, chaired by the Director of Communicable Diseases (CDS), who was an Indian. This same CDS had been very supportive and played a key role in encouraging me to join WHO. We had a good professional relationship even before, during my tenure at NIMR.

However, something unexpected happened during that 2009 planning committee meeting. The meeting included members from various departments, some of whom were also Indian. During the meeting, the Chairman (Director CDS) suddenly treated me very differently, in a way that felt humiliating. I later realized that the tension may have stemmed from his discontent with certain committee members I had invited. After the meeting concluded, I expressed my disappointment and went back to my room. Surprisingly, a few minutes later, the Chair came to my room with a casual pretext, likely realizing how upset I was. Though I appreciated his gesture, my respect for him had diminished. From that point on, he became just another colleague to me. The incident hurt me deeply, and I even considered returning to NIMR. Thankfully, a few colleagues, including many non - Indians, noticed my distress. They came to console me, advising me not to make any hasty decisions. They reminded me that securing a position at WHO was no easy feat and encouraged me to stay. Their words helped me reflect, and I decided to continue with my work.

At the end of 2009, it was time to submit the Performance Management Development System (PMDS) report, where performance is reviewed and rated by a superior and then endorsed by a very senior reviewing officer. Despite the unpleasant incident earlier in the year, the same Director gave me the highest possible rating, noting that my performance had "exceeded all expectations". While the memory of that humiliating meeting remained with me, I was reminded of a quote by E.W. Howe, which states: *"The greatest humiliation in life is to work hard on something from which you expect great appreciation,…"* It resonated with me deeply. Despite the emotional strain, 2009 was an incredibly busy and productive year. I was occupied with organizing and attending multiple international meetings, developing generic protocols for climate change, finalizing the IVM course curriculum, participating in sessions at WHO headquarters in Geneva, and reviewing various country-specific situations related to vector-borne and neglected tropical diseases. I also worked on assessing research capacity across different nations and gaining a deeper understanding of the subjects assigned to me. This year was a true test of both my professional and emotional endurance.

In early 2010, the Department of Communicable Diseases of WHO organized a major public health conference at Hotel Taj, New Delhi, attended by experts from around the world. I was tasked with inviting a central minister as the Chief Guest to inaugurate the conference. At that time, I had a bad experience with the then Health Minister. Therefore, with the help of Prof. N.K. Ganguly, we approached Sri Kapil Sibal, the then Minister for Human Resource Development and Science & Technology, and invited him. He graciously accepted and inaugurated the conference.

The Asia Pacific Malaria Elimination Network (APMEN) meeting was held at the Earl's Regency Hotel in Kandy, Sri Lanka, from February 16th to 19th, 2010. I represented WHO at the meeting. After arriving in Colombo, I was driven to Kandy, a scenic hill station in Sri Lanka. APMEN is a network of 21 Asia Pacific countries dedicated to malaria elimination, along with leaders and experts from key multilateral and academic agencies. With its unique composition of members from governments, public, and private sector organizations, the Network's mission was to support the goal of a malaria-free Asia Pacific. Sir Richard Feachem, APMEN Co-Chair and Director of the Global Health Group at the University of California, San Francisco, co-chaired the meeting. I chaired five sessions covering the following topics: the Sri Lanka case study; surveillance — from passive to active case detection, fundamentals and technical advances; mapping the international limits and population at risk of *Plasmodium vivax* transmission in 2009; Vector Control Working Group priorities and scope of work; and the *Vivax* Working Group priorities and scope of work. The meeting was highly productive. During our stay there, we visited the botanical garden and tea plantations in Kandy. We also had the opportunity to visit the famous Temple of the Sacred Tooth Relic.

Kandy is a key city in Sri Lanka, situated in the heart of the Central Province. It was once the final capital of the ancient Sinhalese kings. One of its most notable landmarks is the Sri Dalada Maligawa, or the Temple of the Sacred Tooth Relic, a significant Buddhist temple located within the royal palace complex of the former Kingdom of Kandy. This temple houses the revered tooth relic of the Buddha. After Gautama Buddha's Parinirvana (final *Nirvana*), the relic was safeguarded in Kalinga (modern-day Odisha) before being smuggled to Sri Lanka by Princess Hemamali and her husband.

The story goes like this: The King of Kalinga, Guhaseeva, fearing backlash from neighbouring kingdoms after his conversion to Buddhism, decided to send the sacred tooth relic he possessed to Ceylon (modern-day Sri Lanka). To ensure its safe transport, his daughter, Hemamala, and her husband, Dantha, disguised themselves as Brahmins and sailed to Lankapatuna (now Ilankeiturei) in 310 AD. The King of Ceylon, Kirthi Sri Meghawanna, received them warmly and placed the relic in the Mahavihara temple at Anuradhapura. Legend has it that Hemamala hid the relic in her hair ornament during the journey. The Tooth Relic was brought to Sri Lanka because it was believed that the Buddha had prophesied that Buddhism would flourish there for 2500 years. King Kirthi Sri Meghawanna, overjoyed, built a palace within the royal complex to enshrine the relic and ordered an annual procession to honour it. As time passed, and the kingdom faced foreign threats, the capital moved several times—from Anuradhapura to Polonnaruwa, Dambadeniya, and others—each time a new palace was built to house the relic. Finally, the Tooth Relic was brought to Kandy, where it remains today at the Sri Dalada Maligawa temple. According to legend, when the Buddha died and was cremated at Kusinagara, his left canine tooth was recovered from the pyre by Arahat Khema. She then gave it to King Brahmadatte, who enshrined it in his kingdom in present-day Puri, Odisha. Kushinagar is a significant Buddhist pilgrimage destination where Gautam Buddha reached his 'Parinirvana' in the 5th century BCE. I had the opportunity to visit Kushinagar in 2023, where I had a meaningful conversation with the priests there.

Chemical control plays a vital role in the integrated approach to managing vectors and pests of public health significance. In numerous vector control programs, countries were using substantial quantities of pesticides; however, a cohesive pesticide management policy was lacking. This highlighted the need for a standardized pesticide management policy for the SEA Region that could be adopted by each member country. I discussed this with Dr Morteza Zaim, my counterpart in Geneva, and we decided to organize an informal expert consultation on public health pesticide management policy.

The consultation was held in Faridabad, Delhi NCR, on April 9–10, 2010, with experts invited from Southeast Asian countries, Geneva, and France. After in-depth deliberations, a comprehensive public health pesticide management policy was developed. This policy outlined the full life cycle of pesticide management—from procurement, storage, and supply to usage and container disposal, emphasizing the safety of spray personnel. The finalized document was subsequently distributed to all countries in the region for implementation and follow-up.

I was extremely busy managing the numerous responsibilities assigned to me by WHO, which required extensive travel to various countries. For lymphatic filariasis, I participated in the Regional Programme Review Group (RPRG), and for diseases such as kala-azar, dengue, and malaria, I contributed to the Regional Technical Advisory Group (RTAG). Annual meetings for each group were organized across different countries, including India. Additionally, I arranged specialized meetings as needed, such as the expert meeting on surveillance and control of insect vectors in natural disasters, held in Jakarta, Indonesia, in July 2010.

While working on neglected tropical diseases (NTDs), we observed limited interest from various countries in prioritizing NTDs. To address this, I organized a Partners' Meeting in Bangkok, also in July 2010, focused on the control, elimination, and eradication of NTDs. This meeting proved fruitful in strengthening the commitment to control and eliminate NTDs across the region.

Since I was tasked with overseeing a wide range of responsibilities—including lymphatic filariasis, kala-azar, dengue, chikungunya, integrated vector management and control, trachoma, yaws, various other NTDs (excluding leprosy), the impact of climate change on communicable diseases, and tropical disease research—I requested senior management for additional technical and administrative support. My request was promptly approved, and I was allocated a few additional staff members. This support allowed me to build an effective team and work more collaboratively to manage these extensive duties.

By the end of 2010, Dr Sangay Thinley from Bhutan joined as the Director of the Department of Communicable Diseases (CDS). He was one of the kindest individuals I had the privilege of working with, and I had known him since my brief assignment as a Temporary International Professional at WHO in 2007. The Regional Director of the South-East Asia Regional Office (SEARO) at the time was from Thailand, and it was widely believed that he held a particular disfavour toward Indians, stemming from India's decision not to support him during his 2003 election as Regional Director. During that election, Maldives had requested the Indian Prime Minister's support for the Maldivian candidate, and India agreed; however, the Thai candidate ultimately won the election. Despite this history, I sensed a slight soft spot from him in my case. I was appointed Editor of the *Dengue Bulletin* published by the SEA Regional Office and was also selected as an editorial board member for the *South-East Asia Journal of Public Health,* with Dr J.P. Narain as Editor-in-Chief. After Dr Narain's retirement, I was honoured to assume the role of Editor-in-Chief for the *SEA Journal of Public Health.*

By 2010, dengue had become a major public health concern in the Region, with Indonesia reporting the highest number of cases. Recognizing the urgent need for comprehensive guidelines on dengue and dengue haemorrhagic fever (DHF) prevention and control; we collaborated closely with leading experts in diagnostics, case definition and management, vector control, and transmission biology. We began by drafting the guideline, refining it extensively with input from the expert panel, which met four times to ensure accuracy and effectiveness. The resulting *Guideline for Prevention and Control of Dengue and DHF* was printed and widely circulated among countries. The initial print run of 1,000 copies was quickly depleted due to high demand, leading to a second printing. The guideline proved so valuable that it was translated into various local languages, including Chinese, to maximize accessibility. Demand for the book remains high to this day. Dr Siripen, Director of a WHO Collaborating Centre for Clinical Management of Dengue in Bangkok, provided invaluable support in developing the guideline.

As dengue became a growing global and regional issue, it required increased attention and effort for effective control and prevention in the SEA Region. Dengue had never been reported in Nepal and Bhutan, but it emerged in these countries between 2004 and 2006, and by 2010, all SEA Region countries except North Korea were reporting cases. With no available effective vaccine or antiviral drug, control efforts centered on vector management and reducing human-mosquito contact. This highlighted the need for comprehensive training in each endemic country on proper vector management, case management, and diagnosis.

Singapore's dengue control program was renowned as one of the most effective in the Asia-Pacific region. Unlike other countries, the program was managed under the Ministry of Environment rather than the Ministry of Health. The Singapore Environment Institute (SEI), the training and knowledge division of Singapore's National Environment Agency (NEA), conducted various courses on dengue control. I represented the SEA Region in these sessions, along with participants from other member countries. The training proved highly beneficial, providing insights we could apply regionally. With support from the WHO Collaborating Centre in Bangkok, we conducted multiple training programs focused on diagnosis and case management, as well as numerous sessions on vector management, to strengthen dengue control across the region.

I was specially invited by the Indian Society of Malaria and Other Communicable Diseases (ISMOD) and the Indian Association of Epidemiologists (IAE) to deliver the keynote address on "Living with Dengue" at their joint annual conference in 2012. During this occasion, I was honoured to receive the Dr A.P. Ray Award for outstanding research on malaria from the Director General of Health Services, Government of India.

In 2011, the Regional Director aimed to establish a flagship institute on tropical diseases, but this initiative did not materialize. During our discussions, we advised him that several research institutes focused on tropical diseases already existed in the South East Asia Region. Instead of creating a new institute, we suggested that it would be more beneficial to establish a strong network among the existing tropical disease institutes in the region. The Regional Director appreciated this idea and entrusted me with initiating the process. Necessary funding was allocated. As a first step, we aimed to map the institutes engaged in research on tropical diseases across different countries in the South East Asia Region, which involved identifying relevant experts from each country. This task was assigned to various experts through the APW mechanism, and appropriate compensation was provided. Prof. N.K. Ganguly was identified for India, Prof. Pratap Singhavasan for Thailand, and several others for countries like Bangladesh, Nepal, Sri Lanka, and Indonesia. Once the reports from each country were received and reviewed, we organized a major event to invite all key experts on tropical diseases from member countries. The experts who prepared the reports for each country were also invited to present their findings. The meeting took place in a well-appointed hotel in Faridabad and lasted for three days.

The meeting was presided over by the Deputy Regional Director of SEARO and chaired by the Director General of ICMR. Following the inaugural session, technical sessions on each country commenced. Each expert delivered a detailed presentation on the various research initiatives in their respective countries regarding tropical diseases, highlighting the different institutes involved and the scientists engaged in that research. These technical sessions were followed by in-depth discussions, and by the end of the meeting, a report with recommendations was drafted and presented to WHO.

Inaugural sessison of the meeting on networking centres on tropical diseases in the SEA Region

The regional meeting on centres of expertise for tropical diseases recommended the establishment of a regional steering committee to facilitate effective networking. This steering committee was formed with eminent experts from each member country in the region. The first meeting of the steering committee took place in 2012 in Kolkata, where a detailed methodology was developed.

The report and recommendations were submitted to the Regional Director for further action. The mapping reports for countries like India and Thailand were excellent, and as a result, these reports were printed for future reference. However, by that time, the Regional Director had lost interest, and no further progress was made.

As I mentioned earlier, I was put in charge of the publication of the Dengue Bulletin alongside Dr Chusak, and I became the sole editor after his retirement in 2010. By that time, dengue was wreaking havoc in many countries in the region, and the responses from these countries were insufficient to match the severity of the problem. It was decided to release the next volume of the Dengue Bulletin as a special issue focusing on the economic impact of dengue. Neither Dr Chusak nor I were economists, so we needed to find a guest editor to help us. Ultimately, we successfully published Volume 37 of the Dengue Bulletin as a special issue documenting its economic impact. This issue generated considerable demand, and following Dr Chusak's retirement, the Dengue Bulletin continued to be published regularly under my supervision. The following year saw a serious outbreak of dengue in Sri Lanka, which resulted in significant infant mortality. In response, we reached out to the WHO Collaborative Centre in Thailand, and its Director, Dr Siripen, along with her team of doctors and nurses, organized field training in Sri Lanka. The country established a national task force on dengue, chaired by the President, and as a result, dengue was brought under control.

The Association of Southeast Asian Nations (ASEAN) is a regional intergovernmental organization comprising ten countries in Southeast Asia. It promotes cooperation in economic, political, security, military, educational, and socio-cultural integration among its members and other countries in Asia. In ASEAN countries, dengue is the deadliest and fastest-spreading disease among vector-borne illnesses. For this reason, during their 10th Meeting on 22 July 2010 in Singapore, the ASEAN Health Ministers agreed to observe ASEAN Dengue Day on 15 June each year. This observance includes simultaneous national activities and regional initiatives to reinforce local efforts, aiming to raise awareness among policymakers, national programs, and communities. The goal is to promote effective and efficient prevention and control measures among various stakeholders in the fight against dengue. ASEAN Dengue Day was officially launched at the regional level on 15 June 2011 in Jakarta, under the leadership of Indonesia, then the Chair of ASEAN. The theme for the inaugural event was "Dengue is Everybody's Concern," highlighting the socio-economic burden of the disease while emphasizing its preventability. I had the opportunity to represent the Southeast Asia Region of WHO at this meeting.

While addressing various issues related to dengue, we recognized in 2012 the need to review the status of dengue in each country within the Southeast Asia Region. Consequently, I organized an inter-country meeting in Bali, Indonesia, in November 2012. To gather comparable data from each country, I developed a template and distributed it to all participating nations. Representatives from each country attended the meeting, and we also invited a few experts from other regions. Indonesia was chosen as the meeting location because it reported the highest number of dengue cases in the Southeast Asia Region, with Bali being the area most affected. Although I have travelled to many countries worldwide, my wife rarely accompanied me; however, she joined me for this trip to Bali. The three-day meeting included an extensive review of the dengue situation in each country, resulting in valuable recommendations to strengthen prevention and control efforts across the region.

Bali is a province of Indonesia, situated to the east of Java and west of Lombok. Unlike most of Indonesia, which is predominantly Muslim, over 83% of Bali's population practices Balinese Hinduism. A DNA study conducted in 2005 revealed that 12% of Balinese Y-chromosomes likely trace back to Indian origins. Interestingly, Odisha has a festival known as *Baliyatra*, which directly translates to 'A Voyage to Bali.' This celebration takes place in Cuttack, Odisha, to honour the maritime history of the region and its ancient trade connections with Bali, Indonesia. *Baliyatra* is celebrated on Kartik Purnima, the full moon day of the Kartik month. Kartik is the 8th month of the Indian calender and falls in October /November, pointing to the strong historical relationship between Odisha and Bali. The Sambalpuri style of weaving and tie-dye has also left its mark on the Patola style in Bali. In Bali, deities such as Shiva, Vishnu, and Garuda are of great significance, and some Balinese Brahmins refer to themselves as Brahmin-Boudha-Kalinga. Lord Jagannath is mentioned in certain Balinese prayers, and the festival of *Masakapam Kapesih* is celebrated. Interestingly, *Masakapam Kapesih* is observed in Bali, where a small boat with burning candles is set afloat. In this ceremony, a child is symbolically sent back to their ancestral land in Kalinga. It's fascinating to see how this ancient bond between India and Indonesia continues to be celebrated in both nations.

Remarkably, Indonesia's national airline is named after Garuda. Having visited Bali on several occasions, I always eagerly anticipate these trips due to the deep ties to Odisha. This connection is why I insisted my wife join me on this trip. During my visit, I learned that 'Ram Lila' is also celebrated in Indonesia, though in their own distinct way. Locals shared with me that the tradition of Ram Lila has been handed down through generations and continues to be a beloved cultural practice today.

Historically, Indonesia, along with other countries in the archipelago like Malaysia and Singapore, was ruled by Hindu-Buddhist kingdoms from as early as the 3rd century AD. The influence of the Ramayana and Mahabharata can still be seen in Java's culture. However, by the 14th century, Indonesia predominantly embraced Islam. One notable exception is Bali, where Hinduism is still practiced in its full form. The Ramayana remains deeply embedded in Balinese culture, celebrated through traditional dances and folk performances. During my travels in Bali, I observed that at the entrance of nearly every home, colourful powder patterns were created, reminiscent of Odisha's *'Jhoti'* (or Rangoli in Hindi), reflecting the region's enduring Hindu tradition

After arriving in Bali, I developed a fever the following day. Despite this, I had to initiate the review meeting, so I took a Paracetamol tablet and proceeded with the meeting, attended by representatives from various national governments including the Indonesian government, particularly from the Health Department. As the fever persisted, I was taken to an international hospital in Bali, where they suspected dengue as my platelet count had dropped below one lakh. I returned to the hotel and continued with my meetings, managing the symptoms with Paracetamol. While they urged me to stay in Bali, I decided to return to Delhi. Our journey to Bali was with Thai Airways via Bangkok, and interestingly, film star Mr. Sunil Shetty was on the same flight with his wife and secretary, seated on our side in the business class. There was no interaction on the way to Bali, but we encountered them again on our return flight and met in the business lounge at Bali Airport. My secretary approached Mr. Sunil Shetty and mentioned that I was in Bali for a dengue meeting as part of WHO, traveling back to Delhi with my wife. Around that time, Yash Chopra's death due to dengue had spurred BMC to fumigate all film studios, which was widely reported in the newspapers. When Mr. Shetty learned of our involvement in the WHO dengue meeting, he approached us, and we had a pleasant conversation. He was very friendly and expressed a willingness to support any dengue control program. He even gave me his personal mobile number, though I later misplaced it.

With the film Star Sunil Shetty at Bali airport,2012

At the Bali meeting in November 2012, country representatives recommended that integrated vector management (IVM) for dengue should be strengthened and that program officers in endemic countries needed training in appropriate methodologies. My immediate task was to arrange another IVM-focused meeting, which I scheduled in Colombo, Sri Lanka, for early 2013. This meeting was successfully conducted.

As mentioned, we at SEARO had developed a comprehensive guideline for the prevention and control of dengue and dengue hemorrhagic fever (DHF) in 2010–11, which included a clear case definition. A year prior, TDR (the Special Programme for Research and Training in Tropical Diseases) had also developed a guideline. However, our experts had some reservations about TDR's definitions. TDR, a global scientific collaboration co-sponsored by UNICEF, UNDP, the World Bank, and WHO, focuses on combating diseases of poverty. In the Bali meeting, we identified that these differing case definitions were causing confusion, so we agreed on the need to synchronize them. To address this, I authored an article in the *Dengue Bulletin* and organized a meeting in Colombo in August 2013, inviting experts from both within and outside the Region. The Government of Sri Lanka was extremely supportive, even hosting an exceptional cultural program for us. The meeting successfully trained representatives from several Southeast Asian countries. It was disheartening, however, to see that while other countries nominated qualified technical personnel, India sent a few irrelevant, non-technical participants for the training.

Visceral leishmaniasis (VL) or Kala-azar (KA) is a serious public health problem on the Indian subcontinent, causing high morbidity and mortality among marginalized communities. It is caused by *Leishmania* parasites and transmitted by sand flies. In the South-East Asia Region, Bangladesh, India, and Nepal are endemic for this disease.

The governments of these three countries launched a VL elimination initiative in 2005, formalized by a Memorandum of Understanding (MoU) signed by the Health Ministers, aiming to eliminate VL as a public health problem by 2010. However, due to a lack of full understanding of vector bionomics at the time, achieving elimination within the specified period was challenging. Each year, a meeting of the Regional Technical Advisory Group on Kala-azar was held. Since the 2010 target was not met, efforts were made to renew the MoU between these three countries. By that time, two additional countries in the Region, Bhutan and Thailand, had reported a few cases of VL. It was decided to include these two countries, and ultimately, an MoU was signed by five countries—Bangladesh, Bhutan, India, Nepal, and Thailand—to eliminate the disease as a public health problem. While the VL issue was less intense in Bhutan and Thailand, Bangladesh, India, and Nepal made substantial progress toward elimination, with mortality rates decreasing drastically. During my tenure at WHO, the drug policy was revised to further support this goal. In Nepal, new cases were reported in hilltop areas, prompting efforts to expedite the VL elimination program in the Region. To this end, in addition to the Technical Advisory Group meetings, we organized an inter-country high-level meeting for VL elimination in 2011. Dr C.P. Thakur, former Minister of Health of India, was a member of our VL Technical Advisory Group. As a specialist in VL treatment and clinical trials of new drugs, he brought valuable expertise. Considering the new cases in Nepal's hilltop areas, we once held a VL RTAG meeting in Kathmandu, a three-day event. At that time, Dr Yadav, then President of Nepal, was a practicing doctor who had treated VL patients. Dr Thakur knew him personally, and when the

President learned about our meeting, he invited us to his residence for evening tea. We had an excellent discussion with him. My last Technical Advisory Meeting on VL as Regional Adviser was held in Bhutan in September 2013. The meeting was attended by experts from across the Region, as well as counterparts from WHO headquarters in Geneva.

With President of Nepal

Lymphatic filariasis (LF), commonly known as elephantiasis, is a neglected tropical disease that primarily affects the world's poorest populations. Infection occurs when filarial parasites are transmitted to humans through mosquitoes. The painful and visibly disfiguring symptoms of the disease—lymphoedema, elephantiasis, and scrotal swelling—can lead to permanent disability. These patients often endure not only physical disabilities but also mental, social, and financial hardships, which contribute to stigma and perpetuate poverty. Of the 1.3 billion people at risk globally for LF, 851 million were in the South-East Asia (SEA) Region. All countries in the Region, except North Korea and Bhutan, were endemic for the disease. LF has been targeted for elimination, and each WHO Region has a Regional Technical Advisory Group (RTAG), previously called the Regional Programme Review Group (RPRG), which meets annually (now biannually) to review progress and provide recommendations for strengthening the program. A particularly memorable meeting was held in Myanmar in 2011.

During my tenure as Regional Adviser, substantial progress was achieved in LF elimination across the Region. The program was intensified in all endemic countries, and I visited numerous villages in Thailand and nearly every major island in Indonesia. Indonesia, the world's fourth-most populous country and the largest island nation, has approximately 17,000 islands, including Sumatra, Java, Borneo (Kalimantan), Sulawesi, and New Guinea (Papua). The LF elimination program was redefined in Indonesia with a comprehensive approach. The Maldives, Thailand, and Sri Lanka made remarkable progress, prompting me to initiate a Transmission Assessment Survey for LF in these three countries, involving WHO experts in 2012. As a result, these countries reached the elimination milestone. Bangladesh and Nepal also advanced toward elimination as a public health program, and India made significant strides in reducing LF cases across many districts. This progress brought me great satisfaction. Bangladesh was certified for LF elimination in 2023 while I served as the Chairman of the Regional Technical Advisory Group (RTAG) for LF, Schistosomiasis, and Soil-Transmitted Helminthiasis for WHO SEARO.

In January 2012, the Director-General of WHO launched a roadmap to accelerate efforts to overcome the global impact of neglected tropical diseases. This roadmap set a target for the eradication of yaws by 2020, marking the second attempt to achieve this goal following the earlier mass campaign led by WHO and UNICEF in the 1950s and 1960s, which remained incomplete. Later, progress was reviewed for each vector-borne and neglected tropical disease. On January 18, 2021; WHO developed and launched a new roadmap (2021-2030) for the elimination of these diseases by 2030, aligning with the Sustainable Development Goals (SDGs).

In January 2012, results from a randomized controlled clinical trial in Papua New Guinea were published, revealing that a single dose of oral azithromycin was as effective in treating yaws as the traditional benzathine penicillin injection. This finding, seen as the most significant advancement for yaws treatment in over 60 years, offered a solution to the operational and logistical challenges associated with injectable penicillin, making it easier to conduct large-scale field treatments. In light of these developments, WHO convened a global meeting to review the yaws elimination strategy, and I participated in this meeting, representing the SEA Region.

CHAPTER – 22

Around Hundred-Thousand Tulips

WHO meetings are typically held in well-connected cities, such as national or state capitals. However, this particular meeting took place in Morges, a charming Swiss town on the shores of Lake Geneva near Lausanne, around 50 kilometers from Geneva. We travelled by road from Geneva airport to Morges, where Dr. K. Asiedu, our counterpart from Geneva, met me at the airport and drove us to the town.

During the meeting, a new yaws eradication strategy was developed, which later became known as the "WHO Morges Strategy". This strategy advocates for large-scale treatment in at-risk communities, beginning with a single dose of oral azithromycin to accelerate the interruption of yaws transmission. Morges, known as the "flower of Lake Geneva," is a beautiful town celebrated for its annual Tulip Festival, featuring more than 100,000 tulips in over 300 varieties. Walking through the town at dawn was a true pleasure, and we enjoyed dinners at a few Indian restaurants nearby.

Participants in the WHO expert meeting on eradication of Yaws, 5-7 March 2012 at Morges, Switzerland

(responsible for Yaws eradication)

Yaws was also endemic in the South East Asia Region, particularly in India, Indonesia, and Timor Leste. While India was declared free from yaws in 2006, the disease continued to pose a problem in the other two countries. During the Morges meeting, I presented India's success story as a model for elimination. Later, the Indian strategy was adopted by WHO for implementation in other endemic countries. Ultimately, India was officially declared free from yaws in 2016.

CHAPTER – 23

A Stately Honour in Thailand

The other programs on soil-transmitted helminthiasis and trachoma also made significant progress in the region. During my tenure at WHO/SEARO, I visited many countries numerous times, but I remember a few memorable stays in less well-known places, one of which was Laos. In 2009, I attended a meeting on intestinal parasites organized by WHO in Vientiane, Laos, traveling there via Bangkok. My experience in Vientiane was very pleasant. Vientiane is the capital and largest city of Laos, located on the banks of the Mekong River near the border with Thailand. The city is home to the most significant national monument in Laos, That Luang, which is a well-known symbol of the country and an icon of Buddhism. Other significant Buddhist temples, such as Haw Phra Kaew, which once housed the Emerald Buddha, can also be found there. Vientiane hosted the 25th Southeast Asian Games in December 2009. The hotel where we stayed was situated right on the bank of the Mekong River, close to the Thai border. The scenery was particularly beautiful in the evenings. During my stay, I worked with Dr Steve Borge, who was in the WHO country office in Indonesia. Although Steve was from the USA and had encountered some serious issues in Indonesia that necessitated his transfer, he joined my unit without any problems and quickly became an asset. Despite being older and single, with his mother still in the USA, he eventually married a Thai lady later on.

We focused significantly on Thailand, as the country was very keen to eliminate lymphatic filariasis as a public health problem. I visited various regions of Thailand, which is officially known as the Kingdom of Thailand and was formerly called Siam until 1939. It is the only Southeast Asian country that has never been colonized by a foreign power, and the Thai people take great pride in this fact. Mainland Thai culture is heavily influenced by Buddhism; however, unlike the Buddhist countries of East Asia, Thailand's Buddhists primarily follow the Theravada school, which is arguably closer to its Indian roots and places a greater emphasis on monasticism. The *Ramakien*, meaning "Glory of Rama," is Thailand's national epic. In 2012, Thailand expressed its desire to honour WHO/SEARO for its significant contributions to the elimination of lymphatic filariasis. I travelled to Bangkok to receive this honour at a colourful event attended by dignitaries from the Thai government and members of the royal family, who recognized our efforts during the ceremony.

Receiving the honour from the Princes of Thailand

Among the many incredible places in Thailand, aside from Bangkok, two that I found particularly memorable were Chiang Mai and Chiang Rai. Chiang Mai, famous for its misty mountain ranges, is a true haven for outdoor enthusiasts. Located about 700 kilometers from Bangkok along the Ping River, it offers breathtaking natural beauty and a rich cultural heritage. On the other hand, Chiang Rai, while smaller and more tranquil than Chiang Mai, is deeply rooted in the history of the Lao-Thai-Lanna kingdom. It also serves as the gateway to the renowned "Golden Triangle," a major tourist destination. During our stay in Chiang Rai, we had the opportunity to walk to Myanmar via a border checkpoint. Each village in Thailand is equipped with a robust healthcare system, and the country's higher education system is also quite impressive. I was particularly struck by Chiang Mai University, established in 1964, which enrols nearly 40,000 students. The university places a strong emphasis on engineering, science, agriculture, and medicine, making a significant contribution to the region's education and progress

CHAPTER – 24

Another Stint with the Who

In the WHO, staff members who joined before 1992 were set to retire at age 60, while those who joined afterward were to retire at 62. This was later extended to 65 for those who joined after January 1, 2014. Since I joined in February 2009, my retirement date was set for March 31, 2013. I had previously worked with WHO temporarily for three months in 2007-2008, which meant I was completing four years, four months, and one week of service. At the time of my joining, I was unaware that a minimum of five years of service was required to qualify for a pension. However, the Director-General (DG) of WHO had the authority to grant extensions of service to deserving professional staff in the regions based on recommendations from the respective Regional Directors (RDs). Unfortunately, the then RD of the South-East Asia Region was not supportive of Indian staff. Nevertheless, he recommended to the DG to extend my service, citing my involvement in managing several important programmes and the lack of personnel to take over my responsibilities if I retired in March 2013. I received an extension of six months, until September 2013. Even then, I was still short of 53 days to reach the five-year mark. I requested the RD to recommend an additional two months of extension for me, but he did not do so.

  All the professional staff in the Regional Office (mainly non-Indians) submitted a representation to the RD, urging him to recommend my extension, but nothing came of it. That year, the election for the next regional director was scheduled, and the Regional Committee meeting was held in Delhi, attended by the DG of WHO. The Government of India hosted the meeting and dinner, overseen by the then Union Health Minister. Ministers from other countries were advocating for their citizens' extensions; this is how a Sri Lankan professional received an extension from the DG, based on their Minister's recommendation. I approached our Minister, who promised to speak to the DG on my behalf. Additionally, during a dinner at the India Habitat Centre in Delhi, a former Minister and the former Chief Minister of Odisha also requested the Indian Health Minister to advocate for my extension and the Indian health minister agreed to do that. The Indian Health Minister attended the dinner along with the DG, but he did not follow through on his promise to mention my case to the DG.

  It was the last week of September 2013, and I was due to retire on September 30. A farewell party was arranged for me, but I chose not to attend and informed the RD of my decision to leave. Shortly after, I experienced a bout of vertigo and was bedridden for about a month. The RD was due to retire in January 2014, with the new RD taking over on February 1, 2014. The new RD was an Indian, marking the first time an Indian held this position through election. She was previously the Deputy Regional Director in WHO/SEARO and was familiar with my work. Once she took office, she moved forward with my reappointment for six months.

Thanks to her sincere efforts, I received the reappointment and rejoined WHO/SEARO in March 2014, working until September 2014. One of my immediate tasks was organizing the celebration of World Health Day in April 2014. Each year, World Health Day has a specific theme, and in 2014, it was "Vector-Borne Diseases." We made all the necessary arrangements for the event, which took place at Hotel Le Meridien in New Delhi. I also provided technical support in areas such as lymphatic filariasis, visceral leishmaniasis, dengue, malaria, soil-transmitted helminthiasis, yaws, trachoma, and tropical disease research.

World Health Day is celebrated annually on April 6, each year focusing on a specific theme. As mentioned earlier, the theme for World Health Day in 2014 was "Vector-Borne Diseases." In conjunction with this event, the South-East Asia Journal of Public Health published a special issue dedicated to Vector-Borne Diseases in 2014. It was particularly gratifying to see an article in the journal authored by Dr Neena Valecha, then Director of the National Institute of Malaria Research (NIMR), and Dr M.R. Ranjit from the Regional Medical Research Centre (RMRC) in Bhubaneswar. The article discussed the origin and evolution of the National Academy of Vector-Borne Diseases, which we had established back in 1994. This publication gained significant popularity throughout the South-East Asia Region.

TDR, or the Special Programme for Research and Training in Tropical Diseases, is a global initiative focused on scientific collaboration to coordinate, support, and influence efforts to combat major diseases affecting the poor and disadvantaged. Established in 1975 and executed by the World Health Organization (WHO), TDR is sponsored by the United Nations Children's Fund (UNICEF), the

United Nations Development Programme (UNDP), the World Bank, and WHO. As mentioned earlier, I was responsible for overseeing TDR activities at WHO/SEARO. We received a special grant under TDR to assist member countries in strengthening their research capacity by sponsoring small research projects. Over time, we noticed that smaller countries like Bhutan, Timor-Leste, and the Maldives were not receiving any research funding from TDR. Consequently, I was sent to the Maldives to conduct a one-man workshop on writing research proposals and research papers. Dr Akjemal Magtymova, currently the WHO representative in Syria, was the WHO representative in the Maldives at that time. She made all the necessary arrangements for the participants and organized the workshop at a hotel on one of the islands.

I arrived at *Velana* International Airport on *Hulhulé* Island, adjacent to the capital, Malé, where the island hotel for our workshop was arranged. After completing the three-day workshop, it was satisfying to see that the Maldives successfully obtained two research projects from TDR during the subsequent funding cycle. Later that same year, there was a WHO meeting on dengue in the Maldives, and I was invited to attend. The newly elected Regional Director was set to inaugurate the meeting, which took place in Malé, the capital city. During our stay, we attended an official dinner in honour of the Regional Director, which was graced by several special invitees, including Dr Abdul Sattar, my former colleague in SEARO, who retired in 2013. After retirement, he moved back to the Maldives and became the Minister of External Affairs. The dinner was also attended by the Minister of Health of the Maldives and the Indian High Commissioner to the Maldives.

In Male with the Regional director, WHO, Minister of Health, Maldives and the Indian High Commissioner to Maldives and Dr Sattar, 2014

I continued my work at the WHO's South East Asia Regional Office. In September 2014, I organized the Regional Programme Review Group meeting for Lymphatic Filariasis, Soil Transmitted Helminthiasis, and Schistosomiasis in Indonesia. The meeting was well attended by programme managers from various countries, as well as experts from different nations and WHO Headquarters in Geneva.

Indonesia, known for its diverse culture and rich traditions, offers a vast array of natural beauty that attracts visitors to its islands. On the inaugural day of the meeting, a cultural program was organized, which was thoroughly enjoyed by all attendees.

In Indonesia in a Cultural Programme, after attending an expert meeting on Filariasis, (Sept. 2014)

My car with UN number (in which I travelled locally)

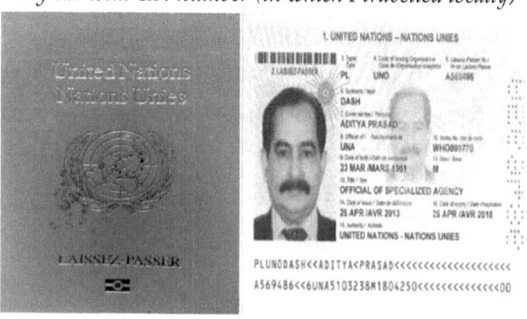

With this UN Passport, I travelled all over the world

By September 2014, I had completed five years and four months and was eligible for a pension. Consequently, I retired from WHO in September 2014 with a pension. My son was also working in Delhi and staying with us along with his family. My wife was heading the Zoology department at a college in Odisha. She joined Delhi University on a UGC assignment and was on deputation. We all initially lived on Haily Road in Connaught Place, New Delhi, before shifting to our own flat in Indirapuram, Ghaziabad, in 2009. At the end of 2014, my son secured a position as an Assistant Professor at a Management Institute in Bhubaneswar. By that time, my wife's tenure at Delhi University had also concluded. Therefore, my wife, son, and his family moved to Bhubaneswar, while I stayed back in Delhi.

Theta Healing

After retiring from the WHO in September 2014, with a pension, I spent some time in Delhi where I met Mr. Amit Kohli. He had a background in engineering and management and offered training in Theta Healing. This was my first exposure to Theta Healing, and I even enrolled in a three-day course with him. However, I found it somewhat unconvincing at first. Theta Healing is a meditation technique created by Vianna Stibal in the United States in 1995. The practice is based on the belief that it helps individuals tap into their natural intuition by altering their brainwave frequency to theta waves. Practitioners claim that this shift allows emotional energy to influence health. At the time, it seemed like a form of New Age meditation, which intrigued me enough to delve into it further.

Theta Healing is a meditation technique rooted in a spiritual philosophy centered around personal growth and well-being. Practitioners believe it merges science and spirituality to help individuals uncover and transform deeply ingrained negative beliefs, emotional barriers, and traumas stored in the subconscious mind. The practice is said to offer benefits like transforming negative thought patterns, empowering individuals to reshape their lives, and even working at a genetic level, down to the DNA. Importantly, practitioners stress that Theta Healing is a technique, not a religion, and is not tied to any specific religious doctrine. It is said to be compatible with any spiritual or religious belief, or even with no belief system at all.

The human brain operates within five primary frequency ranges: Gamma, Beta, Alpha, Theta, and Delta. Although all these waves are present simultaneously, one frequency typically dominates depending on the activity. Theta waves are most prominent during deep meditation, the transition into sleep, and hypnosis. It's believed that the theta frequency can reduce stress, ease anxiety, promote relaxation, enhance mental clarity and creativity, alleviate pain, and even support healing. In Theta Healing, practitioners claim that the brain enters the theta state instantly, allowing for direct interaction with what they call Source, Spirit, the Universe, God, or the Creator of All That Is, depending on personal beliefs. In this state, individuals are believed to be able to undergo significant healing and transformation.

Eventually, I had the privilege of learning Theta Healing directly from Vianna Stibal. I completed two courses with her, including one on training others to teach the technique. I could feel the importancer of Theta Healing while learning from her, although I wasn't able to practice it consistently afterward.

Theta Healing Training from Vianna Stibal

After retiring from WHO and with my family relocated to Bhubaneswar, I decided to rent out my flat and move there as well. I packed everything, arranged for the luggage to be sent, rented out the flat, and moved to Bhubaneswar in November 2014. On my way to the airport in the last week of November, I stopped by NIMR in Dwarka for a cup of tea, where I learned about an advertisement for a Distinguished Scientist Chair. That day was the last date for nomination, and colleagues at NIMR encouraged me to apply immediately. Though nominations were invited by ICMR, I was short on time, so I submitted the application at NIMR for them to send to ICMR that same day.

To designate a laboratory for my work, I contacted the Director of ILS, Bhubaneswar, who readily agreed and provided a certificate via email. I later heard that my application was delivered to ICMR at the last hour. I arrived in Bhubaneswar and, in January 2015, WHO requested my services again, so I accepted an appointment with WHO/SEARO. Meanwhile, my application for the Distinguished Scientist Chair was under review, and in February 2015, the selection committee, chaired by the late Dr Bhan (former Secretary of DBT) and including Prof. Ganguly, Ex-DG of ICMR, and a former CSIR DG, met. I was selected and received an offer in March. Since I was still with WHO, I requested to join ICMR by the end of May, and they agreed. After completing my assignments, I joined ILS, Bhubaneswar, as a Distinguished Scientist Chair in May 2015.

In between, my son completed his MBA in Delhi in 2008 and secured a job through campus recruitment. After two years, we decided to look for a marriage match for him. Since we were based in Delhi, we registered on Oriya Matrimony and received several proposals. We narrowed it down to four options, located in Raipur, Mumbai, Hyderabad, and Halol (near Vadodara). My daughter was also pursuing her MBA, so the whole family—my wife, daughter, son, and I—visited these locations. On one trip, we toured Mumbai, visited the Shirdi Sai Temple, and then went to Halol. Upon returning to Delhi, both my son and daughter favoured the match in Halol.

In our family, it was traditional to match horoscopes before marriage. However, the family in Halol did not believe in horoscope matching. Nevertheless, we obtained the girl's horoscope, but I found it was not a perfect match, which made me hesitant about the marriage. Although I had some knowledge of astrology, I wasn't a strong believer. Considering my family's interest, I eventually agreed, and we conveyed our decision. A few days later, the girl's parents visited us in Delhi, and it was decided to hold the engagement ceremony at the Lord Jagannath Temple in Hauz Khas, New Delhi, with the wedding planned for Bhubaneswar in 2011. The engagement took place as planned, and the marriage was celebrated at Hotel Mayfair, Bhubaneswar, followed by a reception at the Bhubaneswar Club.

Around ten days after the wedding, we returned to Delhi, where we hosted a grand reception with a cocktail dinner for about 800 guests, which was a resounding success. A couple of years later, we welcomed our grandson. Upon hearing the news, my wife, who was in Bhubaneswar, rushed to Delhi. Seeing his tiny eyes, hands, and feeling his soft heartbeat brought immense joy and pride to the family. He instantly became the star attraction. In our Hindu family, it is customary to name children according to their birth star, though our names were not chosen this way. However, I wished to name my grandson according to his birth star, which indicated his name should begin with "Ra." We named him *Raayansh*, meaning "a ray of the Sun." His nickname, *Anmol*, was formed by combining his parents' names, Anjan and Kamolini.

After completing her engineering in 2006, my daughter got a job at Accenture in Bangalore and joined there. Since we were in Delhi, she aimed to move closer and was eventually selected by CSC, an American company, where she joined us in Delhi. During her time at CSC, she met her partner, but we were initially opposed to the match, as the boy was from Kanpur. He was, however, an engineer from BITS and an MBA graduate from IIM. This was our family's first interstate and inter-caste marriage, so we made every effort to dissuade her, but she remained firm in her decision. Despite receiving many promising proposals for her, we couldn't proceed with any of them. My mother-in-law visited us in Delhi, met the boy, and advised us to support the marriage. Though I still had reservations, ultimately, I agreed. The wedding took place in 2013, with the boy's family insisting it be held in Kanpur. We arranged the event there, securing a guest house from a government institute for our attendees. Conveniently, the guest house caterer was from Odisha, ensuring our guests were comfortable with familiar food. We arrived in Kanpur four or five days before the wedding. Our relatives and guests arrived closer to the wedding day, and we were able to accommodate them comfortably in the guest house.

Their wedding customs differed from ours, and I found it a bit unsettling. The night before the wedding, I suddenly felt unwell, and my blood pressure spiked. Fortunately, I noticed it in time and consulted a Professor of Medicine in Cuttack, who instructed me to take a specific tablet immediately. My younger brother rushed to the market to get the medicine, and within three hours, I felt almost normal. It was a memorable and intense experience, as anything could have happened to me that night. The wedding proceeded, and after our guests departed from Kanpur, we returned to Delhi. Shortly afterward, we travelled to Bhubaneswar for another reception.

After the Bhubaneswar event, my daughter and son-in-law moved to Mumbai, where he was working. A few months later, my daughter also found a job there. On November 8, 2016, coinciding with the day of demonetization in India, my second grandson was born. My wife was with my daughter in Mumbai for the delivery. This child felt like a divine gift, a blessing to our family, and he quickly became everyone's darling. His paternal grandmother suggested the name "Annay," a name of Lord Vishnu found in the *Vishnu Sahasranam*.

In March 2015, advertisements were posted for Vice Chancellor positions in several Central Universities. Prof. Ganguly nominated me for these roles, though I soon forgot about it. Meanwhile, ILS provided me with a well-furnished office, and I began my work there. It was a great environment, allowing me to reconnect with many old colleagues and witness firsthand how the institute had flourished over the past 12 years. Seeing the growth and recalling the efforts that had gone into developing ILS was truly satisfying. At that time, Dr Ravindran was the Director, and the late Dr Bhan had retired, with Dr VijayaRaghavan serving as Secretary of DBT.

A few weeks into my tenure at ILS, I received a letter from the Ministry of Human Resource Development (MHRD) stating that I had been shortlisted for the Vice Chancellor position at the Central University of Tamil Nadu. They advised me to attend a personal inteaction with the Search-cum-Selection Committee in Delhi on June 6, 2015. Until then, my idea about central universities was restricted to institutions like Delhi University, JNU, Jamia Millia, AMU, BHU, and Visva Bharati, so I was unaware that Tamil Nadu had a Central University. Upon asking Dr Ravindran, who was from Tamil Nadu, he explained that after 2009, several central universities were established in states without them, and Tamil Nadu was one of these. I was initially uncertain about attending the interview but decided to proceed and experience the process. Arriving in Delhi on June 5, 2015, I stayed at the NIMR guest house. My interview was scheduled for 3:30 PM as the second-to-last candidate, and the venue was the Nehru Museum. Arriving at 3:00 PM, I was called in around 3:45 PM. The interaction went well, and afterward, I received a reimbursement cheque for my airfare. I returned to the NIMR guest house that evening and flew back to Bhubaneswar the next day, resuming my work at ILS.

By the end of July 2015, the interaction meeting for the Vice Chancellorship had faded from my mind. Then, on Saturday, August 1, 2015, while heading to ILS to meet Prof. Padmanaban, former Director of the Indian Institute of Science, Bangalore, and Chairman of the ILS SAC, I received an unexpected phone call. It was from Prof. Sengadir, then Acting Vice Chancellor of the Central

University of Tamil Nadu (CUTN), informing me that I had been appointed as the Vice Chancellor by the President of India, in his capacity as the Visitor of CUTN. He inquired about my joining date, catching me entirely off guard, as I hadn't received any official communication until then. At that time, my wife was in Hyderabad, attending a Board of Trustees meeting for a Trust, so I had no chance to discuss this news with her. I informed Prof. Sengadir that I needed some time to consider. Shortly after, Dr Sengadir sent me the official appointment order, which I also received from Delhi, along with several calls confirming the appointment. I decided that I would first join CUTN and then return to ILS to handle any pending matters.

Dr Sengadir reached out again to confirm my travel arrangements, offering to arrange my tickets. He booked my journey so that I would reach CUTN on the night of August 5, 2015, to join officially on August 6. He briefed me on the route: I would fly from Bhubaneswar to Chennai, change flights to Trichy, and from there, travel by car to CUTN. When my wife returned to Bhubaneswar, I shared the entire story. She wasn't thrilled about my taking up the role at CUTN, but since I had already committed, she did not object further. Before departing, I received welcoming emails from two faculty members at CUTN: Dr Ravindran, a Professor of Physics, and Dr Venkatachelapathy, who was an Executive Council member at the time. Both expressed their support and enthusiasm for my appointment.

I was relieved from ILS on August 5 and boarded my flight from Bhubaneswar to Chennai. In Chennai, I had to change airlines and flights, as Trichy was served by only a few Jet Airways flights at that time. I boarded the flight to Trichy and arrived at 9:30 PM on August 5, 2015. Upon my arrival, I received a warm welcome at Trichy Airport from

Prof. Sengadir and other university officials, who brought me to the CUTN campus. I was informed that the Vice Chancellor's bungalow was nearing completion, but until it was ready, a professor's quarter had been arranged for my stay. We reached the CUTN campus around 12:30 AM, and I was pleasantly surprised to find many faculty members waiting to greet me near the designated house. After a brief interaction with everyone, I was sent to rest. I learned that CUTN occupied around 600 acres of land divided by the Vettar River, a tributary of the Kaveri River. One side housed the residential campus, which spanned over 100 acres, while the other side was dedicated to academic purposes. The next morning, on August 6, I was taken to the academic campus to officially join. It was just a few minutes' drive from the residential campus, and all arrangements had been made for the handover of responsibilities.

Taking over charge of Vice Chancellor (6.8.2015)

CHAPTER – 25

Coming to Temple Town

The Central University of Tamil Nadu (CUTN) was founded in 2009 in Thiruvarur and officially inaugurated on September 30, 2009, by the then Union Minister for Human Resource Development. According to ancient scriptures, being born in Thiruvarur, visiting Chidambaram, passing away in Kasi, or contemplating Arunachala are believed to bring Mukti, or ultimate liberation. Thiruvarur has a long-standing history as a centre of cultural, artistic, and religious significance. It was one of the five historic capitals of the Chola Empire, with one of its emperors making it his seat of power. The town's antiquity is notable, having been governed by various powers throughout history, including the Medieval Cholas, Later Cholas, Pandyas, the Vijayanagar Empire, Marathas, and the British. Thiruvarur is famous for the Thyagaraja temple, which hosts an annual chariot festival in April. The temple's chariot, standing at approximately 90 feet tall and weighing about 300 tons (660,000 pounds), is the largest of its kind in Tamil Nadu.

Thiruvarur is also the birthplace of the famous Trinity of Carnatic music: Tyagaraja, Muthuswami Dikshitar, and Syama Sastri. Until 1991, it was part of the Thanjavur district but was later carved out as a separate district. The region is known for its religious diversity, with notable places of worship such as the Thyagaraja temple, *Nagore Dargah*, and *Velankanni* Church in close proximity to the university. Additionally, independent temples dedicated to each of the nine planets (*Nava Graha*) surround the university, which is a unique feature of the region. The big temple in Thanjavur is about 60 km away, while Kumbakonam is approximately 40 km from CUTN. The first Vice Chancellor joined in March 2009 and served until March 2014. Following this, Dr. Sengadir held the position of Acting Vice Chancellor from March 2014 until I joined in August 2015. The university launched its first academic program, M.A. in English Studies, with eight students selected through an entrance test and two faculty members in November 2009. Initially, the university functioned from the Collectorate building in Thiruvarur before shifting to its own campus in 2014, although construction of academic buildings and hostels was still ongoing at that time.

Immediately after my joining, I convened a meeting with the CPWD officials to assess the status of various buildings. In the afternoon, I held a meeting with all faculty members, who numbered 27 and represented nine departments. During this meeting, I presented my vision for the university. As a newly established institution with limited regular faculty and very few extramural research projects, I announced that each faculty member was expected to generate at least one extramural project. I also informed them that 80% of the overhead charges could be utilized by faculty members for their research work. After a hectic day, I left for home at 7:30 PM. The next day, I arrived at the office by 9:30 AM, but my experience was quite disheartening. Upon my arrival, I noticed that one side of the compound wall of the academic campus was unfinished, allowing cows and goats to graze inside. The progress made by CPWD was extremely slow, and there was no ATM machine nearby, forcing anyone in need of cash to travel to Thiruvarur or Kumbokonam. I began to question my decision to come to this place. Feeling unsettled, I called Dr Ravindran, the director of ILS, to inquire whether he had forwarded my resignation letter for the Distinguished Scientist Chair position. He informed me that he had not yet forwarded it, so I requested him to hold off on doing so, as I was contemplating the possibility of returning to ILS in Bhubaneswar, where I had previously worked.

I joined on 6th August 2015, which was a Thursday. That weekend, Prof. Sengadir took me on a tour of the campus. Initially, I faced a communication barrier with the cook provided to me, as he spoke only Tamil. However, the university arranged for another cook who was from a nearby area and knew Hindi, having worked in North India as well. This solved my food problem. At the time of my joining, there were no statutory officers in place, such as a Registrar, Finance Officer, Controller of Examinations, or Librarian, so I had to oversee everything. The faculty members were very cooperative, and I held frequent meetings with them. Although the non-teaching staff was limited, each member was excellent. Within two weeks, I began to see hope in their eyes. I spoke with my wife, who advised me to stay since I had already taken on this responsibility. After considering her advice, I decided to remain and complete my term. I then called Dr Ravindran again and requested him to send my resignation letter from ILS.

The town housing the university lacked air connectivity, and the road and rail connections were also minimal. Despite these challenges, the university successfully attracted students, faculty, research scholars, and resource persons for national seminars, conferences, and special lectures from all over India. To address the connectivity issues, I wrote a letter to the Airport Authority of India requesting that the Thanjavur airstrip be made functional and also reached out to the Railway Board to propose starting an additional train to Thiruvarur. I handed my letters to the local MP, asking for their assistance in following up on these requests. As Independence Day approached, I planned to hoist the flag on 15th August 2015 at the university. I thought it would be meaningful to perform the first flag hoisting alongside the first Vice Chancellor. I asked my secretary to contact him for an invitation, but he had prior commitments, so I ended up doing it alone.

Flag hoisting at CUTN

The first priority was to advertise the positions for the statutory officers. The advertisements went out in September, and interviews were conducted in November 2015. We successfully selected candidates for the positions of Registrar, Controller of Examinations, and Finance Officer. Additionally, we advertised for the vacant faculty positions and began the recruitment process in early 2016. This was a lengthy process, and we faced a delay when the Tamil Nadu government announced Assembly elections, necessitating a postponement of the faculty recruitment. However, by 2016, we successfully onboarded all the statutory officers along with around 35 faculty members, significantly strengthening the university's academic and administrative structure.

CHAPTER – 26

A (new) AARAMBH (beginning)!

In 2015, the students of CUTN organized a grand cultural event, marking the first of its kind for the year. I was truly touched that they chose to include a segment to welcome and honour me, their Vice-Chancellor, in this festive program. Cultural events are among the most cherished aspects of academic life, reflecting the vibrancy and spirit of the community. They hold immense significance, as culture is what sets humanity apart and shapes the greatness of a nation.

India, with its rich and diverse heritage, is a remarkable contributor to global civilization. As the fortunate inheritors of this varied culture, it was heartwarming to witness the enthusiastic involvement of students in cultural activities. The event was aptly named "AARAMBH," meaning "the beginning," with the theme cantered around "fusion" and "medley." It was a beautiful representation of harmony, unity, and integration amidst the variety and diversity that characterizes our nation. This celebration not only showcased the talents of the students but also reaffirmed the importance of cultural expression in fostering community and belonging within the university.

CUTN attracted a diverse student body and faculty

from nearly all linguistic regions of India, and the cultural event was a beautiful reflection of this diversity. The students showcased an impressive array of performances, including Tamil songs, Western dances, Hindi songs, Malayalam lyrics, Odissi dance, Hindustani music, and even English lyrics. The inclusion of classical songs, duet dances, and various regional art forms enriched the program, aptly described as transcending all "cultural boundaries." Through AARAMBH, the students achieved a remarkable integration and unity at a higher level, representing the university's student body, which comprised individuals from 23 different states. I was genuinely impressed by the breadth of their artistic talents and the depth of their creative abilities. The event illustrated not only the convergence of different parts of the nation into a seamless whole but also a beautiful temporal gliding across eras, where classical traditions met modern and post-modern expressions to create a vibrant medley—a captivating cultural pastiche. In their performances, the students demonstrated that they are worthy successors to the great artists from various regions of India, proving the power of culture to unite and inspire. This event was not merely a showcase of talent but a testament to the spirit of unity and creativity that thrives at CUTN.

I felt immense joy knowing that this cultural event, a true reflection of our nation's diverse heritage, took place in Thiruvarur—a town deeply rooted in the legacy of music, dance, and drama. Situated on the banks of the Cauvery, Thiruvarur has long been celebrated as a hub for the performing arts. In fact, the great Raja Raja Chola once took 400 dancers from this region to Thanjavur, where they were settled to perform in the grand temple he built. The creative spirit of this town, with its deep historical and cultural roots, has consistently inspired musicians and artists for centuries. The legacy of illustrious figures such as Saint Thyagaraja, along with the revered Muthuswami Dikshitar and Syama Sastri, stands as a testament to the artistic vibrancy of Thiruvarur. Understanding the profound importance of art and culture, I was determined to weave these elements into the CUTN curriculum. It was vital for us to nurture the creative potential of our youth, ensuring that all forms of artistic expression and linguistic diversity received the encouragement they deserved. To achieve this goal, I made the decision to establish a School of Performing Arts and Music at CUTN, and I succeeded. This initiative was designed to provide a dedicated space where students could explore their artistic passions, refine their talents, and contribute to the rich cultural heritage not only of Thiruvarur but of India as a whole. The school would serve as a beacon of creativity, creating an environment where the performing arts could flourish, showcasing the diverse talents of our students and celebrating the cultural wealth of India.

In '*AARAMBH*' in 2015

As I perceived it, being a central university, CUTN should have a national character. During my five-year tenure, I tried my best to imbue it with this spirit and make it a mini-India, with students and faculty members from all over the country. When I handed over charge in 2020 and looked back, I felt satisfied that I had achieved this goal.

Shortly after I joined, I was appointed as a member of the India-Australia Education Commission. This commission was co-chaired by the Indian and Australian Ministers and included members from both countries. From the Indian side, there were about four Vice Chancellors from Central Universities. I attended a meeting in Delhi, and at the dinner, I met the Indian Minister for the first time. During our brief interaction, she invited me to meet with her at her office the next morning. Our 30-minute discussion was insightful; I was struck by her dynamism and her ability to make decisions swiftly—key traits of an effective leader.

CHAPTER – 27

A Spellbinding Spell at CUTN

The President of India serves as the Visitor of all Central Universities and is the appointing authority for all Vice Chancellors. In 2014, the President revived the tradition of the Vice Chancellors' Conference, which had last been held in 2003. Vice Chancellors from all Central Universities participate in this meeting, and a few distinguished guests are invited to engage with the group. In November 2015, I attended the Visitor's Conference. The arrangements were meticulously planned—our accommodations and vehicle details were provided to Rashtrapati Bhawan in advance, along with food preferences. The President joins the Vice Chancellors for lunch and dinner. CUTN had a contract with Hotel Samrat (an ITDC hotel), where we stayed. Upon checking in, I received a packet from Rashtrapati Bhawan containing all relevant documents, including a vehicle pass. The designated entry gate for Rashtrapati Bhawan was communicated in advance. These conferences are also attended by the Minister of Human Resource Development, the Secretary, and the UGC Chairman. In November 2015, the Prime Minister also joined to address the Vice Chancellors.

My first experience at this meeting was quite

interesting. Upon arrival at Rashtrapati Bhawan, I met some familiar Vice Chancellors. We were then taken for tea, where we mingled with each other. Suddenly, I noticed a fellow Vice Chancellor approaching the UGC Chairman and nearly falling forward. Thinking he was about to stumble, I instinctively reached out and said, "Oh! You're about to fall!" He looked at me with a serious expression, and another Vice Chancellor quickly pulled me aside to whisper, "What are you doing? He was about to touch the UGC Chairman's feet." I felt awkward and disheartened—was this really the status of Central University Vice Chancellors? Once again, I found myself questioning my decision to take on this role. After tea, we were invited to another hall for a photograph session. Having finished my tea early, I was one of the first to enter. As I stood there, lost in thought, I noticed a tall, strong presence beside me. When I turned, I realized it was the Prime Minister. Soon, everyone else joined us in the hall, and we were directed to our assigned places for the photograph session.

Photograph with the President, Prime Minister, HRD Minister and Secretary & other Vice Chancellors

The meeting began with an address by the Prime Minister and concluded with one by the President. Professor C.N.R. Rao, a Bharat Ratna awardee, was also invited to speak to the Vice Chancellors. Lunch and dinner arrangements ensured that everyone's needs were thoughtfully addressed. The conference lasted two days, and on the final day, the President gave his concluding remarks and met each of the Vice Chancellors personally. I recalled meeting him twice before, back when he was a Union Minister, though I wasn't certain if he would recognize me. During our brief interaction, he spent a few seconds with me.

With President at the end of the meeting

Upon returning to the University, I was reminded of the challenges we faced when I first joined in August 2015. As mentioned, the campus was in a state where cows and goats freely roamed, and essential amenities were lacking. A pressing issue concerned the construction of the guest house. The project had been assigned to CPWD, with an architect from Bangalore. Substantial funds had already been paid, but the construction had suffered a tragic incident about six months prior to my arrival—a portion of the structure collapsed, resulting in the deaths of six workers and injuring around 60 others. When I joined, I was briefed on this situation and visited the site myself. Surprisingly, no internal inquiry committee had been established by the University to investigate the incident, though the CBI had taken up the case, cordoning off the area and halting construction while the inquiry was pending. We coordinated with the authorities to expedite the process, and finally, after the CBI's investigation, the area was released for continued construction. However, we were adamant about ensuring quality before resuming work, and CPWD thoroughly assessed the structure before construction restarted. In 2017, we inaugurated the guest house, a facility with 96 rooms, including 12 VIP rooms, along with a conference hall, VIP dining area, general dining hall, and ample activity spaces on each floor. It was a truly self-sufficient guest house, providing excellent accommodations in the area.

Immediately after my joining, I prioritized the installation of an ATM on campus, coordinating with State Bank of India to have it set up in the academic block within a week. Around this time, all newly established central universities were urged to pursue NAAC accreditation, and the UGC even held a meeting in September 2015, insisting that all new central universities apply before December 2015, even if they anticipated receiving only a 'B' grade. Despite our limited infrastructure—nine departments, 26 permanent faculty members, and around 30 permanent non-teaching staff—we submitted our application for

NAAC accreditation. While the guest house was still under construction, we had fortunately appointed key statutory officers like the Registrar, Finance Officer, and Controller of Examinations. Other new central universities also applied for NAAC accreditation, and NAAC formed committees to visit each institution. The assessment covered the five years up to June 2015, two months before my tenure began. I learned that, unlike other Vice Chancellors, I was not consulted on the committee's composition, likely because my background was in the United Nations, and I had no prior connections with NAAC. Instead, I received a standard letter asking if I had any objections to the committee members, which I did not. Little did I know at the time that the accreditation process could be unpredictable, as was evident in the procedures back then.

The NAAC team arrived in July 2016. With no five-star accommodations nearby, we arranged for them to stay in a quality hotel in Kumbakonam. However, this led to initial grumbling: one member was dissatisfied with the hotel's rating, another wanted better bathroom amenities, and our staff scrambled to fulfil their requests. While we provided files with relevant documents, one member demanded a more luxurious bag, and another requested a new travel bag, claiming his was damaged en route. Upon arriving at the campus, I delivered a presentation on the University. However, it was unclear how much the team absorbed, as one member struggled with English. Over the next two days, the team conducted department visits. On the final day, I had a concluding discussion with them, where some mild disagreements arose, as I didn't agree with certain observations they made. Unfortunately, some team members were unprofessional with faculty members. After their visit, I submitted a form to NAAC with my honest feedback on the team, though I'm uncertain if it was acknowledged. The following year, NAAC conducted a survey on the accreditation process, and I did not hesitate to voice my concern, describing it as a "gamble." Thankfully, by 2019, I saw that the accreditation process had been revised, the impact of which remains to be seen.

In April 2016, the Ministry organized a meeting in Gurgaon with all Vice Chancellors of Central Universities, chaired by the Minister. The main agenda was to identify new and innovative departments for universities. Among the departments identified was Epidemiology and Public Health (EPH). I observed that Public Health as a formal course had developed quite late in India, though by then many institutions, including private ones, offered a Master's in Public Health (MPH). Epidemiology, being an integral component of public health, made it an ideal candidate for a hybrid course in Epidemiology and Public Health. At that time, however, the Life Sciences department at CUTN lacked senior faculty, with an Assistant Professor serving as Head in Charge. I requested her to coordinate the establishment of the EPH department, and she handled the responsibility well. I set up a course curriculum committee, bringing in experts from Delhi, the National Institute of Epidemiology in Chennai, and other institutions. The draft curriculum was reviewed by an expert from the World Health Organization, who made slight modifications before the curriculum was approved by the university's statutory bodies. The department officially launched in 2016, initially staffed with contract faculty. By the end of that year, CUTN had added five new science departments.

The past 50 years have seen a remarkable increase in the complexity of scientific research, with a noticeable shift toward collaborative efforts, often referred to as "team science." Despite this evolution, there remains a significant gap in leadership training across the research landscape. Advancing science, while fostering moral values, is essential for human development. Ethical practice demands the reporting of authentic results. To encourage this ethos, I initiated regular departmental meetings, emphasizing the importance of integrated and collaborative research. Additionally, I began developing lectures on "Mentoring Research," aiming to guide researchers in both scientific rigor and ethical responsibility.

At that time, the faculty and students were equally enthusiastic about the new Vice Chancellor. The students organized a cultural program, *Arambh*, to welcome me, followed by another event, *Meet the VC*. I was genuinely impressed by both programs. In *Arambh*, the students showcased their immense talent, while *Meet the VC* provided a platform for a personal and meaningful interaction with me, allowing us to connect on many levels.

WHO/SEARO was planning to renew efforts for dengue control and prevention, aiming to revise the strategy and develop a comprehensive template for monitoring key parameters with measurable outcomes. They requested me to draft a document outlining this new approach, which would be reviewed at an upcoming expert meeting and by the dengue task force. I worked extensively to create a detailed document for dengue prevention and control, which I submitted to WHO. An expert consultation, along with a meeting of dengue program managers from various countries, was scheduled for early 2016 in the Maldives. By this time, *Zika* was also emerging, so the agenda expanded to include both dengue and Zika. Despite my busy schedule at the university, I attended the meeting and initiated discussions on the new strategy. This sparked an engaging exchange, and the strategy was finalized. Concurrently, the Regional Dengue Task Force convened, where we discussed the need for a technical advisory group on *Aedes-borne diseases* (such as dengue, chikungunya, and Zika) to provide unified guidance given the overlap in transmission by day-biting *Aedes* mosquitoes. I returned to the university from the Maldives and immediately resumed my responsibilities.

The CUTN signed a MoU with Madras School of Economics (MSE) for collaboration for teaching and research in 2011. MSE is a very important institute in south India. Dr C. Rangarajan, former Governor of Reserve Bank of India, former-Chairman, economic advisory group to Prime Minister and Ex-Governor of Andhra Pradesh and Orissa has been the Chairman of MSE for quite some time. The MoU was for five years and was to be renewed in 2016. We renewed the MoU in 2016 for another period of five years. The Ministry of Textiles, Government of India has one institute called as "Sardar Vallabhbhai Patel International School of Textiles & Management" (SVPISTM) at Coimbatore. The Ministry also wanted MoU with CUTN. The MoU was signed in Delhi in presence of the Minister, Mr Santosh Gangwar (now Governor of Jharkhand); Textile, Secretary and myself & the Registrar, CUTN. The CUTN also signed a MoU with the Central Institute of Classical Tamil (CICT), Chennai. In addition, MoU was inked with Indian Institute of Food Technology (IIFT), Thanjavur, Ecole francaise d'Extreme-Orient (EFEO), Pondicherry and Indian Institute of Handloom Technology (IIHT), Salem.

The Trinity of Carnatic music, often referred to as the 'Three Jewels' of Carnatic music consists of the iconic 18th-century composer-musicians Tyagaraja, Muthuswami Dikshitar, and Syama Sastri. Renowned for their prolific contributions, they played a pivotal role in shaping the future of Carnatic music, introducing fresh perspectives and transforming the musical landscape. Each of their compositions is celebrated for its distinctive style and innovative exploration of *ragas*. Intriguingly, all three were born in Thiruvarur, the very place where CUTN is situated. One weekend, I had the opportunity to visit their birthplaces in Thiruvarur, accompanied by my colleague, Prof. T. Sengadir.

 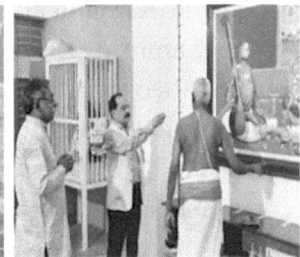

We visited their abodes in Thiruvarur to learn about their glorious histories

Ellalan, a member of the Tamil Chola dynasty, is also remembered as 'Manu Needhi Cholan.' After ascending the throne, he became the king of the Anuradhapura Kingdom in present-day Sri Lanka, ruling from 205 BCE to 161 BCE. According to the *Mahavamsa*, his reign was marked by unwavering justice, applied impartially to both allies and adversaries. One striking example of his commitment to fairness is his decision to execute his own son for the killing of a calf, illustrating his deep sense of duty to the law. In Tamil literature, his name has come to symbolize fairness and justice. His capital, Thiruvarur, was renowned as a beacon of justice. During my travels, I took the opportunity to visit this historic place.

Srinivasa Ramanujan was a brilliant Indian mathematician whose contributions spanned mathematical analysis, number theory, infinite series, and continued fractions. Despite having little formal training, he developed numerous original and profound insights in mathematics largely in isolation. Early in his career, Ramanujan faced difficulties in gaining recognition, as his discoveries were too innovative and unconventional. However, in 1913, he initiated a correspondence with the distinguished English mathematician G. H. Hardy at the University of Cambridge. Hardy quickly recognized Ramanujan's extraordinary talent and invited him to Cambridge, where Ramanujan unveiled groundbreaking theorems that left even Hardy in awe. Hardy later admitted that some of Ramanujan's results "defeated me completely".

A devout Hindu, Ramanujan believed that his extraordinary mathematical abilities were the result of divine inspiration from his family goddess, *Namagiri Thayar*. However, his strict religious practices, particularly his dietary restrictions, posed challenges to his health, especially during his time in wartime England. There, he struggled with the harsh conditions and his inability to follow his traditional diet. Diagnosed with tuberculosis and a severe vitamin deficiency, Ramanujan's health deteriorated, eventually leading to his confinement in a sanatorium. In 1919, he returned to *Kumbakonam*, but sadly, he passed away in 1920 at just 32 years old. Despite his early death, his contributions to mathematics were widely recognized. The journal *Nature* honoured him by listing him among the leading scientific pioneers shortly after his passing. In Tamil Nadu, his birthday on December 22 is celebrated as 'State IT Day,' and India has issued several commemorative stamps in his honour, acknowledging his lasting influence on mathematics and science. His widow,

Smt. Janaki Ammal, later resettled in Madras, supporting herself through a pension and income from tailoring.

Ramanujan's house, located in *Kumbakonam* just 38 kilometers from the CUTN campus, is a place of historical and academic significance. Shortly after joining CUTN, I considered the possibility of the University adopting and preserving this site to honour his legacy. However, by the time we explored this idea, the opportunity had already been taken by Shastra University, a private university near Thanjavur. I have always had a personal interest in mathematics since my school days, and Ramanujan's life and contributions fascinated me. Along with my colleague, Prof. Sengadir, a professor of mathematics, I visited his modest family home on *Sarangapani Sannidhi* Street in Kumbakonam. Born on December 22, 1887, Ramanujan spent his early years in this traditional house before moving to England, where his profound contributions left an indelible mark on mathematical history. Today, his former home has been transformed into a museum, preserving the memory of this extraordinary mathematician.

In Ramanujan's house in Kumbokonam

After leaving WHO in 2015, I was approached by WHO/SEARO to conduct an expert consultation on vector control for Kala-azar, a request I accepted. At that time, the Life Sciences department at CUTN had only a few faculty members—four Assistant Professors, with one serving as Head in Charge. I entrusted the Head in Charge with organizing the conference on behalf of CUTN, and we selected Hotel Crowne Plaza as the venue. Experts from various regions attended, and thanks to her effective coordination, the consultation was a success. The recommendations from this meeting were later integrated into WHO's Kala-azar elimination program. Encouraged by the success of this consultation, we decided to organize a larger Conference on Vectors and Vector-Borne Diseases in Chennai, again choosing the same hotel for the venue. Held in February/March 2017, this conference also proved to be a successful endeavour.

Dr Soumya Swaminathan, Secretary&DG, ICMR with my family at the conference in Chennai

Upon joining CUTN, I found myself regularly attending meetings concerning university affairs, which posed logistical challenges due to the long 14-hour journey to Delhi. For a one-day meeting, this often meant being away from the university for three days. At the time, the faculty was relatively small, and a few members had developed a sense of ownership over the institution, viewing it as their personal domain. As I became more involved in meetings and official responsibilities, a couple of these faculty members began referring to me as the 'Visiting Vice Chancellor.' They were uneasy about having a permanent Vice Chancellor and preferred the interim arrangement of an Acting Vice Chancellor.

After two particular meetings, these individuals began to grow increasingly hostile toward me. They resorted to sending anonymous emails and letters filled with unfounded allegations and fabricated stories, addressed to the Ministry and even the President of India. This experience revealed how envy can act like a magnifying lens, causing some to focus more on others' perceived success than on their own contributions.

To confront the situation, I called a meeting with the Heads of Departments to address the wild accusations. Together, we agreed to disregard such communications. I also raised the issue in the Executive Council (EC), where the consensus was to ignore the anonymous complaints. While I had a good idea of who was behind the allegations—these individuals, who were seemingly friendly with me, often visited my office, offered compliments, and shared casual moments over coffee—I never revealed that I knew their true intentions. I maintained the illusion of camaraderie.

Additionally, there were occasions where these individuals seemed to instigate student protests. I received recordings of conversations where they encouraged student agitation. Twice, protests broke out over issues like hostel food. During these protests, as I interacted with the students, I noticed a staff member discreetly taking photos and videos, which were later uploaded to social media. Unbeknownst to him, I was aware that someone was also recording the situation. This staff member, who was generally loyal to me, had inadvertently become part of the mischief. I found the situation somewhat amusing and chose to let it go, recognizing the complexities and challenges of the environment I was navigating.

I previously mentioned the Institute of Life Sciences (ILS) in Bhubaneswar. I have been a member of both the Governing Body and the General Body of ILS since 2016 till 2021. The annual meeting of the General Body was held in Delhi, where I participated. The meeting was chaired by Dr Harsh Vardhan, the Minister of Science, Technology, Earth Sciences, and Health and Family Welfare. While few members were aware of my contributions to the institute, I still enjoyed attending the meetings.

Seating (L to R): Sri Ashok Panda, Minister Science & Technology, Odisha; Dr Harsh Vardhan.
Standing (L to R): Dr Shekhar Mande, DG. CSIR; Dr A.K. Parida, Director, ILS (3rd from left); A.P. Dash; Dr Pattanayak, VC, Utkal University, (2019)

Shortly after my joining in 2015, we installed an ATM machine on the campus. In 2016, we negotiated with the State Bank of India to open a branch within the academic campus. Additionally, we collaborated with postal authorities to establish a post office on-site. We later opened another ATM in the residential area. The CUTN campus spans two revenue villages in Thiruvarur district, Tamil Nadu, divided by the *Vettar* River, which flows through the Kaveri Delta. A connecting bridge links the two campuses: the academic campus is located in *Neelakudi* village, while the residential campus is in *Nagakudi* village, aptly named as *"Naga"* means "snakes." There are indeed many snakes in the residential campus.

The *Kendriya Vidyalaya* (Central School) is also situated in the residential area, serving students from Class 1 to Class 12. Families residing on the campus often have children, and during 2016-17, we established a play school in the residential campus. To promote awareness about the local snake population, I organized a seminar in collaboration with the Zoological Survey of India (ZSI), Southern Regional Centre in Chennai, inviting Dr A. Aengals from ZSI as the resource person. The Department of Life Sciences facilitated this event in January 2016. We often invited snake catchers to safely relocate snakes to forested areas. During my morning walks, I also observed numerous peacocks on the campus. Their presence likely contributes to the ecological balance, as the snakes help maintain the local wildlife population. I felt a sense of joy seeing the peacocks near my residence, making my morning walks increasingly pleasurable. As I walked through the campus, I would listen to *"Vishnu Sahasranama"* on my mobile, enjoying the sight of peacocks strolling along both sides of the path.

When I arrived on campus, the Vice Chancellor's

bungalow was not yet ready, so I was temporarily accommodated in a professor's quarters for a few months. The bungalow was completed in early 2016. It was quite large for me, especially since I was staying alone while my family could not join me due to various constraints. I was reluctant to move, but during an Executive Council meeting in 2016, a representative from the ministry advised me to take up residence in the VC's bungalow. Following this guidance, I relocated in April or May 2016, when my wife came to visit me.

CHAPTER - 28

Reaching New Heights

Prior to my arrival, the university did not have a Human Ethics Review Board. In accordance with government ethical guidelines for biomedical research involving human participants, CUTN established the Institutional Human Ethics Review Board (IHERB) in 2016. Additionally, in October 2015, we organized a workshop on Intellectual Property (IP) awareness and research methodologies.

We also set up several committees and cells, including a Sports Committee, a Counselling and Guidance Cell, grievance redressal committees for both students and staff, an NSS Advisory Committee, a Service Cell, an Anti-Ragging Cell, a Committee Against Sexual Harassment (CASH), an Internal Complaints Committee (ICC), and initiated the 'Unnat Bharat Abhiyan' program. Later, the government introduced the "Ek Bharat Shreshtha Bharat" initiative, pairing our university with the Central Universities of Kashmir and Jammu. As part of this exchange program, faculty and students from these universities were scheduled to visit CUTN in January 2020, while our faculty and students were to visit their campuses in April/May 2020. Students and faculty from the Central Universities of Kashmir and Jammu did indeed visit CUTN in January 2020. However, the planned visit by CUTN students and faculty to Jammu & Kashmir was unfortunately disrupted by the outbreak of COVID-19

Since 2015, I have been considering the idea of launching a newsletter for CUTN. One day, while having tea in my office, Prof. Sengadir from the Mathematics department and Dr Nirmal Selvamony from the English department visited me. During our conversation, Dr Nirmal mentioned a beautiful bird commonly seen on the campus: the Red-wattled Lapwing (*Vanellus indicus*), a wetland bird. He noted that this bird was quite prevalent across both CUTN campuses and highlighted its distinctive call, "did-he-do-it," as well as its instinct to warn other creatures of impending danger. Inspired by this discussion, I proposed that we name the newsletter "Lapwing" in honour of this remarkable bird. I suggested that the first edition for 2015-16 should be published in early 2016, with Dr Nirmal contributing an article about the Red-wattled Lapwing. Thus, the "Lapwing" newsletter was born.

The Lapwing in the CUTN campus

Until the academic session of 2015-16, CUTN had only a few departments and a limited number of permanent faculty members. I envisioned starting new departments and advertised several vacant teaching positions to support the functioning of these departments. Given Thiruvarur's rich association with the musical Trinity, I believed that establishing a program in Music would be particularly fitting for the university. Consequently, in 2016-17, we successfully launched several new departments, including the Department of Education & Training, the Department of Performing Arts, and the Department of Epidemiology & Public Health.

CHAPTER-29

Transforming CUTN

As part of its commitment to social responsibility, CUTN prioritized community development through community colleges. We launched a 180-day training program aimed at empowering women from six villages adopted by the university for this initiative.

The training programme aimed to enrich the local rural population through knowledge transfer and drive transformational change in rural development. Our *"Unnat Bharat Abhiyan* (UBA) initiatives are designed to create a dynamic relationship between the university and the surrounding society. We provide knowledge and technical support to enhance livelihoods in rural areas and strengthen the capabilities of public and private organisations within the community. The CUTN has adopted six villages around the campus and launched a special training programme for rural women to produce coir products as a source of livelihood, which proved highly effective. We also implemented the *Swachh Bharat Abhiyan* (SBA) with full dedication, extending efforts beyond our campus to include the Thiruvarur district headquarters. This initiative aligns with Mahatma Gandhi's vision, started by the present Prime Minister; now being realized especially in rural areas. We hope India's goal of achieving comprehensive sanitation in the coming years will foster a lasting shift in public behaviour towards cleanliness. Additionally, we aimed to create a green campus, involving the local community in sustainability efforts around the University."

Creating a green campus

All central universities are governed by an academic council responsible for decisions on academic matters, a finance committee that ensures financial discipline, and an executive council, which is the highest governing body. Additionally, there is a building committee to oversee construction-related recommendations. The Vice Chancellor serves as the chairperson of all these committees. The university also has a Court, chaired by the Chancellor, which convenes once a year. However, the Executive Council stands as the primary decision-making authority. The President of India appoints nominees to both the Executive Council and the Court, and the council must meet at least once every three months. Initially, Chancellors are appointed directly by the President of India, and subsequent appointments are made based on the recommendation of the Executive Council. In recent years, I noticed that some central universities were having retired college principals as Chancellors. This trend concerned me, so I ensured that the Executive Council of CUTN recommended distinguished academicians for the role. Our council put forward several renowned names, and after a long wait, Prof. G. Padmanaban, former Director of the Indian Institute of Science, was appointed as the Chancellor of CUTN in July 2018.

From 2016 onward, I prioritized filling vacant teaching and non-teaching positions, understanding that a well-planned recruitment process would attract qualified and enthusiastic candidates who could provide valuable services. Although I oversaw several recruitment processes, one particular experience stood out as disheartening. We advertised the position of Public Relations Officer (PRO) for the second time, as the initial advertisement, issued before my tenure, did not yield any suitable candidates. The second advertisement attracted several applicants, and the shortlisting process was conducted. Unknown to me at the time, one of the applicants was acquainted with a faculty member at CUTN who was part of the shortlisting committee. CUTN follows a transparent recruitment process in which lists of applicants for each position, along with their shortlisted status and reasons for non-shortlisting, are published on the university's website. Applicants are also allowed to raise objections or representations. Despite this transparency, two staff members who had conflicts with the faculty member began raising concerns about the shortlisted applicant, claiming she was unqualified and had connections with the faculty member on the committee. I listened to these complaints, but the PRO position was critical for CUTN due to its importance across central universities, most of which had already filled this role. I had witnessed the value of a PRO in other institutions and was keen to appoint one.

The selection committee, composed of both external experts and internal members, met for the interviews. Experts were asked to submit their scores confidentially on university-provided scoring sheets, which were then handed to me as the chair at the end of the process. Although I chaired the committee, I never awarded scores to any candidate. The candidate who had been the subject of complaints performed exceptionally well and received the highest scores from each expert. However, word of the selection leaked due to the presence of internal members, and the same staff members who had previously raised concerns approached me again, reiterating their objections. During a Kala-azar expert consultation in Chennai, one reporter attended to cover the event, but I did not recall who it was at the time. The staff members suggested that the selected candidate was the reporter, which led to more doubts and even an anonymous complaint against me. The pressure and repeated allegations made me question myself and wonder if I had made an error. Ultimately, we decided to readvertise the position. The next round of interviews did not yield a suitable candidate, nor did subsequent rounds. The post remained unfilled during my tenure, despite multiple attempts. Reflecting now, more than five years later, I still feel the frustration. I know the position will be filled one day, but I am certain that CUTN missed an exceptional candidate who could have made a significant impact.

Bringing smile to everyone:

After recounting the unfortunate incident, I would like to highlight a positive development: the establishment of a "Centre for Happiness" at CUTN. During an invitation from the Amity Group to address their professors and faculty members, I noticed that many expressed concerns about work-related stress. In today's world, stress management has become a critical topic, largely due to the pervasive influence of technology—especially smartphones—that intrude upon our social lives and contribute to the relentless pace of modern life. Stress can lead to serious complications for individuals who struggle to manage their daily responsibilities and maintain a work-life balance. Recognizing this need, I proposed the creation of a 'Centre for Happiness' at CUTN. We successfully inaugurated the first-of-its-kind Centre for Happiness on December 6, 2017. The mission of this centre is to promote the well-being of every member of the CUTN community. It aims to provide valuable resources and initiatives focused on work-life balance, stress management, fostering a positive mindset, effective personal and professional life management, personal development, team building, and minimizing workplace tension—all while infusing joy and happiness into daily routines. The Centre for Happiness serves as a mentor to encourage sensible humour and happiness among CUTNians. It acts as a gateway for the entire CUTN community to awaken and enhance their well-being, ultimately contributing to the betterment of society as a whole.

Establishing Happiness Centre in December 2017

The first convocation of the university took place in early 2014, but students from 2014 and 2015 had not yet received their degrees. Once I established myself at CUTN, we began preparations for the next convocation, scheduled for November 2016. In the first week of July 2016, I travelled to Delhi to invite the Human Resource Minister to be the Chief Guest for the event, and she readily agreed. However, just five days later, there was a change in the ministerial position, and a new minister took office. I returned to Delhi to invite the new minister, who also agreed to attend. Unfortunately, just one week before the convocation, the minister regretted that he would be unable to attend, leaving us in a difficult situation at CUTN, especially as it was the time of Parliament sessions. At a personal level, I reached out to Dr VijayRaghavan, the Secretary of the Department of Biotechnology, who later became the Principal Scientific Adviser to the Government of India. He graciously agreed to serve as the Chief Guest. The convocation proceeded successfully, with Dr VijayRaghavan delivering an excellent address and interacting with our faculty members. After the ceremony, he had to return to Delhi that same day due to the ongoing Parliament session.

CUTN was inaugurated on 30th September 2009. The following year, during the Executive Council meeting, we officially designated 30th September as the convocation date for the university. This decision was communicated to *Rashtrapati Bhawan*, the Ministry of Human Resource Development (MHRD), and the University Grants Commission (UGC).

With Dr VijayRaghaban at 2nd (left) and with Prof Padmanaban and at 3rd convocation (right)

4th convocation   with Dr Renu Swarup, Secretary, DBT
5th convocation

For the third convocation in 2017, we once again invited the Human Resource Minister to serve as the Chief Guest. Initially, he agreed to attend, but five days before the event, he cancelled his participation. As a result, we invited the Vice Chancellor of Assam University. However, we later learned that the same Minister attended a private event in Coimbatore shortly thereafter. This experience led me to decide never to invite any politicians again. The fourth convocation took place in September 2018, by which time our Chancellor had been appointed. We invited the Chairman of the Law Commission of India to be the Chief Guest. For the fifth convocation in September 2019, Dr Renu

Swarup, the Secretary of the Department of Biotechnology, graced the occasion as the Chief Guest.

The first Student Council at the Central University of Tamil Nadu was established during the academic year 2018-19 under the leadership of the Dean of Students' Welfare. The Council represented students and research scholars from all departments of CUTN. Its main objective was to encourage student participation in decision-making processes and engage them in various activities. The Council served as a forum for students to voice their concerns and work collaboratively with the authorities to address these issues. Meetings were held once a month to facilitate ongoing communication and support among the Council members.

Some time ago, in 2019, I visited the Institute of Life Sciences in Bhubaneswar to meet Dr Ravindran, who was also a member of the academic council of the CUTN. After our meeting, as I was leaving his office, I encountered a senior professor who was visiting ILS for another reason. I recognized him, and he greeted me before joining me as I exited the building. He commented, based on his perspective, on my tenure as the first regular director of ILS, as well as on the tenures of Dr Ravindran and the late Dr Parida. I listened patiently to his thoughts. His comments reminded me of a beautiful story that illustrates the concept of partial reality—a narrative found in Buddhist, Jain, and Hindu texts. I shared with him the story of the six blind men and the elephant, an ancient and well-known Indian parable. This tale serves as a cautionary reminder against promoting absolute truths. It highlights how our perceptions and life experiences can lead to limited understanding and overreaching misinterpretations. The central question it raises is: how can someone with a limited grasp of the truth assert their view as the sole reality?

I recall Pandit Nehru's observation: "A university stands for humanism, for tolerance, for reason, for progress, for the adventure of ideas and for the search for truth. It stands for the onward march of the human race towards even higher objectives." In all my addresses during Independence Day, Republic Day, departmental functions, and on occasions such as Teacher's Day, I emphasized that teachers, beyond their routine academic responsibilities, should strive to cultivate students who are not only knowledgeable but also compassionate, dedicated, and committed in their actions. Teaching is a unique profession that offers teachers the opportunity to create an environment that values and uplifts everyone. It is crucial for educators to foster a classroom where both students and teachers learn together to become more fully human. When students are guided to become empathetic individuals, they contribute to a more understanding and inclusive society. At CUTN, we have a Department of Social Work where students are required to engage in field studies across different parts of the country as part of their academic training. This hands-on experience fosters empathy, resilience, and a commitment to social justice in students, empowering them to apply their learning in meaningful ways while growing into well-rounded individuals.

In August 2019, Mr. Banothu Babu, a second-year MA student in Social Work at CUTN, was conducting his fieldwork in *Thiruthuraipoondi*, an agricultural town located south of Thiruvarur district. He was assigned to the Nambikkai Psychiatric Residential Home (NPRH) as part of his project. During his visit, Mr. Babu encountered a 23-year-old woman from Uttar Pradesh who had been residing at the home for over a year after being found lost in Tamil Nadu. Due to her presumed mental illness and a significant language barrier, she was unable to communicate her family details. Mr. Babu, being from Andhra Pradesh and familiar with Hindi, managed to converse with her and piece together her story. He learned that she had been rescued from a bus stand near Mannargudi by the police and brought to the Home. Her family, facing economic challenges, often migrated to different cities for work. The young woman had been taken to Surat, Gujarat, for employment, which she did not enjoy, prompting her desire to return to Varanasi. However, she mistakenly boarded the wrong train and ended up in Thiruthuraipoondi. In addition to fulfilling his fieldwork responsibilities, Mr. Babu played a key role in reuniting the woman with her family in Varanasi. His act of compassion and dedication garnered attention and was reported by major newspapers across Tamil Nadu, India.

    Mr. Babu met with me to share the entire story, and I congratulated him for his outstanding work, encouraging him to continue making a positive impact. He was also an active member of our NSS group and had been shortlisted for participation in the Republic Day national parade in 2020 in Delhi, pending sponsorship by the Government of Tamil Nadu. CUTN formally approached the state government to advocate for his nomination, highlighting his commendable actions as a reason for consideration. Unfortunately, despite our efforts, he was not selected to represent the university in the parade. It was disappointing that, due to other factors, his exemplary work did not receive the recognition it deserved.

    The Hon'ble President, in his role as the Visitor of Central Universities, held meetings with Vice Chancellors from all central universities. Additionally, in 2017, the President extended invitations to several significant events at *Rashtrapati Bhawan*, such as the inauguration of a public museum. I had the privilege of attending these notable events, including an inaugural function presided over by the Hon'ble Prime Minister. Alongside other Vice Chancellors, I toured the various venues. Several Union Cabinet Ministers and Hon'ble Judges of the Supreme Court were also present at these prestigious gatherings.

CUTN began organizing various cultural programs for the students, with the aim of fostering a deeper appreciation for our traditions. One of our key initiatives was the establishment of a heritage club, led by Prof. Madhurima from the Physics department. The club was inaugurated with an event named *"Ayarchi,"* marking the start of efforts to revive and celebrate our rich cultural heritage. The inaugural event featured a variety of traditional games, bringing great joy to students, staff, and faculty alike. I, too, joined in and participated, adding to the collective enthusiasm and spirit of the day.

Transcending Traditions

The Department of Media and Mass Communication, in collaboration with the Committee Against Sexual Harassment (CASH), approached me to organize a program titled "The Trans Art Show." I readily agreed, and the event was soon organized with enthusiasm. We invited Kalki Subramaniam, an accomplished transgender rights activist, artist, actress, writer, inspirational speaker, and entrepreneur from Tamil Nadu, along with a few other notable guests. Kalki, originally from Pollachi, excelled academically and holds two master's degrees: one in Journalism and Mass Communication and another in International Relations. Kalki's art and activism aim to uplift and bring meaningful change to the lives of marginalized transgender individuals. I had the honour of inaugurating the event. During my address, I emphasized that the challenges faced by the transgender community are not due to their own doing but are a consequence of restrictive societal norms. A nation truly prospers when all sections of society progress, making equality and equity the essential foundations for growth.

The Trans Art Show at CUTN, the first of its kind in any central university.

On the night of November 15, 2018, Cyclone GAJA struck the coastal districts of Tamil Nadu, creating a harrowing experience for everyone at the CUTN. Given the university's proximity to *Nagapattinam* and the coastline, the impact was severe. The powerful cyclone hit the campus overnight from Thursday to Friday, causing significant damage to university property and the lush greenery that adorned the campus. Despite the extensive damage, we had implemented effective safety measures, ensuring that no one was injured during the ordeal. Following the storm, we conducted a thorough assessment of the damage and promptly submitted a report to the Ministry and the University Grants Commission (UGC), requesting additional funds for repairs and necessary remedial measures. Unfortunately, despite our efforts, we only received letters of consolation, but no financial support was granted.

The Campus Connect

In September 2017, the *Campus Connect* Wi-Fi project was launched at CUTN, ensuring that the entire campus was equipped with comprehensive Wi-Fi coverage. This significant step enhanced connectivity and modernized the campus infrastructure. During this period.

NCC Comes to Campus

In 2018, CUTN proudly launched Platoon No. 5 and 6 of the 2(P) Independent COY under the jurisdiction of the NCC Karaikal unit. I had the honour of inaugurating the NCC Unit alongside Commodore Vijesh K. Garg, VSM, Deputy Director General of the NCC Directorate of Tamil Nadu, Puducherry, and the Andaman and Nicobar Islands. The National Cadet Corps, recognized as the largest uniformed youth organization globally, unites young individuals from diverse regions, including remote and tribal areas, fostering responsibility, discipline, and a sense of unity among them. I am confident that this NCC Wing at CUTN will provide an inspiring and enriching experience for every cadet, shaping them into committed and disciplined citizens of our nation.

Establishment of NCC in CUTN

Engaging with Nobel Laureates:

In 2017, the Prime Minister of India hosted an interaction meeting with Nobel laureates in Ahmedabad, inviting leading scientists from across the country. Prof. VijayRaghavan, then Secretary of the Department of Biotechnology, was tasked with organizing the event. Among the attendees were a select group of Vice Chancellors from central universities with notable scientific backgrounds, including myself, the Vice Chancellor of Assam University, and the Acting Vice Chancellor of Visva-Bharati University. One of the distinguished invitees was Dr Harold Eliot Varmus, a Nobel Prize-winning scientist renowned for his groundbreaking work and leadership roles as Director of the National Institutes of Health (1993–1999) and later the National Cancer Institute, USA. Dr Varmus's career has been both unique and inspiring. Born in New York, he initially aspired to become a journalist or a doctor, graduating with a B.A. in English literature. He pursued further studies in English at Harvard University in 1962, only to shift paths and apply to medical schools. Despite facing setbacks—Harvard Medical School rejected him twice—he was eventually accepted by Columbia University College of Physicians and Surgeons. His journey included working at a missionary hospital in Bareilly, India, and Columbia-Presbyterian Hospital. To fulfil his military service during the Vietnam War, Dr Varmus joined the Public Health Service at the National Institutes of Health in 1968, where he conducted research on bacterial gene expression with Ira Pastan. His postdoctoral work in Bishop's lab at the University of California, San Francisco, led to the discovery of the cellular origin of retroviral oncogenes, which earned him the Nobel Prize in Physiology/Medicine in 1989. Dr Varmus's scientific contributions and career journey had long fascinated me, so I was particularly eager to attend this meeting and engage in discussions with him and other luminaries.

With Dr Harold Varmus Nobel Laureate in Physiology & Medicine (1989)

*With Dr Venkataraman Ramakrishnan,
Nobel Laureate in Chemistry (2009)*

*With Dr Ada Yonath, Nobel Laureate in Chemistry (2009) &
Dr Hartmut Michel, Nobel Laureate in Chemistry (1988)*

With Dr Harsh Vardhan, Minister Science & Technology (2017)

Journey to my village:

Ever since I joined CUTN, it has been essential for me to visit my village in Odisha to see my mother whenever I travelled there. In November 2017, I went to Bhubaneswar on leave, and one day I set out for my village with my younger brother to visit my mother, who was unwell. My village is 140 kilometers away from Bhubaneswar. While traveling on the highway, a mini truck collided with our car on the side where I was seated. It was a potentially fatal accident. I sustained a severe head injury that caused significant bleeding, and I lost consciousness. Fortunately, my younger brother was unharmed. The accident occurred just before entering Dhenkanal town, where our elder brother lives. My younger brother immediately called our elder brother, and they took me to the Dhenkanal district hospital. To stop the bleeding, the medical team stitched my head and advised my brother to take me to Bhubaneswar right away. My nephew, who is a neurologist at Apollo Hospital in Bhubaneswar, was contacted, and I was transferred there. My family gathered at the Apollo Hospital, where my nephew examined me and also consulted a cardiologist for a health check-up. Eventually, he referred me to a plastic surgeon for further stitching. We also contacted my brother-in-law in Hyderabad, who is a plastic surgeon, for additional advice on proper care. I was kept under observation for a day or two before being discharged.

Unfortunately, I could not see my mother during this visit, and I returned to the university, promising myself that I would visit her next time I was in Bhubaneswar. January 2018 was busy for me. On February 8, 2018, we had a finance committee meeting in Delhi, and I planned to go home afterward. The meeting concluded before lunch, and as I was returning to the hotel from the meeting venue, I received a call from my elder brother informing me that my mother had passed away. I attempted to book a flight that night to Bhubaneswar, but no tickets were available. Finally, I managed to secure a ticket for the morning of February 9, but by the time I arrived, the cremation had already taken place, and I was unable to see my mother. This situation mirrored my experience in 2000 when my father passed away while I was serving as the Director of the Institute of Life Sciences in Bhubaneswar and was away on official duty in Delhi. Both incidents remain unforgettable in my life. I have faced significant personal losses, including my father's death in 2000 and several tragedies between 2017 and 2019, such as my serious accident, my mother's passing without my presence, the death of a beloved co-brother-in-law, the loss of a cousin sister, and finally, the passing of our pet dog in Bhubaneswar in 2019.

Our Beloved Dog, Danny:

The COVID-19 pandemic, particularly after April 2020, rendered me almost non-functional at a professional level. While we were living in New Delhi, we had a pet dog named Danny, whom we brought home in 2007 from a reputable veterinarian with a well-known pedigree. Danny was born on July 31, 2007. When my family moved to Bhubaneswar, Danny stayed with me for a while. Eventually, when it was time for him to join the rest of the family, my wife travelled from Bhubaneswar to Delhi, and my daughter came from Mumbai to accompany him back home by train. Danny quickly adapted to life in Bhubaneswar, fully embracing his role as a family member. He would sleep with us and even sit on the dining chair alongside us during meals. He was loved by everyone in the family, and we felt comfortable leaving the house in his care whenever we went out. With Danny around, no one dared to enter our home uninvited.

In January 2019, Danny developed a stomach problem. He was taken to various doctors in Bhubaneswar and even referred to the Veterinary College and Hospital.

I also consulted a veterinarian in Delhi, but unfortunately, none of the treatments were effective. One morning, he passed away, leaving everyone in deep grief.

Rise of CUTN:

The University made significant progress, increasing the number of departments to 22 by 2018. We had exhausted all faculty positions sanctioned for these departments. In early 2018, the UGC convened a meeting of all central universities to allocate new departments based on necessity and feasibility. During this meeting, I presented the requirements of CUTN, and it was the only central university to be sanctioned six new departments that year, along with 42 additional faculty members. After receiving the sanction letter, we began establishing the new departments and advertising for faculty positions. However, an issue arose regarding the reservation policy. While applying this policy, the total sanctioned strength for the entire university was initially considered. In 2017/2018, the Allahabad High Court ruled that instead of treating the university as a single unit, each department should be treated as an individual unit for reservation purposes. Consequently, all central universities received a circular from the UGC to cancel their earlier advertisements and to re-advertise, applying the reservation policy at the departmental level. We complied, and Indira Gandhi National Tribal University, Amarkantak, was the first to re-advertise, followed by CUTN. This decision led to an article in *The Telegraph* alleging that I was anti-Ambedkar. They could not criticize Indira Gandhi National Tribal University since its VC belonged to a particular category. Meanwhile, the government appealed to the Supreme Court regarding the Allahabad High Court judgment, which led us to pause the recruitment process. Ultimately, the Supreme Court upheld the Allahabad High Court's ruling. In response, the Government of India issued an ordinance stating that the university would be considered as a unit for reservations, overriding the court's decision. This process delayed our recruitment by more than 16 months. Nevertheless, we at CUTN restarted the recruitment process, and by the end of 2019, we had successfully recruited 72 new faculty members. Since my joining, I had recruited around 147 faculty members, bringing the total to 174. By 2019, we had filled nearly 85% of the vacant positions, although around 12 faculty members left—some due to promotions, others for positions closer to their native places, and a few on leave. By 2019, the number of departments had grown to 28.

During the period from 2015 to 2020, CUTN achieved numerous flagship research publications in prestigious journals such as *Nature, Lancet Infectious Diseases, The Lancet*, and many other high-impact journals across the fields of Chemistry, Physics, Material Science, and Geography. As a result, the H-index of CUTN increased significantly. According to estimates by Elsevier, CUTN had the highest number of citations per paper among all new central universities established after 2009. Being a relatively new university, CUTN made notable improvements in its NIRF ranking in 2020, and I am confident that it will continue to rise in the coming years. It secured a commendable position in the Nature ranking, surpassing most of its peers established after 2009.

CHAPTER – 30

Malpractice in Indian Science

Leaders in Indian Science

India has been fortunate to have remarkable scientific leaders and policymakers who have significantly contributed to the advancement of Indian science. Homi Jehangir Bhabha, known as the "Father of the Indian Nuclear Programme," was a pioneering nuclear scientist. He was nominated for the Nobel Prize in the 1950s. Bhabha began his career in Britain but returned to India on annual leave just before World War II. The outbreak of war compelled him to stay in India, where he accepted a position as a Reader (equivalent to Associate Professor) at the Indian Institute of Science (IISc) in Bengaluru, then headed by Nobel Laureate C.V. Raman. This period marked a pivotal point when Bhabha successfully persuaded Indian leaders to initiate an ambitious nuclear programme. With the support of J.R.D. Tata, he was instrumental in establishing the Tata Institute of Fundamental Research (TIFR) in Mumbai in 1945. Bhabha was among the first recipients of the Padma Bhushan in 1954. Tragically, he passed away on January 24, 1966, at the age of 56. Following Bhabha was Vikram Ambalal Sarabhai, who was a decade younger and known as the "Father of the Indian Space Programme." A physicist by training, Sarabhai was pivotal in pioneering space research and advancing nuclear power in India. He died unexpectedly at the age of 52 due to cardiac arrest. Prof. M.G.K. Menon, another influential physicist and policy maker, played a crucial role in shaping India's scientific landscape for over four decades. One of his significant contributions was nurturing the TIFR, founded by his mentor Homi Bhabha in 1945. M.S. Swaminathan, a renowned agricultural scientist, was also a major force, globally recognized as a leader of the Green Revolution. In later years, Prof. C.N.R. Rao emerged as an eminent voice in Indian science. An Indian chemist of high repute, he was honoured with the Bharat Ratna in 2014 for his contributions. In 2024, it was heartening to see the Government of India recognize another distinguished scientist, Prof. G. Padmanaban, with the newly established *"Vigyan Ratna"* award. Prof. Padmanaban, the current Chancellor of the Central University of Tamil Nadu and former Director of IISc, Bengaluru, was the first recipient of this prestigious honour.

India's scientific influence and leadership appear to be waning. Despite significant efforts by the government to bolster the research ecosystem, Indian science has not achieved the momentum it once had. The era when stalwarts like Homi Bhabha and Vikram Sarabhai directed the course of Indian science and wielded significant influence over Prime Ministers and policymakers—who listened to and respected their guidance—seems to have faded into history. This legacy was carried forward to an extent by esteemed figures such as Professors M.G.K. Menon, M.S. Swaminathan, and C.N.R. Rao. With the passing of Prof. Menon and Prof. Swaminathan, and the absence of Prof. Rao from active policy-making, a void in scientific leadership has emerged. Today, India lacks the strong, unified voice and visionary leadership necessary to champion scientific progress and innovation at the highest levels. While the Government of India continues to emphasize research and encourages a culture of innovation and patents through various initiatives, these programs often fall short in terms of effective implementation and strategic oversight. The state of certain research organizations and institutes, unfortunately, reflects these shortcomings, making it a sensitive topic best left undiscussed.

Science Academies

India is home to four prominent scientific academies: the Indian National Science Academy (INSA) in New Delhi, the Indian Academy of Sciences (IAS) in Bangalore, the National Academy of Sciences (NASI) in Allahabad, and the National Academy of Medical Sciences (NAMS) in New Delhi. The first three—INSA, IAS, and NASI—were established prior to India's independence in 1947, while NAMS was founded in 1961. There have been several attempts to merge the three oldest academies (INSA, IAS, and NASI) into a unified body called the "United Academy of Sciences of India," but these initiatives failed to gain momentum due to a lack of enthusiasm from the leaders of the respective academies. The NASI, founded in 1930 in Allahabad by renowned astrophysicist Meghnad Saha, is the oldest. Four years later, Nobel laureate C.V. Raman established the Indian Academy of Sciences in Bangalore. The third academy, originally set up in Calcutta (now Kolkata) in 1935 by Shanti Swarup Bhatnagar, was relocated to New Delhi in 1947. Early efforts to merge these academies before India's independence encountered resistance due to differing perspectives among Saha, Raman, and Bhatnagar, ultimately leading to the collapse of the unification plan.

It is very difficult to gain proper recognition in India, regardless of the effort you put in, unless you have an influential mentor, unwavering supporters, or substantial influence—or are willing to exert pressure on certain decision-makers. When I worked as a grassroots-level scientist, my contributions were not acknowledged, even by my own Director, until a few WHO scientists commended my work. Suddenly, I became a "star scientist." I have never sought recognition. When I worked on the Keonjhar project in 1978, the Director of the National Institute of Communicable Diseases, Delhi, awarded me a certificate conferring the fellowship of the Indian Society of Malaria and Other Communicable Diseases. Similarly, as a scientist at RMRC Bhubaneswar, I received a certificate from the President of the Zoological Society of India conferring the fellowship of the society in 1985. In 1993, I was granted a fellowship from the National Environmental Science Academy, a less prominent institution. In 2000, the National Academy of Sciences conferred a fellowship upon me, followed by the National Academy of Medical Sciences.

When I became a director in 1998, I was so occupied with my responsibilities that I could not consider pursuing other fellowships like FNA or FTWAS. From 2003 onward, I was appointed director of four or five national research institutes, before joining the United Nations. Later, my well-wishers nominated me for the Indian National Science Academy (INSA) Fellowship, with Prof. Ganguly nominating and Dr. V.M. Katoch, then DG of ICMR, seconding it. For five consecutive years, the sectional committees discussed the nominations, consistently recommending me as No. 1 or No. 2. However, due to internal politics, one or two council members manipulated the process, and I was replaced. Each sectional committee recommends five scientists in order of merit, with the top three or four usually awarded the fellowship. The coordinator of the sectional committee presents these recommendations to the Council meeting. In my first attempt, the committee recommended me as No. 1, but one member in the council replaced me with No. 4, as he was working as an emeritus scientist in the laboratory of candidate No. 4. This was clearly bad politics. The next time, I was replaced with No. 5 because that candidate came from the coordinator's institute and was extremely loyal. On another occasion, I was replaced with No. 5, who was a director that had included the coordinator on various committees after the coordinator's retirement. I view these coordinators as a disgrace to Indian science.

FNA was necessary for obtaining the FTWAS fellowship. Although my name was shortlisted in the top five for FTWAS, I did not receive it due to not having FNA. The sectional committees include some members from ICMR and others seeking favours from ICMR, which possibly explains why three successive ICMR Director Generals received FNA during their tenure (2009–2021). the President of INSA presides over the Council meeting where fellowships are conferred, fostering an environment where politics can influence decisions. Some council members prioritize personal benefits over actual scientific contributions. These contributions are measured by metrics such as citation index, H-index, and i10-index. Those who replaced me had far lower metrics than mine, and my credentials exceeded those of the coordinators and, at times, even the President of INSA. Indian science is riddled with such politics. When I was asked to submit an updated CV for the next cycle, I refused. To illustrate the issue, I could compare my scientific parameters with those of an INSA President, not to mention the sectional coordinators and candidates who replaced me, to highlight the unfair politics in Indian science.

Elsevier, through its SCOPUS database, reported the ranking of Indian scientists for the period 2002-2014 based on various evaluation parameters. I was ranked as the top scientist in the subject area of Immunology and Microbiology. Additionally, in the subject area of Medicine, I was ranked 7th among the top 10 Indian researchers. (Source: Department of Science and Technology's publication on *International Comparative Research Base*, December 2015, Page 103 and 104.)

ScholarGPS®, an American company operated by Meta Analytics LLC in California, is recognized as a leading online resource for analysing scholarly activities within academia. It categorizes scholarly work into broad fields and disciplines, providing global rankings of scholars and institutions. The analysis covers a comprehensive profile for each scholar, including their publication history, institutional affiliations, areas of expertise, collaborators, and scholarly ranking metrics. ScholarGPS® identifies top scholars for their exceptional achievements across various fields, disciplines, and specialties. Earlier this year (2024), ScholarGPS® published a list highlighting researchers across disciplines based on their publication records, the impact of their work, and the distinguished quality of their scholarly output. In July 2024, I received an email informing me that I had been ranked within the top 0.5% of all scholars. Out of curiosity, I checked the "Malaria" field and found that 445 scientists were listed globally. I was disheartened to see that only three scientists from India were included — myself and Dr. Neena Valecha among them — compared to 120 from the USA, 112 from the UK, 19 from Thailand, four from Singapore, and two from Sri Lanka.

However, I continued my research activities even while serving as Vice Chancellor of a central university, publishing around 20 research papers in various high-impact, peer-reviewed journals, including *Lancet Infectious Diseases*, *PLoS Neglected Tropical Diseases*, and *Lancet*, during my five-year tenure. I doubt that any sitting vice chancellor has published such papers during their term. Unfortunately, members of our national science academies often prioritize factors other than merit.

Cracks in the Foundation: Rethinking Health Research

According to S.R. Johansson (Health Transition Review, 1996), "Health research produces knowledge about health, and knowledge is essential for improving health; thus, health research improves health." While the underlying philosophy is sound, health research in India over the past three years or so has required considerable strengthening. Increasingly, it has sometimes led to confusion and superficial findings, often shaped by the personal interests and egos of institutional heads. Genuinely valuable insights remain elusive. In many cases, the intellectual and organisational environment has become counterproductive. It is high time for serious introspection and the pursuit of meaningful reform.

There are around ten research councils in India, with all except the Indian Council for Philosophical Research and the Indian Council of Historical Research being scientific councils. The oldest of these councils, established in 1911, now encompasses 26 research institutes across the country and is considered the apex body for biomedical research / health research. When I deliver lectures at various venues, I often discuss the different phases of organizational life cycles, beginning with establishment and progressing through growth, maturity, success, and various peaks, ultimately leading to decay or decline. As I sit at my office desk watching the rain, a thought crosses my mind: has this age-old organization entered the declining phase of its life cycle? Organizational decay is characterized by generalised and systemic ineffectiveness. In such conditions, discussions often become endless, with participants merely trying to sound intelligent in meetings. Scientists may wait for the leader to express an opinion, and then they echo those sentiments. If the leader changes his mind, they too will follow.

The Covid-19 pandemic is still vivid in our memory, having begun in early 2020 amid widespread fear and apprehension. This organization was meant to serve as the nodal authority guiding the country through the crisis. Its spokesperson frequently appeared on television, providing updates and advice on national news channels. In its first advisory, the organization recommended the consumption of chloroquine tablets for the prevention and treatment of Covid-19, leading people to rush to buy chloroquine. Unfortunately, it was not available on the market. While I was at the Central University of Tamil Nadu, some important individuals from Delhi contacted me seeking chloroquine. I attempted to convince them that it was unnecessary, but they insisted on obtaining it for protection against Covid-19, as they had been advised. Ultimately, I collaborated with colleagues in the Public Health Department, and we published an article titled "Role of Chloroquine Sulphate in Prevention and Control of Covid-19." Our conclusion was that it had no effect on either preventing or curing Covid-19. Another advisory recommended taking ivermectin, leading many, including some of my relatives and friends, to ingest it indiscriminately.

To effectively manage a pandemic, three critical areas need to be addressed:
1. **Government Action:** Strong, coordinated efforts from the government are essential for pandemic control. This involves setting clear guidelines, providing accurate and timely information, mobilizing necessary resources, and ensuring that healthcare systems are prepared to handle increased demand.
2. **Scientific Research:** Ongoing research is fundamental to understanding the virus, developing treatments, and creating vaccines. Investing in scientific studies and encouraging collaboration among researchers can drive innovative solutions and ensure informed decision-making.
3. **Public Engagement & Community Support:** Active participation from the public and community involvement are key to a successful response. This includes raising awareness about health measures, promoting vaccination, and fostering cooperation within communities to support one another. Public trust and collaboration play a crucial role in strengthening government actions and advancing research efforts.

The government's efforts during the COVID-19 pandemic were highly commendable. However, it faced challenges in securing adequate technical support from its designated technical bodies and from experts who had effectively managed previous outbreaks such as SARS (2003) and the Swine Flu (2009) in India. Unfortunately, many of these experienced professionals were sidelined by the relevant agencies. The leadership of these technical bodies often lacked backgrounds in public health or virology and failed to consult the appropriate national experts, resulting in misinformed decisions that impacted the effectiveness of the response. Despite these setbacks, the Government of India remained steadfast in its efforts to combat COVID-19. It actively supported and encouraged research by private organizations, ultimately leading to the successful development of indigenous vaccines. India began its vaccination drive in mid-January 2021, and by February 2023, 95% of the eligible population had received at least one dose, with 88% fully vaccinated. This achievement stands as a remarkable success story for the country.

I have been observing the gradual decline of this age-old apex organization for quite some time, with the exception of a brief period between mid-2015 and 2017. Although I served as the Vice Chancellor of a Central University and later another university, I remained actively involved as Chairman or member of several Scientific Advisory Committees, including a Scientific Advisory Group. Over the years, I observed that the guiding principles of the organization often shifted depending on who was in charge. The personal whims—and at times, the immaturity—of its leadership played a significant role in its decline.

Every individual can make a poor decision, but an ideal organization should not. When a bad decision is made, the organisation often fails to recognize it and becomes stuck with the consequences. The individuals selected for these highest positions (except during the mid-2015 to 2017 period) seemed unable to manage their roles effectively. They frequently engaged in work that was familiar and comfortable rather than addressing the more challenging aspects of their responsibilities. Many people view the organization they work for as an "ego ideal." This concept is rooted in psychological involvement, where the ego perceives itself from an imaginary point of perfection, viewing its normal life as vain and futile. As a result, they tend to choose weak executives. It is well known that a weak executive team will struggle with strategy and implementation, which is precisely what we are witnessing now. The primary aim of most scientists and organizations working in biomedical research is to contribute valuable information to improve public health. However, how many biomedical research reports published each year genuinely make a meaningful contribution to this noble cause?

Nevertheless, several flagship institutes specializing in areas such as virology, malaria, tuberculosis, and nutrition have made significant contributions to society. These institutions continue to play a crucial role in advancing research and improving public health outcomes, thereby extending their impact on global well-being. There remains a dash of hope that the inexperience of the organization's chief scientific leader will not undermine the integrity or progress of these esteemed institutions.

I recall a visit in early 2024 from a retired scientist formerly with the World Health Organization in Geneva. During our conversation, he mentioned that an individual who had not been particularly well-regarded at WHO headquarters had resigned and subsequently assumed a senior position here. I am unsure whether this individual currently serves as the head of this longstanding apex organization. However, what is increasingly concerning is the recent appointment of several unqualified and inexperienced individuals as executive heads of key research institutes. The current approach seems to prioritize rebranding and renaming institutions over fulfilling the core responsibilities for which they were originally established.

I have been told that the current chief of this organization, after joining a couple of years back, stated that all experts above 65 are to be replaced. A friend of mine called me and asked, "Does he think that scientists above 65 are brain dead?" I remember attending a meeting where he was invited to inaugurate. He participated online and made some comments that were not quite relevant. He suddenly declared, "I am a secretary to the Government of India, and therefore, I speak on behalf of the Government of India." Of course, yes—the Government is represented by its secretaries. However, I had never heard such a statement from any Secretary before.

I was informed by someone that the then Minister, who was allegedly instrumental in bringing him here, verbally instructed the Chief of this organization and some program directors to replace all experts above 65. That's fine; they have the right to make such decisions. However, the chief of this organization keeps his acquaintances above 65 in various committees. When I checked the scientific advisory committees of different organizations, I was surprised to see that most of the chairpersons lacked relevant expertise but were known to the chief. Regrettably, research is not always conducted well or deemed relevant. Some research falls into a grey area between good and bad—it is simply unnecessary. So, who decides what gets studied? Clearly, this situation is unsatisfactory.

People with even minimal common sense know that age has nothing to do with intellectual pursuits, especially in scientific, academic, and technological fields. Reports indicate that George Whitesides, over 74, is a co-founder of more than 12 companies, including Genzyme, and is named on more than 50 patents. He has developed diagnostics that can be used for tests in developing countries. Carver Mead, at 79, has an implausibly long list of innovations in microelectronics, including the first software compilation for a silicon chip. Barbara Liskov, over 73, leads MIT's Programming Methodology Group. The physician and biologist Leroy Hood helped create the fields of genomics and proteomics by inventing the protein sequencer, protein synthesizer, DNA synthesizer, and the automated DNA sequencer. He later founded the Institute of Systems Biology in Seattle and served as president even after turning 74. Holonyak, over 84, is still a full-time researcher at the University of Illinois, where he works on quantum-dot lasers, which could be used for a variety of novel display and medical technologies. Mildred Dresselhaus, over 82, was the author of 39 papers in 2012, often working in her MIT office by 6:30 a.m. Stewart Brand, at 74, is working on the revival of extinct species. There are hundreds and thousands of examples like these, including in India. Currently, everything in this organization is decided based on h-index-related appointments. While it is indeed a good practice to evaluate candidates based on scientometric indices, the question remains: which indices are the most reliable? Many people in international organizations tend to increase their h-index by publishing more review papers, which complicates the assessment further.

 It seems that the stake holders are expressing concerns about the current chief's lack of experience in government functions and decision-making approach. Erratic decisions, even in small matters like Ph.D guideship sometimes impact the institution's credibility and quality of research. It might be helpful to engage in a dialogue with the chief and other relevant parties to discuss these issues constructively. Such actions, driven by ignorance or poor understanding, can indeed undermine the significant progress and initiatives undertaken by the government in the heath sector. It is crucial to ensure that leadership in any organisation aligns with broader goals and policies of the government, especially in critical areas like health, where decisions have far reached implications. Stake holders could consider raising these concerns through appropriate channels, such as advisory boards or higher authorities, emphasizing the need for proper decision making and alignment with national objectives.

Anyone who reads this chapter, even by chance, may think that I am writing such things because I am over 65 and considered redundant by the present chief of this age-old organization. Honestly, that is not the case. Someone mentioned that the current chief has put a ban on experts above 65, except for a few who are close to him. I have been working on transmission biology and the management of vector-borne and neglected tropical diseases for the last few decades. In early 2023, when this age-old organization considered me redundant, the Government of India included me as a member of the Society of the Council of Scientific and Industrial Research (CSIR), where the Hon'ble Prime Minister is the President, and the Ministers of Science & Technology, Finance, and Commerce are members. It has been very satisfying to witness the tremendous progress in CSIR, which is far ahead of this age-old organization. However, one cannot live a tolerable life without hope. We still hope that this age-old apex organization and similar organizations will regain their originality. This age-old organisation is losing its organizational memory.

India's Eyes on Tomorrow

In 2020, I was engaged as a consultant by a reputed organization to study, analyse, and prepare a report with recommendations on "Strengthening capacity and strategic direction for research and developing an action plan." The primary objective was to provide guidance on the critical policy and strategic shifts necessary to elevate the organization's research agenda to the next level. This assignment took place during the height of the COVID-19 pandemic, a time when the entire world was grappling with uncertainty. Public health experts, virologists, and immunologists became central figures in global response efforts. In this context, I carefully examined available data and resources, with a particular focus on the state of public health infrastructure.

Today, over 80% of the global population resides in developing or under-developed nations. These regions face significant health challenges that put millions of lives at risk. The ultimate aim of health research is to improve the health and well-being of all people. Biomedical and public health research are powerful drivers of progress, leading to improved patient care through innovation and the practical application of scientific discoveries. As societies evolve, so too must our research frameworks and innovation strategies.

Public health, as both a science and an art, is dedicated to enhancing human well-being by preventing disease, promoting health, and prolonging life through collective action. It emphasizes prevention at the population level, seeking to protect and improve community health outcomes. The COVID-19 crisis underscored the urgent relevance of public health, highlighting systemic vulnerabilities and the need for sustainable investment in health systems. As part of my recommendations, I advised that the organisation's country representatives should initiate dialogue with their respective Ministries of Health to explore the establishment of at least one Public Health University per country. A detailed concept note was developed and appended to the final report. In addition, I personally reached out to few central universities in India, urging them to consider establishing a School or Department of Epidemiology and Public Health—similar to the initiative we successfully launched at the Central University of Tamil Nadu in 2016–17.

It was therefore heartening to recently come across a news article dated April 6th or 7th, 2025, reporting that the Government of India is actively considering the creation of a dedicated public health university. The article, titled *"India's First Public Health University on the Cards,"* "….. the proposal under consideration of the health ministry follows an expert group meeting held last month on the public health situation in India. Discussions on the topic of 'advancing public health priorities, innovation and global leadership' focused on the urgent need of an 'Indian public health university'. There remains 'a dash of hope' that this vision will soon take form.

CHAPTER – 31

A Decade of CUTN

On the occasion of the 70th year of independence in 2017, the Government of India began preparations for the 75th year of Indian independence in 2022, terming it *"Sankalp Se Siddhi."* In 2017, nearly 70 higher education institutes, including central universities, state universities, private universities, deemed-to-be universities, IITs, and NITs, were selected by the Government of India to celebrate *"Sankalp Se Siddhi."* The Central University of Tamil Nadu (CUTN) was also selected and supported by the Government of India for this initiative. CUTN initiated the "New India *Manthan*" at the *"Sankalp Se Siddhi"* event in August 2017. It was indeed an inspiring evening at the university.

Both campuses of CUTN are rich in flora and fauna. We published a pictorial book on the fauna of CUTN, which was released on December 28, 2019, after the court meeting. CUTN also celebrated its tenth anniversary in September 2019, and a decennial publication highlighting the university's progress over the past decade was released on the same day. It has turned out to be an excellent coffee table book.

CHAPTER – 32

Cutn During Covid-19

In December 2019, a new coronavirus, now named COVID-19, emerged in Wuhan, China, leading to an outbreak that expanded globally, including in India. It is considered a potential zoonotic disease, with person-to-person transmission occurring through droplets or contact. The mortality rate varied from low to moderate, and no vaccine or treatment was available until 2021. Various organizations worldwide initiated numerous research efforts on diagnostics, drugs, vaccines, and the social and economic impact of COVID-19.

In India, the first COVID-19 case was reported in Kerala on January 30, 2020. Evidence indicated that the incubation period could last from 1 to 14 days, with a mean duration of 5 to 7 days. Peak viremia occurred at the end of the incubation period and before the onset of symptoms, suggesting that transmission begins 1 to 2 days prior to symptom onset. As of June 2024, there were 775.7 million reported cases and seven million deaths worldwide.

After assessing the probability of this potentially damaging phenomenon, CUTN declared the postponement of end-semester examinations as its first step. As a result, all students, except for a few international students, returned to their respective homes. The vulnerable condition was mitigated by ensuring that the CUTN community worked from home and maintained social distance when they came to the office or went outside. Apart from essential services such as estate management, security, and the health centre, all other activities were restricted, and those involved in essential operations diligently followed the safety protocols issued by the central and state governments.

On campus, regular disinfection measures were initiated, and all precautionary steps were taken. With the help of digital technology, learning continued online. A proper timetable was prepared and circulated among the students, facilitating systematic learning without causing mental stress. The faculty team planned various COVID-19 research projects relevant to the current situation. CUTN also supported the state administration by providing necessary space and technical assistance.

On 16th March 2020, I constituted a 'COVID-19 CUTN Task Force,' while the awareness campaign began in the last week of February 2020. The committee consisted of academicians, administrators, medical officers, and an engineer. The task force met periodically to prepare action plans for the university in response to the COVID-19 situation. In March 2020, thermal screening checkpoints were established on both the academic and residential campuses of CUTN. One staff nurse and an attendant were deployed on duty round the clock. Persons entering the campus were checked with a non-contact thermometer and asked about symptoms of coronavirus infection and their travel history. All Health Centre staff were provided with the necessary Personal Protective Equipment (PPE) to manage patients while ensuring the safety of healthcare professionals. The In-charge Medical Officers ensured that

Health Centre staff used the PPE effectively and disposed of used items properly. We constituted a committee with faculty members from the Applied Psychology department and counsellors from the University Health Centre to address the mental health of the university community. The contact details of the counsellors were posted on the University website and communicated to all students, faculty, and staff members. A well-defined helpline for counselling was also established. Although the entire country was in a lockdown state, the essential service staff continued their duties. The university provided necessary masks and gloves to create a safe environment for them. The central library regularly sent emails to all faculty and students regarding various online resources available. Through the dedicated web portal of the Central Library, CUTN, the library staff offered various e-resources to users during the lockdown.

All facilities were provided to international students who could not leave due to the lockdown and cancellation of flights. The university had adopted six villages under the *Unnat Bharat Abhiyan*. During the lockdown period, CUTN extended a helping hand to these villages, including the supply of rations and hand sanitizers. After the COVID-19 outbreak in India, facts and fictions began spreading on social media. In July 2020, I saw a news channel interviewing a high official from a particular scientific organization regarding COVID-19. I was surprised to hear the official statement, "This type of calamity comes once in a thousand years." If such remarks come from the most responsible officers, how can we blame social media? The popular anti-malarial medicine chloroquine is also known to be a broad-spectrum antiviral drug. Since no drug or vaccine was available for COVID-19, repurposing drugs was necessary. I believed there should be a clinical trial with chloroquine. However, without proper clinical trials, that organization recommended the use of chloroquine and hydroxychloroquine (HCQ) for the prophylaxis and treatment of COVID-19. There were a few encouraging preliminary studies in other countries regarding chloroquine and COVID-19, which could have prompted the organization to recommend HCQ for chemoprophylaxis of asymptomatic health workers treating suspected or confirmed COVID-19 cases, as well as for asymptomatic household contacts of confirmed patients. At that time, India had begun proper clinical trials on the efficacy of HCQ for chemoprophylaxis and treatment of COVID-19. Trials were also ongoing in other countries. Meanwhile, in India, self-medication of chloroquine and HCQ by the public without medical advice was a significant concern, as I mentioned it earlier also.

After the outbreak of COVID-19, people around the world recognized the importance of three areas: Life Science, Microbiology, and Epidemiology & Public Health. Fortunately, we had all three departments. In March, we decided to establish COVID-19 testing through RT-PCR. Our faculty was ready; however, some faculty members went home on weekends and could not return due to the lockdown. Nevertheless, we supported the Medical College authorized to perform diagnoses with equipment and chemicals whenever they needed assistance. I expected a lot from the Epidemiology and Public Health (EPH) department. The faculty members in the EPH department could have made significant contributions to the nation during this crisis, especially with the help of the departments of Statistics and Applied Mathematics. I called a few staff members who were available on campus and suggested actions they could take. Only one faculty member came forward, and we submitted an article entitled "Hydroxychloroquine as Prophylaxis or Treatment for COVID-19: What Does the Evidence Say?" to the Indian Journal of Public Health on April 30, 2020, which was published in May 2020. The others chose to disregard my messages and emails, staying in their respective locations. Naturally, I was set to retire in a couple of months.

The Central University of Tamil Nadu has become a premier institution, widely acknowledged for its quality higher education and research in India, with a balanced emphasis on all disciplines and a firm commitment to social justice and rural upliftment. It possesses the tradition, infrastructure, and potential to play a pioneering and leading role in the field of higher education and research. The University takes pride in its achievements, while also recognizing that there are many tasks yet to be undertaken.

The university fosters collaboration and a multidisciplinary approach with a global outlook, helping students develop the well-rounded vision necessary to succeed anywhere in the world. As a 15-year-old yet modern centre of learning in the southern part of our country, it now looks back with pride at the path it has traversed over one and a half decades. I wish and hope that this preeminent institution will continue to grow along sound and modern lines in the years to come, achieving major breakthroughs in frontier areas.

My last month in CUTN

Perception about CUTN

Before my joining, a report was published in the *Times of India* on March 24, 2014, stating that the Central University of Tamil Nadu (CUTN), established in 2009 under an act of Parliament, had turned into a hotbed of inefficiencies and irregularities (http://timesofindia.indiatimes.com/articleshow/32594994.cms?utm_source=contentofinterest&utm_medium=text&utm_campaign=cppst) (Annexure II). This news appeared in March 2014, and I joined on August 5, 2015, for a period of five years. Later, in May 2020, *The Hindu* published an article entitled "Rising CUTN Stature Draws Several Applicants for the VC Post," stating that the university registered significant progress in teaching and research across all disciplines (Annexure II). I retired from CUTN on August 5, 2020, and returned to Bhubaneswar on August 6, 2020. After my return, I was pleased to see an article/news item entitled "VC Hailed for Transforming Varsity into Centre of Excellence," which reported various growth achievements in the university during the last five years (Annexure II).

CHAPTER – 33

Signing off with Satisfaction

While working at CUTN, I faced one of the most complicated periods of my career due to the COVID-19 pandemic and the subsequent lockdowns across the country, states, and towns. University operations were disrupted starting in March 2020. According to norms, we are required to convene the Executive Council (EC) every three months. The EC is the highest decision-making body of a central university and is chaired by the Vice Chancellor. It includes eminent academicians from across the country as members, two nominees of the President of India, one nominee from the University Grants Commission, and five internal members. The Vice Chancellor of a central university is selected by a search-cum-selection committee appointed by the Government of India. As per the rules, the search committee for the selection of the CUTN Vice Chancellor should comprise five members: two nominated by the President of India and three nominated by the EC of CUTN. In early March 2020, I wrote to the Ministry informing them that the EC would send its nominees by the end of April 2020. Accordingly, I convened an online meeting of the EC on April 29, 2020. All internal members participated physically (with social distancing), while all external members joined online. The EC nominated three members, and I submitted the nominations on the same day. I also informed the then Joint Secretary of the Ministry that I was not interested in an extension and that I wanted to be relieved on the afternoon of August 5. Consequently, I advertised the position of Vice Chancellor in consultation with the Ministry in April 2020.

Due to the increase in COVID-19 cases in Tamil Nadu, the government extended the lockdown; however, official movements were permitted. I observed extreme sincerity among the staff at CUTN, who worked diligently while adhering to all COVID-19 protocols, despite the lockdown. Unfortunately, a few individuals took advantage of the situation to evade their responsibilities under the guise of the lockdown. As time passed, I began contemplating my return after handing over charge on August 5, 2020, in light of the ongoing COVID-19 situation. As I write this chapter on July 26, 2020, COVID-19 cases continue to rise. Nevertheless, the work at the university remains unaffected. The next EC meeting was held online on July 24, 2020. After my introductory remarks, a member of the EC, moved a complimentary motion, which read as follows:

"On behalf of all the internal members of the Executive Council of CUTN, I would like to move a Complimentary Motion in appreciation of the Vice-Chancellor, Prof.A.P.Dash for the efforts taken by him, during his tenure as Vice-Chancellor from 06.08.2015 to 05.08.2020 for the overall development of the Central University of Tamil Nadu.

When we reflect on these five years of his tenure as Vice-Chancellor, CUTN has remarkable improvement and significant performance in all the parameters.

I would like to record some of his main contributions in this Executive Council:

i) From nine Departments with 27 Regular Faculty Members in August 2015, the CUTN has now grown into 28 Departments with 162 Regular Faculty Members as on July 2020.

ii) Among the new Central Universities established after 2009, CUTN has fared very well and has been ranked at 103 in the NIRF 2020 overall ranking.

iii) Under his Academic Leadership and Motivation, the Research Publications of CUTN have achieved the H-index of 33 and i-10 index of 925 with a total impact factor of 696.

Resolved to place on record the appreciation of the Executive Council of Central University of Tamil Nadu to Prof. A. P. Dash, Vice-Chancellor (06.08.2015 to 05.08.2020) of Central University of Tamil Nadu for his determined efforts for the holistic development of the University by motivating and guiding the Faculty, Officers, Staff and Students."

The Complimentary Motion was seconded by Prof (Dr) N.K. Ganguly, Dr. Meenakshi Gopinath, Prof (Dr) Subbiah Shanmugam, Prof Neelima Gupta, Prof Aneel Raina and Dr. Subbiah, and the complimentary Motion was unanimously approved and passed as a Resolution No. 32/17 in the EC Meeting dated 24.7.2020. I had to hand over charge of VC to some senior professor on 5th August and it was discussed in the EC meeting on 24th July. The decision was left to the external members of the EC, especially to the nominees of the President. After detailed deliberations, it was resolved that the charge should be handed over to Prof. R. Karpaga Kumaravel, Senior Professor of the University and Ex- Vice Chancellor of Madurai Kamraj University, Madurai.

Due to the ongoing COVID-19 lockdown, most faculty members could not return to the university campus physically after the summer vacation. I was informed that, since I was retiring on August 5, the faculty and non-teaching staff present on campus wanted to arrange a farewell reception for me. They planned to hold it in the university guest house hall. On the morning of August 3, the designated Acting Vice Chancellor spoke to me about the arrangements. Unfortunately, there were strict restrictions on gatherings and meetings imposed by the government, which prohibited larger gatherings. Even meetings of 25 or 30 people were not permitted. Given these circumstances, I did not encourage a farewell meeting and advised them to adhere to government regulations. They adjusted their plans and organized a small farewell gathering for me on August 4, asking the Deans to nominate one representative from each department and one from each section of the university office to represent all departments and sections. Ultimately, the faculty and non-teaching staff gave me a memorable send-off on the afternoon of August 4, commemorating the completion of my five-year term as the second Vice Chancellor of the university and recalling my efforts to transform the institution.

Amidst COVID 19 pandemic, a memorable farewell was given by CUTN on 4th August 2020.

Throughout my career, I had been primarily focused on research, making this my first foray into the higher education sector. It was, without question, the most rewarding role I had ever held in both academia and research. At the end of the farewell meeting, I felt a bittersweet sense of occasion. Some faculty members approached me, remarking that I must be feeling relieved to retire. There was some truth in that — the past five years had indeed been particularly stressful for all Vice-Chancellors of central universities. Yet, it had also been a wonderful, stimulating, fulfilling, and deeply rewarding experience. Throughout my tenure, I spent much of my time alone, as my family remained in Bhubaneswar. I devoted countless hours—sometimes up to 14 a day—to nurturing this new institution. The university, officially established in 2009, began operations on campus in 2014, and I joined in August 2015. The five years that followed were transformative, both for the university and for me. As I returned home after the farewell, I couldn't help but realise how deeply the university had become a part of my life. Leaving felt like the painful loss of something integral to my very being.

As scheduled, I worked on August 5, 2020, until the evening, when I officially handed over charge around 6 PM. I spent a peaceful night at my residence and left the campus the following morning. Due to the lockdown, there was only one flight from Chennai to Bhubaneswar, so I travelled to Chennai on August 6 and stayed there overnight. Mr. Thangaraj, my Private Secretary, accompanied me. Among the faculty members, Dr Venkat from the Physics department also came to Chennai in his car to see me off. I stayed in a hotel in Chennai on the night of the 6th and boarded the flight at Chennai airport on the 7th for Bhubaneswar. Upon my arrival in Bhubaneswar, I entered home quarantine for

14 days, as per the prevailing COVID-19 regulations.

The Central University of Tamil Nadu is situated in a challenging terrain in a rural area of Tamil Nadu. This university is located in the constituency of the late veteran politician Mr. Karunanidhi of the DMK, with the local MLA also from DMK. The local MP belonged to the Communist Party, while the state government was led by AIADMK. Meanwhile, the federal government was under the NDA. There are many untold stories and facts that could be revealed in the next volume, edition, or innings, if any.

CHAPTER 34

Another Innings

In recent years, post-retirement engagement has become increasingly popular among retirees. Those with skills, knowledge, and practical experience are often sought after as consultants, enjoying flexible assignments and attractive remuneration. Nowadays, scientists retiring from research institutions are frequently re-engaged as consultants, as there are often no suitable replacements for their expertise. Similarly, academicians retiring from universities often find opportunities within the university system. While these re-engagements can sometimes depend on the retiree's relationship with the current Director of the institute or Vice Chancellor of the university, they are primarily driven by the need for technical and academic expertise and experience.

Many countries around the globe have adopted the private university system as part of their higher education framework. India, being the country with the second-highest number of private universities in the world, allocates approximately half of its higher education resources to privately governed institutions, while the other half is funded by the federal and respective state governments. Some private universities are owned by industrialists and supported by their Corporate Social Responsibility (CSR) initiatives. Consequently, these private universities strive to attract esteemed faculty members and administrators to enrol the maximum number of students from different states and even abroad.

Many private universities are focusing on research and publication by appointing faculty members with strong research backgrounds across all levels, aiming to achieve top ranks in university rankings and high grades in accreditation. However, some private universities in India have been established by individuals with varying motives—either to serve the nation in the education sector or to create profitable business ventures, often appointing themselves to self-designated positions like President or Chancellor of the universities. Unfortunately, education in India has, for some, become a business that harms the nation both directly and indirectly. While the growing number of private universities has increased access, it has also raised alarming concerns about the overall quality of education in some private universities.

Before I retired from the Central University of Tamil Nadu in August 2020, I received several offers from private universities to join them as Vice Chancellor, accompanied by attractive remuneration. However, my perspective was different. Having served on numerous committees within the Government of India and various research organizations, as well as being an expert member on many technical advisory committees of the World Health Organization, I wanted to devote my full attention to these responsibilities while leading a peaceful life in Bhubaneswar. Although I had previously lived in Delhi for many years, I now wished to settle back in Bhubaneswar and spend the remainder of my life with family and relatives. In this context, I was also approached by a private university, located in Bhubaneswar.

The promoter of the university was a professor at a medical university in the USA, and I knew him casually. The promoter first started a trust / registered society and started an institution. The Government of Odisha recognized it as a university through a Gazette notification on February 26, 2018. After this recognition, the promoter approached me, suggesting that I join this new university as the Vice Chancellor. At the time, I was serving as the Vice Chancellor of the Central University of Tamil Nadu and had already completed half of my term. Numerous initiatives were underway under my leadership, so I declined the offer. However, he hinted that he was looking forward to my retirement. My plans after retiring from CUTN, however, were completely different.

The Indian higher education system comprises both private and public universities. Public universities receive support from the Government of India (Central Universities) and the respective state governments. In contrast, private universities are primarily funded by various bodies, societies, and individuals. These universities are recognized by the University Grants Commission (UGC), which operates under the authority of the University Grants Commission Act of 1956.

Academic freedom

Traditionally, academic freedom refers to the autonomy of educators to teach, study, and engage in research without unreasonable interference or restriction from any source, including the senior management of private universities. It establishes a faculty member's right to adhere to their pedagogical philosophy and intellectual commitments, thereby preserving the intellectual integrity of our educational system. Academic freedom empowers both students and faculty to express their views—through speech, writing, and electronic communication—both on and off campus, without fear of retribution. This freedom, which is essential for the pursuit of knowledge, has faced widespread challenges in colleges and universities across India, particularly in poorly managed private institutions.

Some Private Universities in India has become a business

In the Indian context, particularly in privately owned universities, teachers often receive lower pay, face exploitation, and have limited freedom to advocate for their rights. The higher education system comprises four categories of universities: Central Universities, State Universities, Deemed Universities, and Private Universities. Additionally, there are institutions designated as institutes of national importance. Commercialization of education indeed undermines the core mission of universities: fostering critical thinking, promoting innovation, and serving as centres of knowledge. The trend of prioritizing profit over quality in some private institutions has not only led to compromised academic standards but has also eroded the values that higher education should uphold. Arbitrary appointments, exploitative faculty practices, and excessive administrative interference hinder the pursuit of knowledge and undermine the development of a nurturing academic environment.

I have observed that some highly accredited private universities, rated A++, appoint faculty verbally without providing appropriate appointment letters. According to the University Grants Commission (UGC), a private university is defined as "an institution of higher learning established through a State or Central Act by a sponsoring body," which may include a society registered under the Societies Registration Act of 1860, a public trust, or a company registered under Section 25 of the Companies Act of 1956.

According to the law, for an institution to be granted the status of a private university, the State legislature must pass an Act that confers this status. Private universities must also be recognized by the University Grants Commission (UGC) to ensure that the degrees they award are considered valuable. Many private universities in India encounter serious challenges, such as a lack of quality faculty, inadequate resources and funding for research, difficulties in introducing new courses that enhance student employability, and the need to provide requisite professional skills to meet the demands of the knowledge economy. They also face challenges in attracting meritorious students and developing state-of-the-art infrastructure. Private universities can thrive when faculty members, students, and other stakeholders can make independent and transparent decisions regarding the institution's direction. Staying relevant in an era of high-tech competition is crucial; without quality, no organization can sustain itself in the long run.

Unfortunately, I discovered that the private university where I was working, although established under an Act of the Odisha Legislative Assembly, was run by a person lacking any knowledge or experience in university management. The Vice Chancellor was treated as a puppet and repeatedly reminded by the promoter that he was the "BOSS." The promoter maintained informants at various levels within the university and interfered even in minor details. I soon found the examination system to be equally problematic. The promoter's wife, who claims to have a Master's in Chemistry and a Ph.D., was appointed as Dean of Academics. Despite her lack of teaching or administrative experience, she made decisions regarding academic activities that suppressed the input of professors, deans, and even the Vice Chancellor. Faculty members and staff were appointed based on arbitrary criteria, and erratic payment structures led to frequent terminations. During my brief tenure, I witnessed more people being terminated than appointed. There was no emphasis on retaining quality faculty. Unethical practices were rampant, with faculty members being coerced into writing papers under the promoter's name. Such management practices are a disgrace to Indian academia. While some private universities operate as business ventures, there are a few that genuinely care for their faculty, staff, and students, often surpassing the treatment found in government universities. In the Indian context, many private university teachers are underpaid, exploited, and lack the freedom to advocate for their rights. Toward the end of my professional career, I encountered a private university that was tightly controlled by its promoter and his relatives.

Outspoken views on the ruling establishment or system are met with a resounding "No, No." It is undeniable that the management has demonstrated a particular sensitivity to genuine criticism. However, the resignations raise equally pertinent questions about the management's ability to withstand such pressure and fundamental inquiries regarding the core objectives of the university related to education and research.

Rankings

Only seven Indian universities (six IITs and the Indian Institute of Science) were ranked in the top 400 universities by the QS World University Rankings for 2019. In 1950, there were nearly 20 universities in India.

As of January 2024, the number of universities in India had increased to 1,113, including Central Universities, State Universities, State Private Universities, institutions established through State legislation, Deemed Universities, and Institutes of National Importance. Additionally, there were approximately 45,000 colleges in the country. By 2022, India was home to 35 of the world's top 1,000 universities. Indian universities frequently make headlines for their poor performance in global rankings, prompting criticism from stakeholders for various reasons, including infrastructure deficits, inadequate governance, insufficient teaching capacity, a lack of patent culture, subpar quality research, and poor academic standards. The National Assessment and Accreditation Council (NAAC) was established by the Government of India in 1994 in response to recommendations from the National Policy on Education (1986). However, over time, it has been alleged that NAAC accreditation has turned into a gamble. I have also had my own unfortunate experiences with NAAC accreditation.

I find it perplexing why we in India, place such a significant emphasis on global rankings and NAAC accreditation rather than focusing on building our reputation through a sustained commitment to quality, relevance, and excellence. The global community will inevitably recognize our eminence based on our achievements. Currently, it feels as though we are caught in a frantic race for rankings and accreditations. Despite this, we have excelled in many areas without them. Our IITs and IIMs have produced some of the best professionals, and our IT sector continues to dominate the world stage. Unfortunately, the obsession with rankings has led to unhealthy practices that are detrimental to our universities. It would be beneficial to abandon the relentless pursuit of rankings and accreditation, as exemplified by the IITs and IIMs, and instead concentrate on education for nation-building, as well as research and innovations that promote sustainable development. The Times Higher Education World University Rankings (often referred to as THE Rankings) is an annual publication that evaluates universities, yet many IITs have rightly chosen to boycott these rankings since most were ranked below 300. However, they continue to embrace the QS Ranking, where several IITs are ranked below 200.

I joined the Central University of Tamil Nadu in August 2015, a time when the Minister of Human Resource Development (MHRD) was advocating for an independent Indian ranking system, free from reliance on global rankings. This advocacy led to the approval of the National Institutional Ranking Framework (NIRF), which was launched by the MHRD on September 29, 2015. This initiative created significant buzz in the media and marked an important day in the Indian education system. While the NIRF has laid a foundation for evaluating institutions, it requires further refinement, particularly in establishing proper criteria for assessing research contributions and addressing other pertinent issues. However, the challenge remains: who will undertake this refinement? As a government initiative, many expect that the Secretary of the Department of Education will spearhead these improvements. Yet, it is crucial to note that the Secretary alone is not equipped to enhance the NIRF's credibility and relevance for Indian institutions. It is committed academics who should devise the methodologies necessary for making the NIRF more objective and inclusive, addressing all categories of institutions. The National Education Policy (NEP 2020) aims to foster critical thinking and problem-solving skills, along with social, ethical, and emotional capacities. To enable these goals, we must create an appropriate ecosystem that includes better funding and greater autonomy for universities.

Every year, Stanford University publishes a list of the top 2% of global scientists across various research fields. This list reflects the prevailing research culture and outputs, changing annually. Publication metrics and scientometric indices are widely utilized, though sometimes misused. Stanford has created a publicly accessible database of top-cited scientists, offering standardized information on citations, h-index, co-authorship adjusted h-index, citations to papers in different authorship positions, and a composite indicator. For several years, I consistently found my name among the top 2% of global scientists. However, I chose not to include this in my CV or inform anyone about it, including my wife, who was working at Delhi University and heading a department of Zoology at colleges in Odisha. In recent years, particularly in 2021 and 2022, being recognized as one of the top 2% global scientists has gained prestige. I have observed numerous posts and congratulations on social media regarding this achievement. Furthermore, some private universities now highlight the number of their faculty members included in this prestigious 2% category.

Reputation, whether good or bad, is shaped by both actions and perceptions. In recent years, the appointment of vice-chancellors—who are expected to provide comprehensive leadership, including academic direction—has become increasingly disappointing. A particular Court highlighted this concern in one of its judgments, stating: "The heads of universities, the most visible symbols of the university system, are these days appointed not because they are distinguished academicians, but because they have the right political connections or appropriate political or caste affiliations in the concerned state…" (Dr. Mukhtar Ahmad, AMU, 2019: "What is wrong with the Indian higher education system?" in University World News, February 8, 2019).

A Vice Chancellor (VC) serves as the conscience keeper of any university. As the head of the institution, a VC is expected to act as a bridge between the administrative and academic wings, which is why, in all university acts, the VC is referred to as an 'officer' of the university rather than purely as the academic head. This designation facilitates their multifaceted role, prompting universities to seek individuals with leadership qualities and integrity, in addition to academic excellence and administrative experience. Numerous commissions have made recommendations regarding the role of Vice Chancellors. The Kothari Commission, in 1964, emphasized that "a vice chancellor should be a person with vision. He should command high respect among all sections of society. The vice chancellor should be a distinguished academic… (who) has a commitment to the values for which the universities stand.

In India, we often lament the absence of world-class universities, noting that none of them rank among the top 100 globally. One significant reason for this is the misalignment between the selection processes for world-class universities and Vice Chancellors (VCs). Recently, I read in the newspaper about a former professor from a reputed state University who tragically committed suicide. Reports indicate that he had taken out a substantial loan with a high interest rate to secure a VC position, only to find that his name did not appear on the final list of appointees. This financial burden drove him to despair. Corruption in the appointment of VCs is a topic of open discussion. Many individuals within universities go to great lengths to secure VC positions, often well-versed in the art of lobbying and dealing with middlemen. As a result, universities are losing credibility due to questionable VC selection and a deteriorating academic environment. Appointing a vice chancellor based solely on personal connections or the ability to manage the position constitutes corruption. Additionally, selecting an individual regardless of qualifications, judicial pronouncements, or allegations of plagiarism—simply because of connections—further exemplifies this corruption. (Dr. Prabhu Dev, Ex-VC, Bangalore University (2020): *World-class university and VC selection process are not in alignment!*).

Malpractice in Higher Academics

Education is a transformative force that shapes the world. An effective education system empowers individuals with knowledge and skills, enabling them to contribute meaningfully to society, drive economic growth, foster social progress, and support the holistic development of a nation. As mentioned earlier, the Indian higher education system comprises both private and public universities. Regarding the selection of Vice Chancellors, of late, I believe that central universities are no exceptions to the troubling trends observed in this process. It has come to my knowledge that when many central universities were established in 2009, a search and selection committee was formed to choose the VCs for these newly created institutions. This committee collected CVs of persons known to them and recommended for appointment as VCs for all these new universities. I cannot verify the authenticity of this information, but it was conveyed to me by a highly reputable source.

I can provide an example regarding the VC selection process in one central university, about which I had direct knowledge. After the Vice Chancellor completed his five-year tenure, a search cum selection committee was formed. The committee held three meetings. During the first meeting, they discussed and shortlisted 54 candidates from approximately 250 applicants, aiming to reduce this number to around 20 for personal interactions. However, when around 18 candidates were shortlisted for personal discussions, one individual was added to the list despite not being considered eligible and not being among the initial 54 candidates. This candidate had applied for a professorship at the university but had not even made the shortlist. Surprisingly, he not only participated in the personal discussions but was also empanelled and ultimately appointed as Vice Chancellor. He expressed his gratitude to the members of the search and selection committee. Out of the five committee members, one has passed away, while two are too busy to engage. The VC has included the remaining two experts, who allegedly advocated for his empanelment despite his initial exclusion from the shortlist; in various statutory committees of the university. Additionally, there were anonymous letters alleging plagiarism against him. I have been informed that between 2020 and 2023, three central universities included individuals to be called for personal discussion, who were not initially shortlisted.

Even after 75 years of independence, academic freedom remains elusive in India. The tradition of free speech and thought can be traced back to the *Rig Veda*, with the ancient universities of *Nalanda* and *Vikramshila* serving as notable examples. This legacy continued for many years, reaching a significant point in 1947 with the advent of independence and the establishment of the right to expression enshrined in the Indian Constitution. Traditionally, academic freedom encompasses the liberty of teachers to teach, study, and pursue knowledge and research without unreasonable interference or restrictions, including from senior management in private universities. It establishes a faculty member's right to adhere to their pedagogical philosophy and intellectual commitments, preserving the intellectual integrity of our educational system. Academic freedom grants both students and faculty the right to express their views—whether in speech, writing, or through electronic communication—without fear, both on and off campus. This freedom, vital for the pursuit of knowledge, has faced widespread attacks in colleges and universities across India, particularly in poorly managed private institutions. In these settings, academic freedom for faculty members and students is increasingly under serious threat, often due to the oblique intentions of the promoters. Unfortunately, I have personally experienced this malpractice in one such university.

Staining Vice Chancellors

I came across an article published in August 2024 by an Associate Professor, entitled "Vice Chancellor's Vices." The article emphasized that the Vice Chancellor (VC) is a pivotal figure in a university, serving as the chairman of both the academic and executive wings. The VC must provide effective leadership and act as a crucial link between the university's academic community and the outside world. As the most important functionary of the university system, the VC is essential for creating the right atmosphere for both teachers and students. The article raised pertinent questions regarding the quality of Vice Chancellors being recruited nowadays. It referenced a recent incident where a Vice Chancellor from Delhi University was suspended for "misgovernance." According to University Grants Commission (UGC) norms, both academic excellence and a proven administrative track record should be considered when selecting Vice Chancellors for various universities. The article urged that the role of a Vice Chancellor requires subtle management skills and integrity, ensuring that they do not leave under allegations of impropriety or incompetence, which ultimately reflects poorly on the selection process.

The author cited the eight instances, where VCs had to resign for various reasons. Let me cite a recent example. Following allegations of non-performance, the VC of a newly started university (2009) in south-eastern India had to resign in February 2019, could not complete his term and left half way. Interestingly, after five years (2023-24), he was not only appointed in a prestigious position in a university, but also nominated as the convenor of the search cum selection committee of Vice chancellor of a reputed central university in eastern India. Of course, out of over 1100 universities in India the above can be treated as exceptions. But the universities today are interfered too much. The most a VC can do is to prevent further retrogression. There is a need to select vice chancellors who are scholars with laudable academic and proven administrative abilities.

Choosing Chancellors

In central universities, Chancellors serve primarily as titular heads, with their roles largely limited to presiding over convocations. They are appointed by the Honourable President of India in his or her capacity as Visitor. According to regulations, "the Chancellor shall be appointed by the Visitor (President of India), recommended by the Executive Council from among three persons of eminence in the fields of academic or public life of the country." The Executive Council (EC) is the principal executive body of a central university and comprises eminent individuals, including nominees from the Hon'ble President of India and the University Grants Commission (UGC). This committee deliberates and recommends three names for the Chancellor position, from which the President appoints one. If the President is dissatisfied with the proposed names, he or she has the authority to return the list and request a new one from the EC. This procedure appeared laudable and was initially adhered to with healthy norms for several years, but this has changed in recent times. For instance, an eminent scientist was appointed as the Chancellor of the Central University where I served as Vice Chancellor, and it was a moment of pride when he was awarded the *"Vigyan Ratna"* by the Hon'ble President of India in 2024. However, a change in this scenario has been observed, where principals, even from private colleges were appointed as Chancellors in few central universities. Furthermore, the ministry has begun recommending names from the lists submitted by the respective ECs, sometimes pressuring the EC to provide names to replace the names within a stipulated timeframe.

I have an interesting experience and insights regarding the choosing of Chancellors for central universities. After my tenure as Vice Chancellor of the Central University of Tamil Nadu (CUTN), I decided to settle in Bhubaneswar, my home state, despite owning residences in Delhi NCR. This was during the peak of the COVID-19 pandemic, and I was a member and chairman of several committees for the Government of India and the United Nations (WHO), attending meetings virtually. I had also joined a private university as Vice Chancellor. In 2021, I received a call from a central university in the North East, asking for my consent to include my name among three nominees for the chancellorship recommended by the Executive Council (EC). I agreed and three names were forwarded including mine, but the Ministry of Human Resource Development (MHRD) (now ministry of Education) did not take any action for a very long time and eventually requested another set of names before forwarding the list to the Hon'ble President. This was my first experience with the process. My second experience occurred a year later when the EC of another central university nominated three names, including mine at the top. However, the ministry recommended a different individual, a retired professor; who was appointed as the Chancellor. Later, the EC of another central university in the south recommended three names for chancellorship, again placing my name at number one. As I learned from someone in Delhi, the individual in the second position was chosen by the ministry and appointed as Chancellor instead. Additionally, another Vice Chancellor of a central university in the south sought my consent for consideration by their EC, yet another person was ultimately appointed as Chancellor. In another instance, I was informed by a source in Delhi that I was on the top of list recommended by the EC for Chancellor for a different central university in eastern India. The list was returned by the ministry and the university was asked to send a fresh list. I was told in April, 2025 that the EC of the university had again sent three names including mine at the top in the first week of April, 2025. My last experience was once again with a central university in the North East, where the outgoing Vice Chancellor, during his final EC meeting, deliberated and recommended my name at the top of the list for chancellorship. Ultimately, I feel I failed to meet the personal criteria of the decision-maker(s). Unfortunately, current practices surrounding these appointments are suffocatingly powerful, leaving little room for genuine meritocracy.

India once held a prominent position in the global landscape of education and innovation, with ancient institutions like *Takshashila* and *Nalanda* standing as centres of knowledge and learning. The National Education Policy (NEP) of 2020 aims to revive this rich heritage by promoting a holistic, multidisciplinary approach to education, fostering research and innovation, and integrating technology. There is 'a dash of hope' that, when fully realized, the NEP has the potential to propel Indian academia to new heights of excellence and global acclaim.

CHAPTER 35:

Looking Back

My academic life has been a journey of many ups and downs. While I was never a brilliant student, I never failed at anything I attempted. My academic journey has resembled a see-saw, marked by several upward feats and downward challenges. Now, when I reflect on my experiences, I realize that the events in my life were guiding me toward a shift in specialization from Zoology, through Biomedical Sciences, to Epidemiology and Public Health Science as I approached the end of my professional career.

My grandmother and mother sowed the seeds of spirituality in my mind during my childhood, but they remained dormant until I got married and had children. My first religious trip was to Shirdi with my family and students in the late 1980s. Despite his busy professional schedule, my father-in-law taught me how to recite the *Gayatri Mantra* 108 times every day in the early morning. The *Gāyatrī Mantra* is a highly revered mantra from the *Rig Veda*, and *Gāyatrī* is the name of the Goddess associated with the *Vedic* meter in which the verse is composed. The *Gayatri mantra* is widely cited in Hindu texts and plays an important role in the thread ceremony among Brahmin families in India. Modern Hindu reform movements have popularized the practice of the mantra, making it widely accessible. It is considered one of the most important and powerful *Vedic* mantras.

I began reciting the Gayatri Mantra in 1982, starting with ten recitations a day for around 6 to 8 months, before increasing it to 108 times each morning after my bath. However, when I faced serious challenges in my life and career between 1988 and 1990, and when the Indian judiciary failed to protect my family, I turned to spirituality for solace. I started reciting the *Gayatri mantra* three times a day (morning, noon, and evening), 108 times in each session, which continued for several years. As my professional and personal responsibilities increased, I found it challenging to maintain this routine. Eventually, I returned to reciting it once in the morning, a practice I continue even today. I never fail to recite it, even when I was down with Covid-19.

During my time as a scientist at the Regional Medical Research Centre in Bhubaneswar, I was awarded an enviable international research project in the early 1990s. Among five global projects focused on lymphatic filariasis (LF) transmission control, one was designated for India, and I was leading it. This project focused on the biocontrol of LF vectors and involved 80 project staff, two well-equipped vehicles, and all necessary resources. However, this success became an eyesore for many of my colleagues. The then Director, late Dr Kishnamachari, supported me fully, but some of my colleagues were intent on undermining my peace. Unfounded allegations and anonymous letters were sent against me daily. A few individuals even approached politicians to obtain letters of complaint, which were then sent to the ICMR Headquarters and the Ministry.

A close friend of mine, the late Pitambar Mohanty, took me to a pandit near the Chilika Lake area, who advised me to recite the *Baglamukhi Mantra* every day. *Baglamukhi* is the eighth goddess among the *Dasha Mahavidya* and her name is derived from *Bagla* and *Mukhi*. The term "Bagala," a distortion of the original Sanskrit root "Valga," means bridle—the headgear used to control a horse. Thus, *Baglamukhi* represents the Goddess who has the power to control and paralyze her enemies. I began reciting the *Baglamukhi Mantra* daily in the late 1990s. Coincidentally, I was later selected as the Director of the Institute of Life Sciences, Bhubaneswar, leaving the Regional Medical Research Centre, Bhubaneswar, behind for good. The rest is history, as I have already detailed in this book.

There has been considerable discussion and debate regarding the National Education Policy (NEP) 2020. The NEP was approved by the Union Cabinet of India on July 29, 2020, and subsequently launched by the Hon'ble Prime Minister. At that time, I was serving as the Vice Chancellor of the Central University of Tamil Nadu (CUTN), with only seven days remaining until my retirement. On that day (29th July, 2020), I received a call around 8:45 PM from national *Doordarshan*, informing me that the Honourable Prime Minister would be launching the NEP and would speak on national television at 9 PM. They had selected two academicians to comment on the policy: the then Director of IIT Mumbai and myself. In a rush, I quickly changed from my night suit into a T-shirt, as there was no time to turn on my computer. I joined the broadcast via my mobile phone and shared my comments on the NEP, particularly emphasizing the research aspects and the multiple entry and exit provisions. Since then, numerous meetings and discussions have taken place regarding the NEP, both online and offline. As I write this, nearly three years later, it appears that hardly any university has fully implemented the NEP in its true sense (as of July 2023). Nonetheless, NEP 2020 represents a significant and positive development for the Indian education system.

As of July 2024, there are nearly 54 Central Universities in India, including 10 in the North-East, 7 in Delhi, and 6 in Uttar Pradesh, in addition to various state and private universities. Central universities, also known as union universities, are public institutions established by an Act of Parliament and fall under the purview of the Department of Higher Education in the Ministry of Education. Each year, a Visitor's Conference is held where all Vice Chancellors of CUs convene to discuss various issues. The Hon'ble President has shown great magnanimity during these conferences. In some states, there are also higher education councils that provide opportunities for Vice Chancellors to meet and engage in discussions. These meetings should encourage open debates grounded in verifiable facts and data regarding many reforms, including the NEP, without fear or prejudice.

I am particularly concerned about how Vice Chancellors are often unable to exercise their powers "within the statutes granted autonomy" due to excessive governmental control. Simply publishing a few high-impact papers by a limited number of faculty members is insufficient to elevate our universities to a position of excellence. Mr. Amitabh Kant, the outgoing CEO of NITI Aayog, addressed the poor quality of research in our institutions for the first time, and I wish he had raised this issue with our Honourable Prime Minister much earlier in his tenure.

It is not desirable for our institutions to become mere printing presses for producing large volumes of low-quality publications, which would only serve to hinder our nation's progress, despite the abundant young talent present in our universities. We often prioritize our personal and self-interests over national interests and the future of the next generation. My dedication to my life's goals has not only enriched my own life but, I believe, has also left a lasting impact on society. By seeking excellence and performing my duties with conviction, I have been able to inspire others to dream boldly, take ownership, and pursue their passions confidently. I have always believed in the spirit of teamwork and have contributed to collective progress.

Throughout my life, like many others, I was relatively unknown. However, at the age of 70, in 2022, I gained recognition as a notable Indian when I was awarded the civilian honour of *"Padmashree"* in Science and Engineering by the Honourable President of India. Interestingly, *"Aaj Tak"* mistakenly (?) published that I had received the *Padma Bhushan* (Annexure VI). What had I achieved in my life up until that point? I had successfully established five national-level research institutes under the Ministry of Health and Family Welfare and the Ministry of Science and Technology in India. At the age of 57, I joined the World Health Organization's Regional Office for South-East Asia, where I spearheaded programmes for the control, elimination, and eradication of vector-borne and neglected tropical diseases that affect marginalized communities and the poorest of the poor. I made significant contributions to the elimination of lymphatic filariasis as a public health problem and studied the impact of climate change on vector-borne diseases. I played an important role in the control and elimination of dengue, kala-azar, malaria, yaws, and trachoma. Additionally, I investigated the changing patterns of vector behaviour and the ecological succession of vector species.

By the time I turned 64, I nurtured a newly established central university. I have published over 300 research papers in highly reputed journals such as *The Lancet*, *Lancet Infectious Diseases*, *Nature Genetics*, *Nature Medicine*, and many others. My work has earned me an H-index of 62 and an i10-index of 206 (as of January, 2025). Dreamed boldly through my actions and achievements, I have contributed to collective progress and paved the way for future generations to build upon their aspirations, perpetuating a cycle of growth and empowerment. I had the opportunity to travel extensively to many countries around the world for work – ranging from USA to Sri Lanka, the UK to South Africa and Europe to South America, I had an excellent time in each place.

CHAPTER 36:

Padma Politics

I never compromised in my professional life, often prioritizing my career over my family. As a result, I neglected my family responsibilities, while my wife took on the full burden of managing our household. I could hardly spend time with my family during those years. My wife worked as the Head of the Department of Zoology at a college in Bhubaneswar, but I had to leave Bhubaneswar in February 2003 to take on the role of Director at the National Institute of Research for Tribal Health in Jabalpur. This was followed by moves to Delhi and then to Tamil Nadu. Ultimately, I returned to Bhubaneswar in mid-August 2020, during the Covid-19 pandemic. The nearly two decades of separation from my family was no easy feat.

I have never sought Padma awards, even as I witnessed many recipients, particularly from metro cities like Delhi and Mumbai. Many of these individuals were doctors who had the opportunity to treat VIPs or were recommended by politicians and people in power. I personally know a few who received the "Padma Bhushan" in science without making any significant contributions. This has shaped my perception of the Padma awards: if you know someone influential, you may receive one; otherwise, it's best to forget about it. Ideally, Padma awards should be occasions to honour our icons, performers, artists, and scientists—those who have achieved extraordinary success and made significant contributions to society. However, politics has often influenced the selection of recipients, even in fields like science and engineering. Initially, two civilian awards were established in January 1954: the Bharat Ratna and a three-tier system of Padma awards. The Padma awards were classified into three categories: Class I, Class II, and Class III. However, in January 1955, the Padma Vibhushan was reclassified into three distinct awards: the Padma Vibhushan, the Padma Bhushan, and the Padmashree.

It was September 14, 2013 or 2014, when my wife read something in the newspaper and called to advise me to apply for a Padma award. The deadline was September 15, and I had no clue how to proceed. Some previous Padma recipients informed me that I needed to be nominated. Since I was in Delhi and time was running out, I went to Odisha Bhawan. I met with two MPs from Odisha, both of whom happily agreed to nominate me. On the final day, September 15, I learned from someone in Delhi that there was a specific format for the nomination. He sent me a copy of the required format, so I forwarded the forms to the two MPs who had nominated me, requesting them to renominate me using the correct format and sent it. I'm not sure if that was done because I did not receive any further information afterward, and I chose to put it out of my mind. The complexities and nuances around awards like the Padma seem deeply intertwined with politics and societal perceptions, reflecting both the achievements of individuals and the broader context of governance and recognition in India. However, my perception of the Padma awards began to change in 2017-18 when I saw many genuine individuals from remote areas receiving these awards, even without any political backing.

In August 2015, I joined the Central University of Tamil Nadu (CUTN) as the Vice Chancellor. The university's statutory committees were reconstituted during my tenure. In 2019, Prof. N.K. Ganguly, the former Director General of ICMR and former President of JIPMER, Pondicherry, became a member of the Executive Council. Additionally, in 2018, Prof. G. Padmanaban, the former Director of the Indian Institute of Science, Bangalore, was appointed as the Chancellor of the University by the Honourable President of India. Both distinguished individuals were Padma Bhushan awardees and nominated me for the Padma Bhushan in Science & Engineering for 2020. Later, I learned that the central intelligence agency visited CUTN for verification, which I understood was part of the procedure for potential Padma awardees. The entire CUTN community was hopeful, eagerly watching television on January 26 to see if my name would appear. Unfortunately, all disappointed when it did not happen. Undeterred, they nominated me again for the Padma Bhushan for 2021. I retired from CUTN on August 5, 2020, and returned to Bhubaneswar. Colleagues from CUTN informed me that in December 2020, the central intelligence officers came again to CUTN for another verification for my Padma award. I also heard that verification took place in Odisha, where I was residing at the time. With double verification completed, I felt hopeful once again, but ultimately, it did not materialize, leading me to decide to step back from pursuing the nomination for the award. Enough was enough. It was disheartening to observe that after 2016, hardly anyone had received the Padma Bhushan in Science & Engineering. If anyone did receive it, they were either from space science or were awarded posthumously.

Then came 2021. I was working as the Vice Chancellor at a private university in Bhubaneswar, feeling a great deal of dissatisfaction with the academic and research ethics practiced there and my inability to effect any meaningful changes. My interest in the Padma award diminished, and I had not received any messages regarding intelligence verification like I had in the previous two years. On January 25, 2022, while I was in my office, around 11 AM, I received a call from an officer at the Home Ministry of the Government of India. They informed me that the Government of India had decided to confer the Padma Shree in Science and Engineering to me. The officer was very polite and requested me to keep this information confidential until the official announcement later that evening. I felt a mix of emotions; I was pleased to finally receive some recognition after all my hard work, but slightly disappointed that it was the Padma Shree instead of the Padma Bhushan I was nominated for in previous years. At the time, my wife was in home isolation due to COVID-19. I called her to share the news, and she was happy for the same reason—at least there was recognition. Later that evening, I had a scheduled Zoom meeting. During the meeting, I received a call from a former Chief Secretary of Odisha congratulating me on the Padma award, which informed me that the announcement had already been made. I switched on the television to see coverage of the Padma awards. Every channel in Odisha was showcasing the names and photographs of the Padma awardees from the state—except mine. Only my name appeared, without a photo. Having returned to Odisha in late 2020, during the COVID-19 pandemic, I realized that most people in Bhubaneswar did not know about my return, except for my family. Later that evening, around 9 PM, the media managed to collect my phone number and reached out for interviews. The next morning, some local political leaders visited my home to congratulate me. I learned that the Honourable Chief Minister of Odisha congratulated all Padma awardees from the state via Twitter. Among five awardees in India for the Padma Shree in Science and Engineering, I was the only one from Odisha and likely the fourth or fifth to receive it since independence. Both the Honourable Minister of Home Affairs and the Home Secretary of the Government of India sent personalized letters of congratulations to the awardees. My perspective on the Padma awards highlights the challenges that often come with meritocracy, particularly in fields as impactful as science and public health. It was heartening to see that I eventually received the Padmashree award. Recognition can serve as an important affirmation of one's work, especially in fields where contributions are vital for societal advancement.

CHAPTER – 37

Nobel Leaurates of Indian Origin / Connection

I clearly remember that during my early college days, my Physics lecturer told me about C.V. Raman – his work and his Noble Prize; and two years later my Botany Lecturer explained about the Nobel award-winning contribution of Dr Har Govind Khorana. Later when I started my career as a Senior Research Officer in a field operational research project on malaria, I clearly came to understand about the epoch-making discovery of Sir Roland Ross on 20th August, 1897 and then his noble prize in 1902. While working as the Vice Chancellor of the Central University of Tamil Nadu, I got an opportunity to interact with a dozen of Nobel Laurates along with other eminent scientists of the country including Dr VijayRaghaban, the then Secretary, Department of Biotechnology and later who became the Principal Scientific Adviser to Government of Inia. This interaction meeting was organized in 2017, by the Hon'ble Prime Minister of India and around 40 to 50 Indian scientists were invited for interaction with these Nobel laurates at Ahmedabad. Among these scientists, three Central University Vice Chancellors (who were also scientists) were invited. These privileged Vice Chancellors were, myself, Prof D.C. Nath, VC of Assam University, Silchar and the Acting VC of Viswa Bharti. In the opening session, an official from the Nobel Foundation mentioned about the number of Indians got Nobel Prize till date. I was trying to identify all the Indian Nobel Laurates, but always missing someone. Finally, I could summarise below the Indian Nobel laurates till date:

1. Sir Ronald Ross (1902): Nobel Prize in Physiology and Medicine. He was born in Almora district of India. His father was Sir Grant Ross, a general in the British Indian Army.
2. Rudyard Kipling (1907): Nobel Prize in Literature - born in Mumbai in 1865. Kipling wrote of Bombay "Mother of Cities to me, For I was born in her gate".
3. Rabindranath Tagore (1913): Nobel Prize in Literature - Indian poet, philosopher, and polymath.
4. C. V. Raman (1930): Nobel Prize in Physics - Indian physicist known for the discovery of the Raman effect.
5. Har Gobind Khorana (1968): Nobel Prize in Physiology or Medicine - Indian-born scientist who became a naturalized citizen of the United States.
6. Mother Teresa (1979): Nobel Peace Prize - although not Indian by birth, she worked extensively in India and received Indian citizenship.
7. Subrahmanyan Chandrasekhar (1983): Nobel Prize in Physics - Indian-born American astrophysicist.
8. 14th Dalai Lama (1989) : Nobel Prize in Peace
9. Amartya Sen (1998): Nobel Memorial Prize in Economic Sciences - Indian economist and philosopher.
10. V.S. Naipaul (2001): Nobel Prize in Literature

11. Venkatraman Ramakrishnan (2009): Nobel Prize in Chemistry - Indian-born American-British structural biologist.
12. Kailash Satyarthi (2014): Nobel Peace Prize - Indian child rights activist.
13. Abhijit Banerjee (2019): Nobel Memorial Prize in Economic Sciences - Indian-born American economist.
14. Esther Duflo (2019): Nobel Memorial Prize in Economic Sciences - French American economist of Indian descent.

While mentioning these facts, I remember Srinivasa Ramanujan, a self-made mathematician from *Kumbokonam*, Tamil Nadu. He did not have any formal degree or any training in mathematics, but made a substantial contribution to mathematical analysis, number theory, infinite series, and continued fractions. He got Fellowship of the Royal Society in 1918, but passed away in 1920 at the age of 32. He could not get any other recognition in his life time. I had a chance to visit his home in *Kumbokonam* in 2020.

CHAPTER-38

The CSIR Connection

In the 1930s there was a growing need for establishing research organisations. Prominent scientists such as C.V. Raman and J.C. Ghosh proposed and an advisory board of scientific research was constituted. It was when Arcot Ramaswamy Mudaliar recommended to have a Board of Scientific and Industrial Research and his recommendation paid off when the Board of Scientific and Industrial Research (BSIR) was created on 1 April 1940. Mudaliar was made chair of the board. Then the constitution of the Council of Scientific and Industrial Research (CSIR) as an autonomous body was prepared under Mudaliar and Bhatnagar. Thus, CSIR came into operation on 26 September 1942 when a decision was made to create an organisation to further the advancement in industrial research.

The Council of Scientific and Industrial Research (CSIR) came under the Ministry of Science and Technology. Now the CSIR has a dynamic network of 37 national research laboratories with a pan India presence. According to the SCImago institutions ranking world report of 2021, CSIR is the only Indian organisation among the top 100 global institutions. CSIR holds the 7th position in Asia and is ranked as the top institution in the country. The CSIR

Society is the Apex body of CSIR, the functions of which includes to: review the progress and performance of CSIR, give the policy direction to Governing Body and approve the annual report and yearly accounts of CSIR. Hon'ble Prime Minister of India is the President of the CSIR Society. Hon'ble Ministers of Finance, Commerce and Science & Technology are members. Also, few eminent people from Industry, administration and science and technology are members of the society of CSIR. The Society is reconstituted every three years. In 2023, I was nominated as a member of the CSIR society. It was desired in the 2022 Society meeting that one member will mentor at least one research institute of CSIR and I have to mentor the Indian Institute of Chemical Biology (IICB) at Kolkota. The institute was established in 1935 as a biomedical research centre in Kolkota, West Bengal.

A report was published by the Science & Technology Department of Government of India in December, 2015 on "International Comparative Performance of India's Research Base 2009 – 2013" and identified top 10 researchers in different areas. As per the data published the contribution of major research organisations in India was as follows at that time.

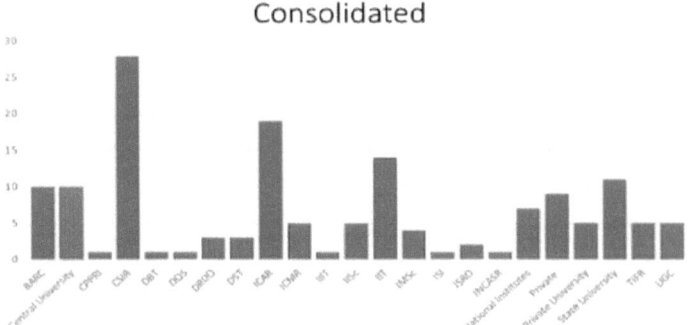

The IICB is engaged in research on diseases of national importance and biological problems of global interest, employing sophisticated state-of-the-art technology. It carries out researches in variety of areas including chemistry, biochemistry, cell biology, molecular biology, neurobiology and immunology which promotes productive interdisciplinary interaction. IICB is one of the major laboratories in India to carry out multidisciplinary concerted efforts to conduct basic research on infectious diseases. It offers exciting opportunities to students who are keen on research career in Biological and Chemical Sciences leading up to the award of a PhD degree.

On the invitation of the Director, IICB, I visited their institute in August, 2023. On their request I delivered a talk on "Research in the National Education Policy-2020". I also discussed about strengthening the patent culture and other issues that we are facing today. IICB has proved to be a flagship institute in CSIR. I found that IICB has published nearly 1000 research papers in peer reviewed journals during the last five years till July, 2023. A journal is judged by it's impact factor. In biological sciences, a paper published in a journal with impact factor more than 3 is considered as good. During the last five years, it published 750 papers in journals having impact factor more than 5 and 15 papers in journals having impact factor more than 10. There are many research organisations in India dealing with such areas, but are far behind IICB. However, since my job was to mentor, I highlighted on the following issues:

- Research agenda should be related to sustainable development goals (SDGs), so that India should be among top 5 countries in achieving SDG goals
- Focus on studies related to Severity of Climate change impact

> Translate research evidence into Policies, Practices and Products and Develop knowledge to action research and Policies
> Strengthen Visibility: Dissemination and outreach programmes
> Further strengthen the patent culture to have meaningful products

Fruitful outcomes of an organisation largely depend upon good policy making and good governance along with few other issues. Governance is fundamental. I have seen organisations fail because of problems at the governance level. Ineffective governance compromises the ability of the organisations to succeed. Effective governance, in contrast, greatly assists the organization. Effective governance includes efficiency, simplicity, is focused, allows a respectful conflict of ideas, is integrated and synergistic, has good outcomes and preserves community interests.

CHAPTER-39

Vanishing Scientists

According to a report published by the Department of Science and Technology titled "Scientific and Development Statistics (1978-79)," total annual expenditure on science and technology increased from 11 million in 1948-49 to 726,140 million in 1980-81. This significant growth led some to predict that India would become a scientific superpower by the year 2000. However, the scientific community in India remains fragile, as our scientists often lack the respect they deserve. While we are recognised globally for our brilliant minds, a large portion of the Indian population is unaware of what scientists do, apart from the more visible aspects of science.

According to NDTV on 8th October 2015, 11 Indian nuclear scientists experienced unnatural deaths between 2009 and 2013. One notable case was L. Mahalingam, a 47-year-old nuclear scientist who went for a morning walk in June 2009 and never returned. His decomposed body was later found, and the incident was concluded to be a suicide. Two months prior, another scientist, Ravi Kumar, was found dead in his flat. In December 2009, two young scientists, Umang Singh and Partha Pratim Bag, lost their lives in a fire accident at BARC, despite not being directly connected to the incident. Additionally, in February 2010, Mahadevan Padmanabhan Iyer, a 48-year-old mechanical engineer working at BARC, died in South Mumbai. We are all familiar with the story of Dr. Nambi Narayanan, the renowned Indian scientist whose remarkable journey was powerfully portrayed in the 2022 film *Rocketry: The Nambi Effect*.

Reflecting on the case of Dr Nambi Narayanan inevitably brings to mind the suspicious and untimely deaths of other key figures in India's scientific community—most notably Dr. Vikram Sarabhai and Dr Homi Bhabha, both of whom were instrumental in shaping India's space and nuclear energy programs, respectively. I remember reading about these events as a young student, and they have lingered in my memory ever since. Dr Homi Bhabha tragically died in an Air India plane crash over Switzerland in early 1966, at the age of 56. Dr Vikram Sarabhai, meanwhile, passed away at the age of 52 in a room at his favourite resort in Kovalam. While these cases stand apart in terms of circumstances, their timing and the strategic importance of their work have long invited speculation. Adding to this unsettling narrative was the 1972 suicide of Dr. V. H. Shah, which raised many unanswered questions. In 2013, two senior engineers involved in the development of India's first nuclear-powered submarine were found dead on railway tracks—an incident that deepened concerns. Around the same time, another woman scientist, Dr Uma Rao, was also discovered dead under mysterious circumstances.

Another deeply poignant story is that of Dr. Subhash Mukherjee, a pioneering medical scientist who, in 1978, created India's first in vitro fertilization (IVF) baby—just 67 days after the birth of the world's first IVF baby in the United

Kingdom. Despite this groundbreaking achievement, he was reportedly denied the opportunity to share his work with the international scientific community. Subjected to bureaucratic indifference and professional isolation, Dr. Mukherjee faced relentless harassment. Tragically, he died by suicide on 19 June 1981, at the age of 50.

The lack of adequate mental health support remains a pressing issue across the globe. In the post-COVID-19 era, this crisis has become even more visible, with distressing reports of suicides emerging from premier institutions. Unfortunately, such cases are not isolated. There are numerous similar instances that point to deeper systemic issues within academic and research environments. As someone aptly observed, conducting scientific research in India—whether in universities or government-funded institutions—can often be "too rigid, too hierarchical, and too authoritarian," creating a challenging environment for many scholars and scientists. At least, I experienced it firsthand—many times—during my career as a scientist.

But why am I writing this chapter? Just a few days ago, on 25th August 2024, I learned of the sudden and tragic passing of a senior scientist from the Institute of Life Sciences (ILS) in Bhubaneswar, where I had served as director in the early years. This scientist joined ILS in 2007, after relocating from the USA. Around 2015, a small committee was formed by ILS to investigate his alleged irregular attendance, and I was included in that committee. If I recall correctly, I travelled from Tamil Nadu, where I was serving as Vice Chancellor at the time, to Bhubaneswar for the meeting, but the scientist did not attend and I returned. When I came back to Odisha in August 2020 to join a private university in Bhubaneswar, he often visited me, and we communicated frequently through WhatsApp and phone calls. I would share my articles with him, and he would do the same. We both appreciated each other's work. In response to an advertisement for the position of Director at ILS, he applied, was shortlisted, and invited for an interview. However, the late Dr. Ajay Parida, who had completed a five-year term as Director, was reappointed. A few months later, following Dr. Parida's sudden passing, the position was advertised again in October 2022. The advertisement specified an age limit of 58 years, and this scientist, being just over 55, requested that I nominate him for the position, which I did. However, the short-listing committee only considered candidates under the age of 55, for reasons known only to them. This scientist expressed his frustration to me on several occasions. I also recall a tragic incident from around 2008, when Dr P.C. Supakar, a colleague of mine at ILS, passed away suddenly at his residence. Dr Supakar was an exceptional scientist who worked closely with me throughout my tenure. He was deeply dedicated to his research and had no desire to take on an administrative role. Therefore, after my departure from ILS, he chose not to apply for the position of Director. It is truly disheartening to reflect that, in the past decade, three scientists from ILS have tragically passed away unexpectedly.

It is high time we address the growing issue of vanishing scientists in India, which can stem from a range of factors including harassment, frustration, depression, work-life imbalance, overwork, and health issues. Mental health in the workplace is of paramount importance, yet we live in a world where mental health support remains inadequate. Every organization, especially universities and research institutions, should prioritize resources to support the mental well-being of their employees. This includes providing easy access to counsellors for timely psychological support whenever needed. My reflections on the mental health challenges faced by scientists, as well as the systemic issues within research institutions, are especially pertinent today. Addressing these concerns is essential for cultivating a healthy scientific community—one that can not only thrive but also contribute positively to society.

Looking back, I often wonder how I managed to survive the challenging times during the early days of my career in the 1980s and early 1990s. Despite having a couple of prestigious international projects, I faced intense criticism from both colleagues and superiors. I endured threats at the Bhubaneswar railway station about being transferred to a remote location, and I witnessed the injustice when my wife was selected for a position, only to be denied the appointment. One of my significant projects was not even forwarded, while another director at a different institute received an international grant for a project that was strikingly similar to mine. Today, I look back and congratulate myself for overcoming these hardships and the harassment I faced throughout the early years of my scientific career.

CHAPTER-40

Experiencing Spiritualism

As I mentioned earlier, my grand mother and mother were pivotal in my spiritual upbringing. I grew up in a large joint family, where my uncle, a Sanskrit *Pandit*, taught us numerous *Slokas* and *Mantras* in Sanskrit. Among these were the *Bojan Mantra*, recited before meals and *Surya Namaskar* – though I must admit I have completely forgotten now. However, my grandson Annay, who attends a *Gurukul* – style school called *'Bodhi Vidyalaya"* in Mumbai, has learned these practices, and I plan to relearn them from him. We were educated about the cultural significance of Lord Jagannath and how Adi Shankaracharya recited Jagannath *Ashtakam*. In my childhood I also learned that the *'Geeta Govindam'* was composed by Jaydev in the 12th century, beautifully depicting the relationship between Krishna & Radha. It is said that Lord Krishna himself composed the final stanza of the *'Geeta Govindam'*. According to tradition, when *'Geeta Govindam'* is recited, an 'asana' should be set out, as Lord Krishna comes to listen to its verse.

When I was working as a scientist at the Regional Medical Research Centre, Bhubaneswar, I was in close contact with a senior person, Late Shri Dwarika Mohan Mishra; who was an ardent devotee of *Shirdi Sai Baba*.

Through him I came in contact with the philosophy of *Shirdi Sai Baba*, who always said *"Sabka Malik Ek Hai"* (Everyone's God is One). This attracted me. I also visited Shirdi several times at the shrine of *Sai Baba* and every time, I had a unique experience. I read several books on Shirdi Sai Baba to understand his philosophy. He was indeed a great Saint, as people can still experience.

From my child hood, I heard about Lord Jagannath from my grandmother, mother, father and uncle etc. My mother used to spend a month every year in Puri to visit Lord Jagannath every day and my wife was visiting Lord Jagannath temple very often. Now a days, I visit the temple sometimes with my wife, Vijayalakshmi. But my every visit was arranged by someone from the Government. My last visit to Lord Jagannath with my wife was in September, 2024. Even if we were provided with someone to help us, it was so difficult to have the *"Darshan"* of Lord Jagannath that I doubt if it will be possible for me to visit again to have His *"Darshan"*.

In chapter 24, under "Theta Healing", I mentioned about a type of meditation, which may be called as a new age meditation or theta healing, developed by Vianna Stibal in USA in 1995. It is said that 'Theta healing' technique helps one to improve mind, body, and spirit. Theta state is a state of mind that has been studied for decades by neuroscientists, psychologists, and other researchers, as claimed by them. This state of mind is characterized by a low-frequency brainwave pattern that is claimed to be associated with deep relaxation, meditation, and creativity. It claims to change a practitioner's brain wave pattern to the theta pattern. After being trained in this procedure by Vianna Stibal herself during 2014-15, I started practicing it for some time, but now a days, unable to make time to continue that.

I came across an article written by Andrea Jain of the Indiana University-Purdue University, Indianapolis (DOI: https://doi.org/10.30664/ar.67499). The summary of the article was "In October 1989, long-time yoga student, John Friend (b. 1959) travelled to India to study with yoga masters. First, he went to Pune for a one-month intensive postural yoga programme at the Ramamani Iyengar Memorial Yoga Institute, founded by a world-famous yoga proponent, B. K. S. Iyengar (b. 1918). Postural yoga (De Michelis 2005, Singleton 2010) refers to modern biomechanical systems of yoga which are based on sequences of asana or postures that are, through *Pranayama* or 'breathing exercises', synchronized with the breath. Following Friend's training in Iyengar Yoga, he travelled to Ganeshpuri, India where he met *Gurumayi* Chidvilasananda (b. 1954), the current guru of the path Siddha Yoga Meditation, at the *Gurudev Siddha Peeth Ashram*. The encounter profoundly transformed Friend, and *Gurumayi Chidvilasananda* initiated him into Siddha Yoga".

But before that, there is some co-incidence regarding this. While working at the Institute of Life Sciences (ILS), Bhubaneswar, I had a colleague, a scintillating scientist, named Dr B. R. Das. He used to visit USA every year for his scientific activities. During one of his visits, he went to Shree Muktananda Ashram, New York, where he received the divine initiation, *shaktipat-diksha*, from Gurumayi Chidvilashananda, the head of Siddha Yoga path (www.siddhayoga.org). Since then, he became a serious practitioner of *Siddha Yoga* teachings and practices. During those days, I think in late 1990s, he organised *"Satsangs"* at Bhubaneswar and I participated a couple of times. Soon my wife and daughter became followers of Siddha Yoga and now they are deeply involved. Now a days, since the last couple of years, my wife has started *Satsangs* every month, at least twice. When I am here in Bhubaneswar, I participate those *satsangs* along with other Siddha Yoga followers, and experience peace, tranquillity and immense satisfaction. I have realized that the philosophy behind *Siddha Yoga* is highly laudable and powerful. This is a path based on the grace and teachings of the *Siddha Yoga Gurus*. This form of yoga has been passed down through a lineage of enlightened masters. For last more than 50 years *Gurumayi Chidvilashananda* has been the spiritual head of Siddha Yoga.

Elizabeth De Michelis is a scholar of religion specialising in the history of modern yoga. In 2006, she was instrumental in creating the Modern Yoga Research website. She categorized modern yoga into three types: Modern Postural Yoga (stressing on physical exercises), modern Meditational Yoga, (stressing) concentration & meditation, and modern denominational yoga, (includes religious and philosophical doctrine). According to her description, Iyengar Yoga is an example of modern Postural Yoga, whereas *Siddha Yoga* is an example of modern denominational Yoga.

According to the Wikipedia *"Siddha Yoga"* is a spiritual path founded by Swami Muktananda (1908–1982). According to its literature, the *Siddha Yoga* tradition is based mainly on eastern philosophies and draws many of its teachings from the Indian yogic texts of *Vedanta, Kashmir Shaivism*, and the *Bhagwat Gita*. According to Dr Raj Nehru, Vice Chancellor, Shri Vishwakarma Skill University; Kashmir Shaivism is a profound non-dual philosophy that emphasizes the primacy of Universal consciousness (*Chiti*). In Kashmir Shaivism, everything in existence is a manifestation of this consciousness. Siddha Yoga is a spiritual path that incorporates meditation, chanting, serving selflessly and *Dakshina*. The mystery of the Siddha Yoga practices is that they are enlivened with the awakened energy of the *Siddha Yoga Guru*. Thus, our own effort is magnified as we apply ourselves to the practices. *Gurumayi Chidvilashananda* received the authority and the power of Siddha Yoga from her Guru Swami Mukatananda before he passed away in 1982. As a Siddha Guru, she carries out her mission of awakening seekers to their own potential for enlightenment by bestowing **Shaktipat Diksha**. *Shaktipat diksha* is the transmission of spiritual energy from a guru to the student, believed to awaken the student's dormant *Kundalini* energy. In *Siddha Yoga*, the relationship between the student and the Guru is central. The Guru is seen as a guide and an enlightened being who helps the student progress on the path toward self-realization. The present head of Siddha Yoga is *Gurumayi Chidvilasananda*who is affectionately called as *Gurumayi,* which means 'Guru Mother'. I have seen *Gurumahyi*"s picture, seen her on the screen. She is full of grace radiating lots of positive & spiritual energy.

Siddha Yoga Ashrams and Meditation Centres are available all over the world and provide opportunities to the seekers for in-depth study and practices. They hold retreats and courses and mainly conduct *Satsangs* where the power of collective Siddha Yoga teachings and practices support seekers to progress in their sadhana leading to great transformation.

Swami Muktananda (affectionately called as Baba) who established the path of Siddha Yoga was a disciple of *Bhagavan* Nityananda who was a giant among the Siddha Masters of his time. He is known as a *'Janam siddha'*- who is born with full realization of his own divine nature.

There have been very few who have equalled his stature throughout history. After traveling the length and breadth of India, Bhagavan Nityananda (affectionately called as *Bade Baba*) came in mid 1930s to the famous holy place of Ganeshpuri which is a small village about 80 km north of Mumbai. It was home to Bhagavan Nityananda from 1936 until he left his body in 1961. It is a holy land since ancient times. It is said that Sage Vashishta, Lord Rama's Guru, held a great yagna here. The great Guru *Bhagawan Nityanand* further sanctified this place. Thanks to Dr B.R. Das, through whom I had the great good fortune to visit Ganeshpuri with my wife some 15 years ago. I came back to Odisha after almost two decades and my wife has started a Siddha Yoga meditation Centre here in Bhubaneswar. She organises two *Satsangs* every month and I get the opportunity to participate. But I continue to do my daily spiritual routine which gives me maximum satisfaction. Meditation and Yoga increase one's capacity, skills and qualities. The ability to take responsibility beyond one's capacity and manage it with inner richness and outer dynamism come from these.

CHAPTER-41

On Deck - Post Retirement

After serving a full term as Vice Chancellor of the Central University of Tamil Nadu, I completed my tennure as Vice Chancellor of a private university on 31st August 2023. I had joined the private university reluctantly and faced continuous disagreements with the management. From 1st September 2023 onwards, I decided to focus on contributing to my field of science in ways that I could make the most impact. I have actively participated in various meetings of the World Health Organization, serving as a member or chairperson, and have delivered lectures at numerous universities and research institutes on relevant topics. On 15th September 2015, during the 17th UN General Assembly, the world adopted the Sustainable Development Goals (SDGs), which aim to end poverty in all its forms by 2030. The SDGs consist of 17 goals and 169 associated targets, addressing a wide range of issues including poverty, hunger, armed conflicts, energy, water, climate change, and equality. These goals are global in nature and universally applicable to all countries. Achieving the SDGs on time is not feasible without controlling, eliminating, or eradicating vector-borne and neglected tropical diseases. My extensive experience and research in the transmission biology and control of these diseases have enabled me to provide technical support whenever needed, and I continue to do so. The main objective is for India to be among the top ten countries in achieving the SDGs.

I have also published scientific articles to raise awareness, including a couple of opinion pieces in op-eds and magazines focused on malaria, a disease that has been with us for a very long time. Malaria has been the subject of three Nobel Prizes: Ronald Ross, born in India, in 1902; Charles Laveran, a French army doctor, in 1907; and Tu Youyou from China in 2015. The history of malaria extends far back, with references in Chinese bronze inscriptions dating from 1562 to 1066 BC, and in Indian texts since the 6th century BC. However, modern research began only in the 19th century, following the discoveries of Laveran on 5th November 1880 and Ross on 20th August 1897. One of the articles I co-authored, focused on malaria treatment, emphasizing the need for a drug regimen that could reduce the pill burden on patients. The historic discovery by Ronald Ross in India paved the way for significant progress in malaria control and elimination. To date, over 40 countries have been certified malaria-free using existing strategies and tools for case management and vector control. Malaria is now targeted for elimination by 2030, and efforts should be framed from an elimination perspective. In an opinion piece co-authored with Professor Y.K. Gupta, we argued that new and improved medical tools are needed to enhance the efficiency and effectiveness of malaria elimination strategies. Specifically, there is a need for better rapid diagnostic tests for *Plasmodium vivax* that are highly specific and sensitive, as well as an antimalarial drug regimen that reduces the pill burden to improve patient compliance (Annexure-III).

The COVID-19 pandemic significantly increased awareness of the critical role of public health. In 2023, *Outlook* magazine interviewed me about the importance of public health, and our detailed discussion was published (Annexure-IV). Public health focuses on improving and protecting the health and well-being of communities, with a strong emphasis on prevention across large populations. Its scope is multifaceted and extends beyond health sciences to include areas such as mental health (clinical psychology), social work, mass communication, geography (remote sensing and natural disaster prediction), and health economics, among others. Translating research evidence into products, policies, and practices (the "3 Ps") is essential for advancing public health. In India, public health has traditionally been a neglected field. Given the country's vast population and diverse health challenges, there is a pressing need for a substantial number of public health specialists and virologists.

As mentioned, my expertise lies in transmission biology and the management of vector-borne and neglected tropical diseases affecting marginalized communities. In India, three major vector-borne diseases—malaria, lymphatic filariasis (LF), and Kala-azar (KA)—are targeted for elimination by 2030. Both LF and KA disproportionately affect the poorest populations, making their elimination crucial for achieving the Sustainable Development Goals (SDGs). These diseases, caused by different parasites, share a common factor: transmission via vectors. Strengthening vector control, an essential component of disease elimination, requires skilled entomologists—a resource India currently lacks.

The Southeast Asia region, including India, accounts for 54% of the global burden of neglected tropical diseases

(NTDs), with LF and KA being key targets for elimination. LF, a chronic and disabling disease, remains endemic across 328 districts in 21 states and union territories. KA, or visceral leishmaniasis, is a potentially fatal illness that affects some of the world's most underserved communities.

The branch of science dedicated to the control of insect vectors is known as entomology. India has a rich tradition in this field, dating back to the early 20th century. The country was a leader in the global fight against malaria during the 1950s and 60s, pioneering DDT-based indoor residual spraying (IRS) programs. However, the current capacity for vector control research and surveillance has weakened, making the country more vulnerable to threats from malaria, LF, and KA.

In 2014, the World Health Organization highlighted the significance of vector-borne diseases by making them the theme of World Health Day. While renewed commitments to preventing and controlling these diseases have led to significant progress, targeted interventions still require the expertise of medical entomologists. Ending deadly vector-borne diseases in India will demand sustained, coordinated efforts from all stakeholders—including government, communities, researchers, and industry. By rebuilding our entomological capacity, investing in research and innovation, and working together, we can create a healthier future for all (Annexure-V).

Back in 2006, when I was the Director of the National Institute of Malaria Research, New Delhi, malaria dominated the headlines in Indian newspapers due to an outbreak in Assam in February of that year, which resulted in several deaths. At the time, the national malaria drug policy designated chloroquine as the first-line treatment for presumptive cases, as well as for radical treatment of

Plasmodium falciparum malaria in "low-risk" areas. Initially, chloroquine had been the drug of choice, but over time, malaria parasites had developed widespread resistance to this popular medication. We documented numerous locations across India where chloroquine was no longer as effective as before, which led us to advocate for a change in the drug policy. However, there was significant resistance to updating the policy. In response, I wrote an article titled "Malaria Malpractice" in 2006, highlighting the issue. This article drew the ire of the national malaria program and the government, leaving them quite displeased with me. Fortunately, the then-Director General of the Indian Council of Medical Research supported me during that challenging time (Annexure-VII).

Some people view my life as successful and filled with achievements. My wife describes me as a workaholic. However, I have never been motivated by money; I find contentment in meeting my basic needs. For me, happiness comes from skilfully discharging my responsibilities while fostering strong relationships with stakeholders, along with maintaining a harmonious work-life balance.

Enduring dengue

Dengue is the most significant mosquito-borne viral disease affecting humans, and in India, its spread has dramatically increased over the last few decades. The epidemiology of dengue in India has been complex and has substantially evolved over the past half-century, with changes in prevalent strains, affected regions, disease severity, and case management approaches. The number of reported cases is directly influenced by effective surveillance, monitoring, and reporting, as dengue cases can only be documented if they are actively sought. Mortality due to dengue was very high until the mid-1990s; however, in recent years, it has decreased to 0.1% or less in some states in India. According to WHO, the global incidence of dengue has risen sharply, with reported cases increasing from 0.5 million in 2000 to 5.2 million in 2019. In 2023, the world recorded the highest number of dengue cases, with 6.5 million reported across 80 countries. Although 6.5 million cases were reported in 2023, the estimated total infections may have reached 390 million, with 96 million exhibiting clinical symptoms. Effective reporting is contingent on robust surveillance in any given region. While working at WHO, I observed that some countries lacked proper surveillance systems for certain diseases, and as a result, they could not report the actual number of cases.

    I returned to Bhubaneswar, Odisha, in late 2020, considering it an upcoming city with amenities catering to senior citizens. I received a senior citizen card, and I recall being addressed as a senior citizen and asked about my wellbeing during 2021–2022. Eventually, I sold my flat(s) in the Delhi NCR and settled in Bhubaneswar. Dengue is a climate-sensitive disease, and given Bhubaneswar's climate, I anticipated cases to start rising from mid-April through the end of October. When I arrived, I observed some precautionary measures being taken to prevent dengue. However, this year, I noticed a lack of visible preventive actions. By June and July 2024, I saw a rise in dengue cases, including in areas where I live. On July 11, 2024, I sent a message to the Health Secretary regarding the increase in cases and urged for preventive measures, including insecticide fogging. When I learned that the wife of a central minister had lost her life to dengue, I also expressed my concerns to the Hon'ble Health Minister. In October 2024, I wrote to the Bhubaneswar Municipal

Corporation (BMC) authority for dengue prevention and received the following reply:

"Thanks for your concern, let me apprise you that BMC is working continuously with all its machinery to tackle the dengue issue. It's mainly awareness and destruction of breeding sources. We have been quite successful this year. Last year the detected cases in September were around 4000 which are only 1000 this year. We closely monitor every new case and try and sanitise areas where we see some patterns. I don't know if your assessment about rise in cases is based on any survey or any scientific study but it seems to be only perception. The situation was comparatively quite grim in other Indian cities. We had team of health ministry visiting the city after the death of the honourable minister's wife. They expressed satisfaction with our efforts.

Once again appreciate your concern but kindly see some scientific data before pressing Panic button. Warm regards."

This reply genuinely surprised me, and I decided it wasn't worth my time to pursue the matter further. Life is indeed a continuous learning journey, and even at this stage, I learned something valuable from this gentleman. It was a lesson in how certain individuals in administrative positions perceive public health, surveillance, monitoring, and the science that supports it. Having worked in several countries, I have encountered various approaches to public health, but this experience will certainly stand out as a memorable one.

In September 2024, despite my concerns, I still saw no preventive measures for dengue. That month, I noticed two hospital-admitted dengue cases in my area. Then, on October 22, my grandson developed a high fever, which I immediately suspected to be dengue. He tested positive on the 23rd. The following day, my wife, daughter, and son all developed fevers and also tested positive, as did my driver, who had been helping us. In total, we had five cases in our family and close circle. By the morning of October 26, my son and grandson's conditions were worsening. I rushed them to AIIMS that afternoon, where they were admitted, one on the first floor and the other on the sixth, later being moved to private rooms. My son fainted three times. On October 28, they were both near critical and one required platelet transfusions. I spent five days and four sleepless nights, filled with anxiety, at the hospital. Thanks to God's grace and the dedicated care from the doctors and staff at AIIMS, both my son and grandson recovered and were discharged just before Diwali. It was an incredibly harrowing experience; one I would not wish on anyone.

Sometimes, I question my decision to settle in Bhubaneswar. With the recent changes in Odisha's government, I sincerely hope the new administration will establish a strong foundation to address key issues, including public health. It's crucial that they appoint trained and experienced personnel in critical positions to better serve the public. I still hold onto the hope that Bhubaneswar can transform into the "pensioner's paradise" I initially envisioned—a city where senior citizens feel valued and well cared for.

CHAPTER-43

Witness to History: The Ram Mandir Consecration Ceremoney

The grand Consecration ceremony of the Ram Temple in *Ayodhya*, marked by the *Prana Pratistha* ritual on 22nd January 2024, was a historic and spiritually profound event. The sacred ceremony infused life into the deity's idol, officially consecrating the temple as a divine abode of Lord Ram. Devotees and dignitaries from across India and beyond gathered on invitation to witness this monumental moment, which symmbolises devotion & cultural heritage. The consecration ceremony of the *Ram Mandir* in Ayodhya was successfully completed on 22nd January 2024 by 1 PM. The grand event was organised by the temple Trust, which extended invitations to eminent personalities from various fields. Attendees included actors, politicians, industrialists, bureaucrats, spiritual leaders, Padma awardees, athletes and other distinguished individuals, making it a momentous and diverse gathering. Top industrialists like Mr Ambani, sports persons like Mr Sachin Tendulkar; Mr Amitabh

Bachchan, Ayushman Khurana, Hema Malini, Kangana Ranawat etc from film industry were invited.

A few distinguished guests were invited from Odisha for the *Ram Mandir* consecration ceremony. As a Padma awardee, I had the privilege of receiving an invitation. The eminent representatives who handed over the invitation to me had earlier invited the *"Gajapati"* and the then Chief Minister of Odisha. I was genuinely delighted and honoured to be a part of this historic moment.

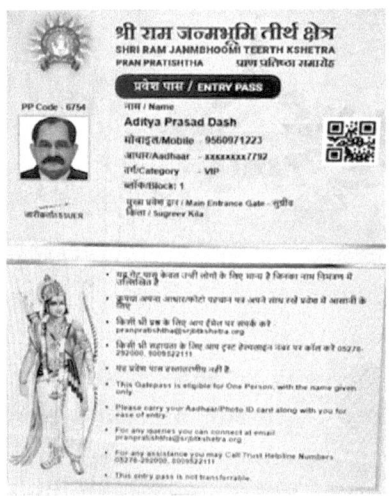

There was only one Indigo flight from Bhubaneswar to Lucknow via Raipur and I traveled on it for the Ram *Mandir* consecration ceremony. Interestingly the couple seated next to me was none other than the esteemed *"Gajapati"* and his wife., who were also traveling for the same historic occasion. It was truly an honour to share the journey with such distinguished company. I was received at the Lucknow airport and was taken to hotel Holiday Inn. One Law student from Lucknow University was assigned the job to take me there in his car. The young man who drove the car was very kind and graciously offered to assist me with transportation to Ayodhya. Since I already had other arrangement in place, I politely declined his offer. He then shared his contact number with me and encouraged me to reach out to him if I faced any difficulties during my journey. His thoughtfulness left a positive impression on me.

My stay in hotel Holiday Inn near Lucknow airport, provided a comfortable base for attending this once-in-a-life time event in the holy city of Ayodhya. Early the next morning, we departed for Ayodhya, with the hotel arranging breakfast as early as 4:30 AM. As we prepared to leave, the hotel played Ram Bhajans from 4 AM, filling the atmosphere with a deep sense of spiritualism. After breakfast, we embarked on our journey to Ayodhya, which turned out to be a truly memorable experience. The impeccably clean roads gave the impression of traveling through Europe, setting a remarkable tone for the day.

Entering Ayodhya town was thrilling, with a warm and vibrant welcome awaiting us on both sides of the road. The streets came alive with music, dance, and jubilant celebrations. At the entrance, numerous volunteers offered their services (Seva) with great devotion. They carefully took our shoes, kept them in proper places, and guided us to our designated seating area. The seating arrangements were divided into eight blocks, and I was in Block-1, alongside notable personalities from Bollywood and sports. The arrangements were excellent, ensuring everyone was comfortably seated. The highlight of the ceremony was the Indian Air Force helicopters showering flowers over the *Ram Mandir* during the Prana Pratishtha, adding a majestic touch to the event. Meanwhile, a group of 30 artists played various Indian musical instruments, creating a mesmerizing and spiritual ambiance.

We returned to Lucknow in the late afternoon, where the entire locality continued to resonate with *Ram Bhajans*. Upon entering the hotel, we came across a wedding ceremony in progress. Interestingly, even at this joyous occasion, only *Ram Bhajans* were played, reflecting the profound impact of the day's events. After spending the night in Lucknow, we returned to Bhubaneswar the following day, carrying with us cherished memories of this historic and spiritually uplifting experience.

After attending the consecration ceremony on 22nd January, 2024, we returned home. During the flight to Bhubaneswar, I had the opportunity to meet some distinguished individuals onboard. Upon arriving at Bhubaneswar Airport, we were greeted with an unprecedented and heartwarming welcome, making the experience even more memorable.

A few days after the consecration ceremony, we received Prasad along with small stones carved from the larger stone used to sculpt the idol of Ram Lala. Receiving these sacred items felt like a divine blessing, a cherished reminder of the historic event we had the privilege to witness.

ANNEXURE - 1

Resolution No. 32/17 in the Executive Council Meeting dated 24.7.2020

The Complimentary Motion moved by Prof. R. Karpaga Kumaravel was seconded by Dr.Ganguly, Dr.Meenakshi Gopinath, Prof (Dr) Subbiah Shanmugam, Prof Neelima Gupta, Prof Aneel Raina and Dr.Subbiah, who joined Prof.Kumaravel in the complimentary Motion, which was *u*nanimously approved and passed as a Resolution No. 32/17 in the EC Meeting dated 24.7.2020.

I had to hand over charge of VC to some senior professor on 5th August and it was discussed in the EC meeting on 24th July. The decision was left to the external members of the EC, especially to the nominees of the President. After detailed deliberations, it was resolved that the charge should be handed over to Prof. R. Karpaga Kumaravel, Senior Professor of the University.

ANNEXURE – 2

Central University of Tamil Nadu News (Before joining of A.P. Dash)

The Times of India
Central university falls short of expectations
Dennis Selvan | TNN | Mar 24, 2014, 13:24 IST

TRICHY: The Central University of Tamil Nadu (CUTN), which was established in 2009, under the act of Parliament, has turned in to a hotbed of inefficiencies and irregularities. The varsity which has spread over two revenue villages in Thiruvarur district, has not lived upto its expectations, said academicians. The UGC has reprimanded the administration for its lack of vision and for not making any progress o on the anaemic front. While irregularities are noticed in the appointments, the University has lost its charm for the students. ... Alarmingly during the last five years no controller of examinations and Librarian were appointed.. Read more at: http://timesofindia. indiatimes.com/articleshow/32594994.cms?utm_source=contentofinterest&utm_medium=text&utm_campaign=cppst

Central University of Tamil Nadu News (AFTER joining of A.P. Dash)

The Hindu
Rising CUTN stature draws several applicants for VC post

SPECIAL CORRESPONDENT
TIRUCHI, MAY 26, 2020 23:28 IST
UPDATED: MAY 27, 2020 03:48 IST

There are many aspirants from amongst senior and retired professors of Bharathidasan University, Tiruchi, for the post of Vice-Chancellor of Central University of Tamil Nadu (CUTN), Tiruvarur, that falls vacant later this year.

As the tenure of the current Vice-Chancellor, A.P. Dash, is coming to an end during August, the Ministry of Human Resource Development (MHRD) released an advertisement on May 17, inviting applications for the post in order to complete the appointment process beforehand.

Last time, there were at least 20 applicants from Bharthidasan University. This time, the number could be much more, it is learnt.

The requirements specified for applicants constitute the highest level of competence, integrity, morals and institutional commitment; a distinguished academician, with a minimum 10 years of experience as Professor in a University or 10 years of experience in a reputed research and/or academic administrative organisation with proof of having demonstrated academic leadership; and preferably not more than 65 years of age as on June 17, 2020.

The choice of the candidate will be made from a panel of names recommended by a committee constituted under the provisions of the Central Universities Act, 2009.

The progress made by the CUTN since its inception

in 2009 is stated to be a driving factor for attracting many applications for the top post.

The CUTN, in its 11th year now, has registered significant progress in teaching and research in the disciplines of social sciences and humanities, basic and applied sciences, mathematics and computer sciences, behavioural sciences, commerce and business management, communication, education and training, technology, and performing arts.

The uniqueness of CUTN is the great opportunity for students for increased cross-cultural understanding, say faculties.

Last year, the university received over 80,000 applications for the 1,100-odd seats.

The varsity has also made its mark in research with several flagship publications in high-impact peer-reviewed international journals such as Nature and Lancet.CUTN's citation track is also strong, with some of the faculty members having over 8,000 citations and an h-index of 47.

(After I retired on 5th August, 2020 and left the University on 6th August morning)

The Hindu
Special Correspondent, Tiruvarur
AUGUST 11, 2020 21:18 IST
VC Hailed for transforming Varsity into Centre of Excellence
UPDATED: AUGUST 11, 2020 21:18 IS

The institution, they said, has become the talking point for academics for the strides it has made to become a prominent centre for advanced learning and research. Several positions he had held prior to his posting at CUTN was a vital factor for establishing the presence of CUTN at the national level, senior faculty members said.

Prof. Dash, who belongs to Odisha, had served as Director, Institute of Life Science, Bhubaneswar; Director, National Institute of Malaria Research, New Delhi; Director, Centre for Research in Medical Entomology, Madurai; Director, Desert Medicine Research Centre, Jodhpur; and President of National Academy of Vector Borne Disease. He was a Distinguished Scientist, Chair and Adviser of World Health Organisation, and President of Odisha Science Academy.

He recounted how he spent most of his time on the campus, engaging all stake-holders for progress of the institution. The institution, which had just nine departments at the time of his joining on August 5, 2015, saw the start of 19 new departments offering job-orientated programmes during his tenure.

Prof. Dash was also instrumental in signing MoUs with front-ranking institutions. The last was signed, despite the COVID 19 pandemic, with Institute of Textile

Technology, Salem, Tamil Nadu, for offering B.Tech course in Textile Technology.

Faculty members lauded the progress made in improving infrastructure, academic atmosphere and campus placement during his tenure. "Under Prof. Dash's leadership, CUTN had ensured publication of research articles by the faculty in high impact journals including Nature and Lancet," Professor and Head, Department of History, CUTN, said.

Recruitment and selection procedure for teaching and non-teaching posts were conducted in a fair manner during his tenure. "The work culture cultivated by him in CUTN has inspired all stake-holders," Professors added.

ANNEXURE - 3

Malaria cure: Need a drug regimen that reduces pill load
21st July, 2023; Dr Y.K. Gupta & Prof. A. P. Dash

(https://h-leads.com/malaria-cure-need-a-drug-regimen/)

To eliminate malaria from India and the Asia-Pacific region by 2030, we need an unwavering commitment of technical, programme, policy and private sector centred around impacted communities.

Our understanding of malaria dates back to 1897, when Sir Ronald Ross in India demonstrated the involvement of mosquitoes in transmission of malaria parasites. This historic discovery allowed for remarkable progress towards malaria control and elimination. To date, 42 countries have been certified malaria-free through the use of existing strategies and tools of case management and vector control.

The Asia-Pacific region has significantly reduced the malaria burden, with a 64 percent decrease in confirmed cases and 88 percent decrease in reported deaths in the last decade. However, in 2021, the region reported only a 2.5 percent decrease in confirmed malaria cases — in contrast to the 10 percent decrease reported in 2020. Today, just six countries carry 95 percent of the region's malaria burden: Afghanistan, India, Indonesia, Pakistan, Papua New Guinea, and Solomon Islands.

The sustained burden of *P. vivax* — a form of malaria that is more difficult to detect, diagnose, and treat compared to the more common but deadly *P. falciparum* — in Asia-Pacific is another growing concern. While relatively rare outside of the region, *P. vivax* accounted for 48 percent of all malaria cases in Asia Pacific in 2021. This poses a unique challenge, especially in the Greater Mekong Subregion (GMS) where *P. vivax* contributed to 81 percent of the malaria burden — a 5 percent decrease from 2020.

Despite these challenges, Sri Lanka, Maldives, and China were able to eliminate malaria using the existing time-tested tools and strategies. Bhutan, Nepal, Republic of Korea, Thailand, Timor-Leste, Vanuatu, Democratic People's Republic of Korea, and Malaysia are also making accelerated progress.

India has a special role to play.

India's private sector is one of the leading manufacturers of the World Health Organisation's pre-qualified Rapid Diagnostic Tests (RDTs), Artemisinin-based combination therapies (ACTs) and Long-Lasting insecticidal nets (LLINs). These are the key malaria tools for domestic and global malaria programmes. In India, the impact of these tools on malaria elimination efforts is clear. In 2021, the National Center for Vector Borne Disease Control (NCVBDC) reported 161,753 cases, registering a 88 percent reduction since 2010.

The impact of existing tools and techniques is also evident in achieving malaria elimination, as demonstrated by national and sub-national initiatives. This approach was tested as part of the Malaria Elimination Demonstration Project (MEDP), which was an indigenous public-private partnership project between the Government of Madhya Pradesh, Indian Council of Medical Research and Foundation for Disease Elimination and Control, India which is a CSR subsidiary of Sun Pharmaceutical Industries Ltd.

The key strategy behind MEDP was to utilize existing

tools and strategies for malaria elimination in the tribal district of Mandla, with special emphasis on monitoring and accountability. This project achieved its objectives and eliminated indigenous transmission of malaria from the district in about four years.

We argue that there is a need for new and improved medical tools that would enhance efficiency and effectiveness of malaria elimination strategies. There is a need for improved rapid diagnostic tests for *P. vivax* that are highly specific and sensitive. There is also a need of an antimalarial drug regimen that reduces the pill load to improve compliance.

For the treatment of uncomplicated *P. falciparum* malaria, Synriam is a fixed-dose combination (FDC) drug indigenously developed in India and approved by regulatory authorities in India and several African countries. Two noteworthy features of Synriam are that 1) the drug uses synthetic Arterolane maleate that removes the requirement of agriculturally-acquired artemisinin and 2) it is a low-dosage pill, which leads to better treatment compliance and more successful malaria control and elimination campaigns.

Tafenoquine has recently obtained marketing authorisation approval for the radical cure of uncomplicated *P. vivax* malaria, as the treatment has been shown effective in preventing relapse. As a single-dose cure, tafenoquine can improve compliance and therefore could potentially supplant, primaquine, the only other approved medicine for radical cure of *P. vivax* malaria, which needs to be taken over 7 or 14 days.

When existing vector control tools are used properly, they are extremely effective in reducing malaria transmission. However, the recent findings from Papua New

Guinea of reduced bio efficacy of long-lasting insecticidal nets have been attributed to resurgence of malaria after a change in coating formulation was shown to result in the inferior performance of the nets.

We propose that new and improved antimalarial drugs should be subjected to expedited WHO Pre-qualification and national regulatory approvals. We also propose that any evidence of reduced efficacy of drugs or bed nets should be immediately and appropriately investigated by national and global funding agencies and regulatory agencies.

To eliminate malaria from India and the Asia Pacific region by 2030, we need an unwavering commitment of technical, programme, policy and private sector centred around impacted communities.

Dr. Aditya Prasad Dash, currently Vice Chancellor of the Asian Institute of Public Health University was the Vice Chancellor of the Central University of Tamil Nadu and the Director of the National Institute of Malaria Research, New Delhi. He was also the Regional Adviser of the World Health Organisation for the South-East Asia Region. He was conferred with Padmashree in Science and Engineering in 2022.

Professor Yogendra Kumar Gupta is the Principal Advisor, India Strategy Development at Global Antibiotics Research and Development Partnership (GARDP). He serves as the President of AIIMS, Bhopal and AIIMS Jammu.

ANNEXURE –4

OUTLOOK

OUT LOOK SPORLIGHT: OUTLOOK FOR BRANDS; 23 MAY 2023 5:43 PM

The Public Health Question: Ways Forward

(https://www.outlookindia.com/outlook-spotlight/the-public-health-question-ways-forward-news-288791)

With the Covid 19 pandemic having created a greater awareness about the critical role of Public Health research and experts, Outlook speaks to Professor A. P Dash, Vice Chancellor of Asian Institute of Public Health University, the premier Public Health institution in India, to understand some key ways forward.

The recent pandemic has created a greater awareness about the aspect of public health. But we still remain woefully unaware of the scope of the term. Could you please elaborate?

Perhaps no better time in current history demonstrates the critical role of public health than now. With the world still recovering from the devastating effects of the COVID-19 pandemic – economic, social and political, we have learnt many things. Foremost among these is the importance of public health.

Now coming to your question, Public Health (PH) focuses on improving and protecting community health and well-being, with an emphasis on prevention among large groups of people. The World Health Organization defines public health as "the art and science of preventing disease, prolonging health through the organized efforts of society." Public Health is significant in aiding and prolonging life.

The scope of public health is manifold. It is not confined to Health Sciences alone. It encompasses, mental health (clinical psychology), social work, mass communication, geography (remote sensing and predicting natural disasters etc), health economics, among others. Translating research evidence into products, policies and practices (3 Ps) is very important.

What disciplines does the study of public health draw from? An ideal Public Health University may have disciplines such as Public Health, Epidemiology, Data Science, Bioinformatics and one health centre under the School of Public Health. Disciplines such as Biological Sciences, Microbiology /Virology, Climate Change and Environmental Health and Molecular Health Sciences under a School of Biomedical Sciences; disciplines like Clinical Psychology, Health Economics, Social Work, Mass Communication under the School of Social Sciences.

What are some research focus areas at AIPH?

Health is a stepping stone to achieving virtually all other human development goals. Many of the advances in healthcare that we enjoy today are based on research. Recent improvements in life expectancy; in the prevention, diagnosis and treatment of disease, and in healthcare delivery and outcomes have their origins in research that was carried out over many decades. AIPH University aims to carry out research that can be converted into deliverable products. It aims at productive research in areas of public health and related fields that can be used in products, polies and practices (3 Ps). In addition to areas like health system strengthening, the research agenda would include RMNCH+A (Reproductive, maternal, neonatal, child health plus adolescent), Non communicable diseases and infectious diseases, and one health.

Where does India stand with regard to public health delivery in respect to international and regional standards?

Public Health was a neglected area in India. A country like India needs a large number of public Health specialists and virologists. Handling of pandemic needs three things: government's effort, research and people's participation. India, we had seen the strong government's efforts at national and sub-national levels. Research in India was productive in a way that we got two vaccines and supplied to many countries. Public health delivery is not a simple thing. In handling Covid-19, India demonstrated better skills than many countries. WHO has declared India freed from Yaws in 2017. India is also heading towards elimination of Malaria and elimination of lymphatic filariasis, kala-azar and leprosy as public health problems. The case fatality rate of dengue has drastically come down. Therefore, now India is in a better position with regard to public health delivery in respect to many other countries.

What is the near-term and long-term vision that you have for AIPH?

AIPH University will be a vibrant University in the country addressing all public health issues and targeting their solutions with single-minded commitment.

ANNEXURE –5

THE TIMES OF INDIA

Opinion, India: May 26, 2023, 4:25 PM IST **Prof Aditya Prasad Dash** in Voices, India, TOI (https://timesofindia.indiatimes.com/blogs/voices/why-we-must-ensure-more-scientists-are-at-the-helm-of-indias-fight-against-malaria-dengye-filariasis)

Why we must ensure more Scientists are at the helm of India's fight against malaria, dengue, Filariasis?

Every year, diseases such as malaria, dengue, Kala Azar (KA) and Lymphatic Filarias (LF) impact the lives and livelihoods of hundreds and thousands of people across India. According to World Health Organization estimates, India contributed 79% of malaria cases and 83% deaths to the Southeast Asia Region in 2021; over one lakh dengue cases were reported in the country between January and October 2022.

The Southeast Asia Region bears 54% of the global burden of neglected tropical diseases (NTDs) and LF and KA are the key focus for elimination in the region. LF, a disabling, chronic disease, is at present endemic across 328 districts in 21 states and union territories in the country. Kala Azar, or visceral leishmaniasis, is a potentially fatal disease that affects the world's most underserved communities.

What each of these diseases has in common is that they are transmitted by vector – animals or insects that spread disease-causing organisms. India's unique geospatial features make it a hotspot for vector-borne disease. The country's geographic and climatic diversity also means that it is home to a wide variety of vectors, including multiple species of mosquitoes.

Scientists have made great leaps in developing solutions such as insecticides, long lasting insecticidal nets

(LLINs), and larvicides, to combat the threat to human life by disease-bearing insects. However, emerging challenges, including insecticide resistance and climate change, has led to resurgences in diseases that were previously controlled.

The consequences of these diseases are manifold – illness, disability, loss of productivity, poverty, and even death in certain diseases. It is imperative that we take a targeted approach to eliminating these diseases and one of the most efficient and cost-effective ways of addressing the biggest challenges in insect-borne disease control is by improving scientific capacity to survey insect populations and diving corresponding context-specific solutions to eliminate their ability to transmit disease.

The branch of science associated with the control of vector insects is known as "entomology". India had a rich tradition of entomology, dating back to the early 20th century. The country was at the forefront of the global fight against malaria in the 1950s and 60s, with the development of DDT-based indoor residual spraying (IRS) programs. However, the present capacity for vector control research and surveillance in the country is weak, leaving us susceptible to the increased threat of malaria, LF and kala azar.

An acute shortage of medical entomologists has meant that the monitoring and surveillance of disease-causing insects, and resulting strategies to control outbreaks, have been overlooked. Large discrepancies in capacity building have also meant that those who are interested in entomological research have not been equipped with the tools and information required to tackle the significant burden on safeguarding communities from the threat of vector-borne disease.

To build back our capacity to meet emerging threats

in insect-borne disease control head on, it is critical that we invest in building entomological capacity and expertise. By training more biologists in entomology, increasing research funding, and establishing a network of disease surveillance systems and insecticide resistance, we can ensure well equipped ecosystem for training and research at national and sub-national levels in India.

In 2014, World Health Organization focussed the world's attention on vector-borne diseases by making it the theme of World Health Day that year. Renewed commitments to the prevention and control of these diseases have resulted in significant gains but targeted interventions require the expertise of medical entomologists.

Entomologists can ensure a targeted, evidence-based approach to control vectors, ensuring that available resources and efforts are maximized. Integrated Vector Management, a comprehensive approach that includes a range of interventions suited to specific environments is an important method for managing vector borne diseases.

In order to achieve WHO's goal of eliminating neglected tropical diseases (NTDs) by 2030, it is crucial to gain a better understanding of the transmission dynamics of these diseases. Measures such as integrated vector management can reduce vector populations and limit their contact with humans, ensuring that a disease can no longer be spread. Ensuring that water does not stagnate and otherwise eliminating insect breeding sites can also be an important way of controlling their populations.

The Covid-19 pandemic added a tremendous burden to the country's public health infrastructure, which meant that insect-borne diseases have been on the rise in recent years. To make up for lost time and safeguard the health and wellbeing of large populations across the country, we must ensure that greater investments be made in building India's entomological capacity.If we prioritize and invest in training, research and development, we can ensure the advancement of new solutions to address specific challenges. This could lead to the sharing of best practices within Southeast Asia, making India a leader in vector elimination innovation. By equipping a new generation of entomologists with cutting-edge technology, tools, and skills we can drive efforts to free India of preventable insect-borne diseases.

Ending deadly insect-borne diseases in India will require sustained and coordinated efforts from all stakeholders – government, communities, researchers, and industry. By building back our entomological capacity, investing in research and innovation, and working together, we can create a healthier future for all.

Prof Aditya Prasad Dash
Vice Chancellor, Asian Institute of
Public Health (AIPH) University

Annexure - 6

MALARIA MALPRACTICE
(From Frontline, June 30, 2006)

India has reported about 2 million malaria cases every year since the mid-1990s. There are two predominant strains: Plasmodium vivax and Plasmodium falciparum. The disease caused by the former is milder, results in death rarely and can be treated with chloroquine. The latter leads to complications, including cerebral malaria. Almost all malaria-related deaths are cases of falciparum; the reason for its deadly nature is that the parasite has become increasingly resistant to chloroquine in almost all malaria endemic regions of the world.

The authors allege that on six occasions in 2004, the Bank approved the purchase of over 100 million tablets of chloroquine, worth $1.8 m, for its project in India knowing full well that the medication would be used to treat drug-resistant falciparum malaria. According to WHO's revised recommendations of 2003 for treating falciparum malaria, chloroquine should not be used when treatment failure exceeds 15 per cent. "The quantities make it probable that millions of patients with falciparum malaria received such treatment inappropriately. Both money and lives are wasted by these decisions," the paper said.

In a rejoinder, published in the same issue of the

journal, Jean-Louis Sarbib and associates from the Bank rejected the charge of "medical malpractice" and defended the Bank's Enhanced Malaria Control Project (EMCP) in India. According to them, the Bank's aim in India, as elsewhere, is to provide credit to the ongoing government-led strategy. This tailored the malaria drug policy to match the distribution of different malaria parasites in various parts of the country. The EMCP covered 1,045 Primary Health Centres (PHCs) in 100 districts over the States of Andhra Pradesh, Chhattisgarh, Gujarat, Jharkhand, Madhya Pradesh, Maharashtra, Orissa and Rajasthan at a cost of about Rs. 120 crores.

Malaria has already made the headlines in Indian newspapers this year. An outbreak in Assam in February, earlier than the usual June-July period, has seen 170 deaths in the State to date, the highest in recent years. Though outbreaks in the northeastern region have now become an annual occurrence, the World Bank controversy has once again brought the government's malaria control programme, its drug policy in particular, into sharp focus.

India's total number of malaria cases has declined to a steady 2 million. However, the parasite profile has been changing significantly over the years with a steady increase in the percentage of falciparum cases across the country. According to the Health Ministry's National Vector Borne Diseases Control Programme (NVBDCP), formerly known as the National Anti-Malaria Programme (NAMP), falciparum accounted for 50.56 per cent of the cases in 2005 (see graph) and is present in all parts of the country (see map). Areas with more than 30 per cent of falciparum cases are categorised as high-risk. These include much of the northeastern region (with Assam and Meghalaya over 70 per cent), Orissa (over 80 per cent), Jharkhand, Chattisgarh and even parts of West Bengal, Madhya Pradesh, Maharashtra and Andhra Pradesh.

Only about 0.5 per cent of falciparum cases develop into complicated malaria in the country as a whole. However studies conducted by the National Institute of Malaria Research (NIMR), formerly Malaria Research Centre, in several hospitals in Orissa, Assam and Jharkhand have shown that 25-30 per cent of patients develop complicated malaria. According to its director A.P. Dash, about 30 per cent of complicated falciparum malaria cases become fatal if treatment fails. Annually, Orissa accounts for the largest number of deaths due to malaria in the country. There is also a noticeable increase in the number of complicated falciparum malaria cases and consequent deaths, which indicates of falciparum's increasing drug resistance, Dash points out. In 2003, the total number of cases was 1.87 million of which falciparum accounted for 0.86 million and there were 1,006 deaths.

But, more pertinently, these reported cases are only indicative of a trend. According to WHO, the actual disease burden is about 6-7 times the reported number. Correspondingly there is a wide gap between estimated deaths and the number actually reported. Any malaria control programme, the drug policy in particular, should take this into account, Dash points out.

According to India's Malaria Drug Policy, formulated in 2002, chloroquine is the first-line drug for presumptive treatment. It is also the first-line drug for radical treatment of falciparum malaria if the patient is in a `low risk' area. In `high risk' areas however, the policy advocates a regimen of chloroquine plus primaquine.

Second-line treatment, a combination of sulphalene / sulphadoxine and pyrimethamine (the SP combination) followed by primaquine, is recommended at the block/PHC level only in 'chloroquine resistant' areas (treatment failure of 25 per cent or more) and in specific cases where a patient does not respond to chloroquine. In severe and complicated falciparum malaria cases, the policy recommends intravenous quinine irrespective of chloroquine resistance status of the area (with a quick switch over to oral quinine) or injectable artemisinin derivatives.

Black Eagle Books

www.blackeaglebooks.org
info@blackeaglebooks.org

Black Eagle Books, an independent publisher, was founded as a nonprofit organization in April, 2019. It is our mission to connect and engage the Indian diaspora and the world at large with the best of works of world literature published on a collaborative platform, with special emphasis on foregrounding Contemporary Classics and New Writing.

www.ingramcontent.com/pod-product-compliance
Lightning Source LLC
Chambersburg PA
CBHW060547080526
44585CB00013B/471